SYLVIA FRANCKE studied for the st.
of drama at Rose Bruford College in Ke
a trustee of RILKO (Research Into Lc
Any spare time she has is taken up with
grandchildren.

£4-50

THE
TREE OF LIFE
AND THE
HOLY GRAIL

THE TREE OF LIFE AND THE HOLY GRAIL

*Ancient and Modern Spiritual Paths
and the Mystery of Rennes-le-Château*

Sylvia Francke

TEMPLE LODGE

Temple Lodge Publishing
Hillside House, The Square
Forest Row, RH18 5ES

www.templelodge.com

This edition published by Temple Lodge 2007

First published in an earlier edition in 1996

A catalogue record for this book is available from the British Library

ISBN 978 1902636 87 0

Cover by Andrew Morgan
Typeset by DP Photosetting, Neath, West Glamorgan
Printed and bound by Cromwell Press Limited, Trowbridge, Wiltshire

For Helen
(Pipy)
27 January 1971
11 April 1982

Contents

Colour Plates

1. View of Rennes-le-Château from La Pique
2. Magdalene Tower, built by Bérenger Saunière with money from the mysterious fortune he acquired
3. Bérenger Saunière (1852–1917), parish priest of Rennes-le-Château from 1885 to 1915
4. 'The Shepherds of Arcady' by Nicholas Poussin, from the Louvre, Paris
5. The last of the clues leading to the Jean Vié tomb; an inscription on the plinth of a wrought iron cross with Virgin and Child outside the door of the church at Rennes-les-Bains. Underneath 'In Hoc Signo Vinces' ('By This Sign Thou Shalt Conquer') are written the words 'Domino Vie Rectore' which Gérard de Sède has translated as: 'To the master who shows the way'
6. Jean Vié tomb in the cemetery outside the church at Rennes-les-Bains
7. The Apprentice Pillar at Rosslyn Chapel near Edinburgh in Scotland (left); image of DNA (right)
8. Cymatic patterns on the arches of Rosslyn Chapel
9. 'Twelve-year-old Jesus in the Temple' by Ambrogio Borgognone (1450–1523)
10. 'Vitruvian Man' by Leonardo da Vinci
11. 'Our Lady Under-the-Earth' in the crypt at Chartres Cathedral
12. 'The Last Supper' by Leonardo da Vinci
13. Fern patterns in the fan-vaulting of Exeter Cathedral
14. Fern patterns in frost figures
15. Standing stone on Orkney. The angle of the top is 42°
16. Dr Rudolf Steiner (1861–1925), founder of anthroposophy, or spiritual science
17. 'The Group' wooden sculpture by Rudolf Steiner and Edith Maryon
18. Aurora borealis
19. The Globe Playhouse (1599). Schematic design from 'The Byrom Collection'

20. A very impressive example of the Fibonnacci Series leading to fractals within plant growth is reiterated by the florets of broccoli 'Romanesco'. The spirals displayed here lead in alternate opposite directions, having the successive numbers of the Fibonacci series

Preface

In the autumn of 1983 my husband came into the house with some new paperbacks he had just bought. He took one of them from the pile and threw it to me saying: 'This isn't my subject, looks historical—perhaps you should read it.' I turned the book over, recognizing the title immediately: *The Holy Blood and the Holy Grail* by Michael Baigent, Richard Leigh and Henry Lincoln. I began to read and from that moment on became one of the many thousands of people captivated by the complex mysteries surrounding the enigmatic village of Rennes-le-Château in south-western France. However my own involvement in this mystery was not to be confined to reading the seemingly endless stream of books and articles that flowed in the wake of *The Holy Blood and the Holy Grail*. Almost as soon as I had decided to research the mystery for myself, information began to find its way into my hands. Suddenly flights and train journeys took on significance as new friends entered my life who were also synchronistically involved in various aspects of the story, until a sizeable band of seemingly very old friends were interacting with one another almost forgetting that we had all met by chance! In hindsight, it is very interesting to review this element of 'chance' that seems to crop up in the story of all these books. In both the public and private accounts given by some of the authors involved, a similar thing seems to have happened. But in some cases these experiences may have had human origins rather than synchronistic ones!

In writing the first edition of my contribution to the growing pile of information on the Mystery of Rennes-le-Château, I somehow found time to research and write in the very early mornings before seeing my very lively family of four to school for nine o'clock. Because of the lack of time experienced in my particular life-style, it wasn't until 1996 that *The Tree of Life and the Holy Grail* was eventually published, with the help of Thomas Cawthorne, who began as editor but to whom I eventually gave joint authorship. That might have been the end of the story. I discussed the possibility of a rewrite with a literary agent I met at a party in 2002; her answer was that the whole Rennes-le-Château affair was already 'a long way down the road'. So I forgot about it until 2003! This time I joined millions worldwide and was so caught up in the plot of *The Da Vinci Code* by Dan Brown that, reading it at Gatwick Airport in the summer, I was delighted when my flight to Turkey was delayed by two hours, so that I could carry on reading. It took a long time to get going again and Thomas Cawthorne had moved on to other subjects. Realizing that interest in the Rennes mystery, fuelled by *The Da Vinci Code*, has reached an even wider readership, the sense of urgency in explaining its enigmas from my original viewpoint, Rudolf Steiner's spiritual science, has become even more acute than before. The enormous popularity of *The Holy Blood and the Holy Grail* and *The Da Vinci Code*, this recent publishing phenomenon, is proof that humanity is hungry for something new which somehow resonates with information that has its roots in the distant past. This 'something new' is encapsulated in the findings of Rudolf Steiner's spiritual science or anthroposophy, which has its origin in the ancient mystery wisdom and which, as a continuation of the tradition of esoteric Christianity, brings this updated esoteric knowledge to bear on the most urgent problems of our present time.

My thanks are due to Sevak Gulbekian for agreeing to republish the original book and so patiently waiting for this edition to be finished. At the eleventh hour Linda Greenslade, as a representative of the world 'outside' anthoposophy, valiantly agreed to take on long pages of dense material which she has very skilfully edited into a new version. Also many thanks to Thomas Cawthorne for his original input, which still survives in pockets of the extensively reformulated original material. Martin Wacey was initially responsible for introducing the first draft of the manuscript to Thomas who passed it on to Sevak, so many thanks to Martin. As we mentioned in our first edition, Margaret Jonas, author, researcher and Librarian at Rudolf Steiner House, had provided us with invaluable material which has since been corroborated by more recent publications. Also very many thanks go to Eileen Lloyd for her tremendous patience and meticulous attention at the editing stage, and for compiling the index. In addition, there is the still-growing band of new friends, who are not only related to the story behind this book, but also to its connection with my fifth child, who avidly watched Henry Lincoln's original *Chronicle* programmes with me in the late 70s but died on Easter Day in 1982, the year that *The Holy Blood and the Holy Grail* was first published. Last of all my thanks go to the rest of my family who have somehow put up with my preoccupation with the subject. Their feelings are probably accurately recorded in a statement made by one of my daughters who once said, 'I can't promise what I'll do if I have to hear about Cathars and Templars one more time!'

1 January 2007

1.

The Scene is Set

Rennes-le-Château is a place with a mysterious secret. It is situated in an area of south-western France that has been the focus of much activity for many thousands of years. Numerous Druid stone circles and dolmens are scattered about on the surrounding slopes, indicating that this has been a centre of ancient religious significance through the centuries. There are many springs and the land is rich in minerals which brought the Romans to established gold mines in the area. This initially provided some of the speculation for the original mystery of the 'treasure' of Rennes-le-Château, which has been thought by some to have been the ancient capital of the Visigoths, then named Redae or Rhedae, said to have a population of around thirty thousand people, which gave the name of Razès to the area.

For nearly four decades an increasingly vigorous stream of information has fostered an industry which turned this tiny village high in the foothills of the Pyrenees into a location rivalling Disneyland. In the warm months of the tourist season it has barely been possible to move down the few narrow streets of Rennes as crowds of people jostle shoulder to shoulder looking hopefully around, expecting instant answers to the questions posed by a book that many of them are holding. Some rush into the eleventh-century church, now embellished with bizarre nineteenth-century symbolism, gaze around blankly, then rush out again, the book still open in their hands—and none the wiser.

It all began with the publication of *The Holy Blood and the Holy Grail*. There have been numerous reprints since the first paperback copy came out in 1982. A plethora of titles followed for the next 20 years, then the flow seemed to ebb slightly until a new gripping novel catapulted Rennes-le-Château and its mystery into the limelight once again. It seems that there can't be many people left worldwide who don't know about *The Da Vinci Code* by Dan Brown which came out at the beginning of 2004.

Random House in the USA sent out ten thousand review copies, and by the summer of 2005 ten million copies had been sold in America alone. The book has, to date, been translated into 28 different languages, and a feature film came out in the spring of 2006. A very publicized court case between Dan Brown and two of the authors of *The Holy Blood and the Holy Grail* temporarily put the release of the film in jeopardy—but also gave increased publicity to both of the books, thus giving their version of the Grail story the greatest possible worldwide coverage.

While on the way to a holiday in France in 1969, television producer and writer Henry Lincoln made the casual purchase of a paperback, *Le Trésor Maudit*, by Gérard de Sède[1] which might have remained consigned to the post-holiday oblivion of all such reading had he not been deeply drawn into a mystery which has now captivated millions around the world.

The publication of *The Holy Blood and the Holy Grail* released unprecedented shockwaves of controversy and speculation on an ever-expanding readership. It began as an exploration into the possible sources of incredible wealth bestowed upon the obscure and relatively unimportant priest of Rennes-le-Château, Bérenger Saunière. It ended, having followed a convoluted path through a historical thicket involving Cathars, Templars and Freemasonry, with a sweeping challenge levelled at the historical basis of orthodox Christianity. The authors claimed that at the heart of the Rennes-le-Château mystery lay forbidden knowledge concerning Christ's survival of the crucifixion and his marriage to Mary Magdalene and that from this union descended a bloodline running through the Merovingian kings of France and, later, through many of the royal houses of Europe. A typical reaction came from a man who turned to a friend of mine in a bookshop shortly after its publication and, pointing to a copy, announced: 'I was a Christian before I read that, now I don't believe in anything.'

In *The Holy Blood and the Holy Grail* and subsequently in *The Da Vinci Code* there is frequent reference to an 'underground stream' of hidden knowledge stretching back to the distant past. The various authors identify this esoteric stream as an ancient source of hidden knowledge that was suppressed by the growing Church of Rome. This underground stream of esoteric Christianity originated in the early mysteries and progressed as Gnosticism, through the Cathar heresy and Knights Templar to the mysterious Rosicrucian brotherhood of the fifteenth century. In *Collins English Dictionary* 'Gnosis' is described as: 'Intuitive knowledge of spiritual truths'. I have come to believe that the reason why so many people have resonated with certain information put forward in *The Holy Blood and the Holy Grail* and *The Da Vinci Code* is because the authors occasionally came into contact with *genuine* mystery knowledge. Also, interest in Gnosticism has been increasing since the discovery of the Nag Hammadi library in 1945 and the Dead Sea Scrolls at Qumran in 1947. However, the interpretation given to the cryptic esoteric writings they contain by the investigators of most of these best-selling books has often proved to be more materialistic than the *exoteric* Christianity that they challenge! As Andrew Welburn, a leading scholar of Gnostic writings, points out:

> Some of the books used by particular groups and communities within the earliest Christianity were never intended for public display; they were books for the circles of the initiated, and their contents were intended to be preserved in secrecy. It is to these that we owe the term apocryphal, since *apocryphon* in its original connotation means 'a secret book'. Gnostic literature provides many instances—for example, the Nag Hammadi *Secret Book (apocryphon) of John*. The *Gospel of Thomas* also contains secret teaching...[2]

The initiates would have only been instructed in these writings after they had experienced arduous and sometimes dangerous preparation for deeper understanding of the spiritual content of these mysteries which were hidden from physical experience. 'Mystery' language therefore carries a different meaning to its apparent material interpretation. From these misinterpretations of esoteric writings have arisen the main flaws in understanding that now lead to a materialistic picture of the 'historical Jesus'. Elaine Pagels, a major authority on Gnosticism, makes the possibility of this misunderstanding clear when she describes the orthodox Christian approach:

> In its portrait of Christ's life and his passion, orthodox teaching offered a means of interpreting fundamental elements of human experience. Rejecting the gnostic view that Jesus was a spiritual

being, the orthodox insisted that he, like the rest of humanity, was born, lived in a family, became hungry and tired, ate and drank wine, suffered and died. They even went so far as to insist that he rose *bodily* from the dead. Here again, as we have seen, orthodox tradition implicitly affirms bodily experience as the central fact of human life. What one does physically—one eats and drinks, engages in sexual life or avoids it, saves one's life or gives it up—all are vital elements of one's *religious* development. But those gnostics who regarded the essential part of every person as the 'inner spirit' dismissed such physical experience, pleasurable or painful, as a distraction from spiritual reality—indeed as an illusion. No wonder, then that far more people identified with the orthodox portrait than with the 'bodiless spirit' of gnostic tradition. Not only the martyrs but all Christians who have suffered for 2,000 years, who have feared and faced death, have found their experience validated in the story of a *human* Jesus.[3]

The countryside around Rennes-le-Château is alive with Gnostic overtones. 'The Black Castle' and 'The Village of Light', 'The Priest's Canyon' and 'The Devil's Ramparts' continue the theme of dualistic powers in perpetual war. Long before the development of Christianity the spiritual life of communities all over the ancient world was maintained by the ancient mystery centres. These mysteries were received by those who were initiated and given out to the wider public in the form of stories and legends. The initiate gained direct knowledge of the spiritual world through the experiences he gained in these ancient centres. Thus he became a 'Gnostic', or 'Knower'.

To begin with Christianity gradually developed together with this ancient knowledge. However, this situation was not destined to last. At the Council of Nicaea in AD 325 Gnosticism was declared heretical by the developing Church, under the leadership of Constantine, the first Roman Emperor to champion Christianity. This would seem to mark the root cause of the great divide that has followed the course of Christianity down the centuries.

One of the forms that Gnosticism took was developed in the Cathar heresy. This was a belief in a 'dualism' that held that the creation of the world was due to forces of darkness acting together with forces of light. As one travels near Rennes-le-Château large roadside placards announce that one is now 'in Cathar Country'! The Cathars flourished there in the eleventh and twelfth centuries until they were effectively exterminated by the Roman Church in the middle of the thirteenth century.

The origins of this dualism arose from Manichaeism, a powerful early Christian belief system which, in turn, grew out of the ancient Zoroastrian view of the world. Not only Cathars, but Templars, Rosicrucians and Freemasons developed under the influence of the Manichaean impulse.

The Austrian thinker and seer Rudolf Steiner (1861–1925) has described his spiritual science or anthroposophy as a continuation of Gnosticism in a new form. Many of his lectures and writings referred to facts that were not to be discovered in Gnostic texts until the findings at Qumran and Nag Hammadi 20 years after Steiner's death.

Rudolf Steiner referred to Gnosticism in many of his lectures and books. He described how it had grown out of the original mystery wisdom, which was guarded in sacred locations of the ancient world. His descriptions were based on an understanding that creation had proceeded from a purely spiritual existence, and that early mankind was originally in very close contact with its spiritual origin but has subsequently progressed in varying degrees through an 'evolution of consciousness' that has gradually alienated humanity from the spiritual source of its creation. Steiner refers to the wisdom gained in the early mysteries as,

> something which up to this day has been completely exterminated from human evolution, rooted out by currents running counter to the deeper Christian revelation: this was Gnosis, a wisdom into which had flowed much of the ancient knowledge revealed to men in atavistic clairvoyance. Every trace of the Gnosis, whether in script or oral tradition, was exterminated root and branch by the dogmatic Christianity of the West—after this Gnosis had striven to find an answer to the question: Who is the Christ?[4]

However, in his description of the original Gnosis, he continues by saying:

There can be no question today of reverting to the original Gnosis—for the Gnosis belongs to an age that is past and over... There is no question of reviving the Gnosis, but of recognizing it as something great and mighty, something that endeavoured, in the time now lying nineteen hundred years behind us, to give an answer to the question: Who is the Christ?[5]

This question 'Who is the Christ?' could be a question that is simmering under the surface for many of us today. In the above statement by Elaine Pagels the identity of 'Jesus' as a 'spiritual' being is under discussion. In the first quotation from Rudolf Steiner, he is asking the question 'Who is the Christ?' In the second quotation from Steiner, he emphatically states that 'There can be no question today of reverting to the original Gnosis' because in his understanding this 'spiritual being' to whom Pagels refers, and of whom the ancient mysteries and the Gnostics taught, is predominantly *Christ* not *Jesus*.

Before the inner eye of the Gnostic lay a glorious vista of spiritual worlds, with the Hierarchies ranged in their order, one above the other. How the Christ had descended through the worlds of the spiritual Hierarchies to enter into the sheaths of a mortal man—all this stood before the soul of the Gnostic ... This majestic, sublime concept of Christ has fallen into the background, but all the dogmatic definitions handed down to us as Arian or Athanasian principles of faith are meagre in comparison with the Gnostic conception, in which vision of the Christ being was combined with wisdom relating to the universe. Only the merest fragments of this great Gnostic conception of Christ have survived.[6]

Steiner's statement that 'Gnosis belongs to an age that is past and over' underlines the fact that human consciousness is constantly changing. For the last few thousand years we have woken more and more to the impressions of the physical world around us. Today we are ready to begin to wrestle with the concept of a connection between *Christ* as a spiritual being incorporated in a *human Jesus*. This concept then leads to a thought that within all of us is a higher, spiritual nature working through and eventually transforming the part of us that is subject to purely physical laws. 'Who is Christ?' could be the question that prompted both the writing and avid acquisition of the procession of books that began with *The Holy Blood and the Holy Grail* and currently culminates in *The Da Vinci Code*. For this reason, when I first read *The Holy Blood and the Holy Grail* I felt that there might be a genuine desire on the behalf of the authors to unravel this perplexing question. From this point onwards I would like to attempt both to answer the question first posed by the Gnostics, over two thousand years ago, and to delve deeper into the mystery of Rennes-le-Château as it appears in *The Holy Blood and the Holy Grail* and *The Da Vinci Code*, with the help of research carried out with insight gained from Rudolf Steiner's spiritual science.

2.

The Underground Stream and the New Mysteries

The underground stream

It is possible to trace threads of mystery knowledge that run through ancient times to the present day. These threads when put together form what is sometimes referred to as an underground stream of esoteric knowledge. This knowledge was worked with and passed on by dedicated people regardless of the prevailing attitudes. Like water flowing in the rock structures beneath our feet, its presence is unknown to all but a few.

Rudolf Steiner has described how there were many mystery centres in the ancient world, into which those who were ready to receive knowledge of the spiritual realities underlying physical existence were initiated. Even in the time of Jesus, Judaism possessed a genuine esoteric doctrine. Rudolf Steiner says, 'This mystery teaching was full of hidden knowledge about the "spiritual man" and provided ample indications of how human cognition could find a path to the spiritual world.' He further says, 'The essence of the Palestinian mysteries found no place in Romanism, for Rome had evolved a special form of community or social life which was only possible if the spiritual man was ignored.'[1]

Steiner describes how at Jesus' trial, the Sadducees, one of the Jewish religious sects, played a leading part. They joined forces with Rome because they shared a common aim, 'to eradicate, to suppress everything that proceeded from the ancient Mysteries'.[2]

Later, in the fourth century, the Emperor Constantine carried out an effective programme of extermination that was directed against all the sacred institutions and places of the Roman world, which also encompassed areas of previous Greek culture. After a short respite under the rule of Julian the Apostate, the purge continued under subsequent Emperors.

In AD 377 the sanctuary of Mithras in Rome was destroyed. From 390 to 395 the 'Temple War' was raging, fanned by Theodosius, in which among much else the most glorious mystery centre of Alexandria, the Serapeum with its priceless library, fell victim. In 396 the Eleusinian Mysteries were closed. In 415, the brilliant woman philosopher Hypatia was torn to pieces by the Christian mob.

This suppression of the original mystery knowledge was to continue, for Gnosticism, which retained the essence of the pre-Christian mysteries, was persecuted through the ages. Whole communities followed Gnosticism, which was incorporated into the beliefs of groups such as the Cathars. The mystery of Rennes-le-Château is closely linked with the history of the Cathars. They claimed they belonged to an older, truer form of Christianity than the Catholic Church. A very strong influence in Cathar belief was that of Manichaeism. Rudolf Steiner speaks of Manichaeism as:

> a spiritual movement which although at first only a small sect became a mighty spiritual current. The Albigensians, Waldenses and Cathars of the Middle ages are a continuation of this current, to which also belong the Knights Templar ... and also—by a remarkable chain of circumstances—the Freemasons.[3]

Manichaeism arose in Asia Minor in the third century AD.[4] Mani, its founder, was born in AD 216 in Babylon and lived mostly in Iran. Manichaeism began to address the enigma of the relationship between the original source of spirit and fallen matter, which includes creation in the material realm, leading to problems caused by incarnating in a physical body. Walter Johannes Stein says of Mani's teachings that: 'In true Manichaeism there lives a wonderful moral impulse, a true Christianity; but with a special and peculiar concept of sin. That sin is something that can be made good again, this is the faith of Manichaeism.'[5]

But various influences made it impossible for these Gnostic concepts to continue to filter through the early development of Christianity. What happened at the hands of Constantine illustrates this graphically.

In addition to the effects resulting from the Council of Nicaea and from the destruction of the ancient mystery centres at the hands of Constantine, there were several influences which prevented deeper understanding of the relationship between spirit and matter. These influences, among others, were caused by the interference of a being described by Rudolf Steiner as Sorat the Sun Demon, the two-horned beast, the adversary of the Lamb, mentioned in the Book of Revelation. Sorat, identified by Steiner as an opposing being of great power, is called 'the Sun Demon', because he works against the Beings of the sun who Steiner sometimes refers to as 'the Sun Intelligence'.

Mani was one of the first teachers at a centre of learning which was founded in the early third century AD, by King Shapur I of Persia. There Mani taught his version of Christianity, which while retaining the Zoroastrian view of Christ as a Sun Being, taught of his subsequent involvement in Earth evolution. This view would later be absorbed by the Cathars.

> After the death of King Shapur, Mani was no longer protected and other priests, who wanted to introduce ancient pre-Christian sun worship, rebelled against him. Mani suffered a similar death to Christ on Golgotha two and a half centuries later. However, as the true Sun Spirit, the Christ was no longer to be found in the sun sphere, but rather in the surroundings of the earth. Thus the priests of Ghondi Shapur, knowingly or unknowingly, became worshippers of the 'Sun Demon'.[6]

Steiner has described the centre in which Mani taught, Ghondi Shapur, named after King Shapur I of Persia, as a university that flourished west of Baghdad just as that ancient city first came into being. Remains of its location are still visible through aerial photography. One can only understand the great danger of what was prevented from happening at this centre and how through it Sorat intended to destroy the future development of humanity if we consider the complicated enigma connected with the progressing degrees of soul development through which humanity passes in unfolding evolution.

> With the entry of the Graeco-Roman epoch the old instinctive clairvoyance of humanity changed into a more conceptual cognition. This came about in different ways in the various peoples. Among the Greeks there evolved an artistic thinking full of fantasy, among the Hebrews a calculating, combining one. The Semitic family of nations pressed rapidly and one-sidedly forwards in the development of the intellectual head thinking.[7]

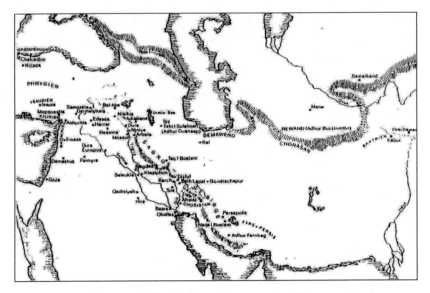

Map of location of Ghondi Shapur (in present-day Khuzestan, Iran)

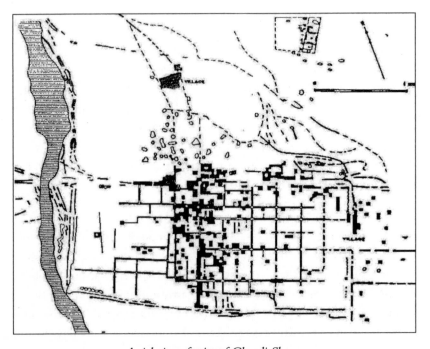

Aerial view of ruins of Ghondi Shapur

At the time of Ghondi Shapur, which reached its peak of activity around the year 666, while the Semitic peoples were already reaching a more intellectual form of consciousness, the prevailing consciousness of those involved in the Academy of Ghondi Shapur was, as yet, too immature to understand the great dangers that were being prepared in the inspiration behind its research and teachings. Humanity as a whole *was not* (and, in the twenty-first century, *is still not*) capable of developing the faculty to handle them safely. What were these teachings, and what were the dangers? The interaction of spiritual energies within the physical laws of matter were studied and used at Ghondi Shapur, while those working with them there were still at an immature stage of development. In the ancient mysteries, similar teachings had only been given in the inner mysteries, where initiates received them after long and dangerous preparation. Towards the end of this chapter we will see how the awakening forces of the individual would not begin to stir until the beginning of the fifteenth century. Only after this time, and not for a long time after, would it be safe to approach knowledge of the spiritual powers active in nature. To attempt this prematurely, it would seem to me, would be working across the frontiers of the spiritual world into the realm of black magic.

The Semitic peoples, who reached a more intellectual form of consciousness ahead of the Greeks and people of the west, included, on the one hand, the Jewish race, who particularly developed intellect in an inward direction, towards the fostering of their soul life. On the other hand, the Arabs directed the development of their intellectual activity towards increasing understanding of the outer world, of nature in all its forms.

Ghondi Shapur had opened its doors to the Gnostics and to those carrying Aristotle's teachings in the original Greek language. Aristotle was a pupil of Plato. He was given the task of conveying the ancient mysteries, which Plato taught in a richly pictoral and symbolic way, into the more intellectual concepts used in western thought. It was at Edessa in the fifth century that Aristotle's writings were translated into Syrian, before reaching Ghondi Shapur and from there taken to the newly established Baghdad where they were again translated into Arabic.

This process was what Steiner has referred to as 'the Arabianizing of

Aristotelianism',[8] which demonstrates one of the many examples of currents running counter to the true Christian revelation. In essence, the more esoteric nuances of Aristotle's writings were lost when translated from a viewpoint of greater materialism.

In this way much of the original inspired mystery-content of Aristotle's writings never found its way to Europe. Rudolf Steiner refers to this as a tragedy of enormous magnitude. The new Islamic culture was already immersed in a more conscious intellectualism, so that the spiritual value of Aristotle's original writings was, to a great extent, lost in translation. Rudolf Steiner describes how the Arabic impulse penetrated Aristotle's work, which then in this form was bereft of most of its original mystery content and so became the basis of modern materialistic science.

What happened to the pre-Christian mystery stream at the hands of the Romans, to the early Christian mystery stream at the Council of Nicaea, and the writings of Aristotle at Ghondi Shapur are all examples of the workings of influences that run against the progressive stream of human evolution.

These influences also infiltrated the Catholic Church via the Eighth Ecumenical Council of 869 in Constantinople. About this Council Rudolf Steiner's pupil, the historian Dr Walter Johannes Stein, writes:

> The living spirit died when doubts of the Trinity arose. The Council of 869, through which Trichotomy was abolished—the teaching that body, soul and spirit are to be considered as distinct from one another in man—is only a completion of a long series of events. The Council merely expressed what had been accomplished within human evolution. The path to the spirit was no longer accessible in the old way. At the same time Ahriman, the Spirit of Lies, was drawing near . . . that Spirit of Untruth then entering humanity. But upon this fact hangs world history; for how could the modern age approach—the age of the machine, of printing, of the power of the newspaper—without the entry of this spirit? It had to enter.[9]

It has also been considered that Manichaeism had an affinity with Celtic Christianity. The same influence behind the fate of Aristotle's original writings may also have been operative in the impulse behind the obliteration of Celtic Christianity in Britain at the Council of

Whitby. It is therefore fascinating to connect the dates of the height of the power of the University at Ghondi Shapur, the year 666, with the date when the Council of Whitby reached its culmination in 664. If Celtic Christianity had continued, there would surely never have been the enmity that now exists between pagans and Christians. Celtic Christianity was the automatic transition from all that was sound and holistic in the pagan beliefs that immediately preceded it. The Culdee Church never accepted the Church Council of Nicaea as does Christendom today.

It is fascinating to note that the number 666 is the 'number of the Beast', the two-horned beast already referred to. The number 666 represents the year 666 when Sorat's attack on the Sun Intelligence was at its height.[10] In his lectures on the Book of Revelation given in Dornach, Switzerland between 5 and 22 September 1924, Steiner shows how these attacks are repeated in multiples of 666.

> ... it was there for a second time after a further 666 years had passed, in 1332, in the fourteenth century. At that time once again the Beast rose up out of the waves of world events ... It was the time when ... the Order of the Knights Templar wanted to found a sun view of Christianity, a view of Christianity that looked up again to Christ as a Sun Being, as a cosmic being, a view that knew again about the spirits of the planets and stars, a view that knew how in cosmic events Intelligences from worlds that lie far apart from one another work together, not only the beings of one particular planet, a view that knew about the mighty oppositions that are brought about by such obstinate beings as Sorat, the Sun Demon, who is one of the most mighty demons in our system. What is at work in the materialism of human beings is, fundamentally, the demonic work of the Sun Demon.[11]

Esoteric Christianity has been persistently attacked since its early prefiguration in the pre-Christian mysteries. These attacks led to the destruction of the ancient mysteries by Rome, the 'Arabianizing of Aristotelianism', the overruling of the Gnostics at the Council of Nicaea, the genocide of the Albigensian Crusade, the arrest of the Templars and the suppression of the Rosicrucians in the seventeenth century.

Rudolf Steiner has very often spoken of the Rosicrucians, not as a shadowy Renaissance group existing only in realms of conjecture and speculation but as a hidden and very powerful current in the evolution of esoteric Christianity. Their mission was to foster the development of the human individuality in the physical world without losing the spiritual substance, which is the human being's birthright, to teach the finding of spirit through the senses. To better understand the significance of the Rosicrucian mission we need to take a detailed look at basic spiritual teaching. We shall shortly see how man had begun as a being who had originated in a purely spiritual world; through the Fall he was increasingly distanced from it. In one of his fundamental books, *Theosophy*, Rudolf Steiner describes this changing relationship between the human being and the spiritual world of his origin, now mediated by the activity of the 'soul':

> Through the body we belong to the physical world. With our spirit, we live in a higher world. Our soul binds the two worlds together during our lifetime ... Between the body and the spirit the soul lives a life of its own. It is served by its likes and dislikes, its wishes and desires, and places thinking at its service.[12]

An aspect of the soul is the 'astral' body. The 'ego' or 'I' are alternative names for the spirit.[13] Rudolf Steiner named the different stages through which the soul developed in this relationship between the ever more conscious activity of the human body and the spiritual world. Each stage lasted for over a thousand years, and that period was subsequently named after the stage through which the soul was passing. The unfolding of this changing relationship was charted as follows:

Sentient soul	1900 BC	*orektikon*
Intellectual soul	747 BC	*kinetikon*
Consciousness soul	1413 AD	*dianoetikon*

Later we shall see how humanity lost its direct awareness of the spiritual world as a result of the Fall. As this connection faded, so human beings gained independence and began to develop individualized thinking bound to the material brain. It was because of this limitation that they could advance in freedom to nurture their innermost forces which could eventually be turned outwards to grasp the spiritual in nature and by so doing begin to gradually rediscover their relationship to the spiritual world from which they had been alienated by the Fall. This alienation has intensified through the time when the intellectual and consciousness souls were developing.

The consciousness soul has to do with the awakening activity of human individuality, the eternal spiritual core of our being, the human ego just mentioned. Since its first feeble activity began, this ego has the task of transforming the subtle human sheaths whose effective activity has been impaired by the Fall. The ultimate goal of the consciousness soul stage of development has to do with the eventual transformation of the astral body which will then become an effective tool for reversing the damaging effect of the Fall on all of the human bodies, both subtle and physical.

The first Rosicrucian writings were printed in 1614, 1615 and 1616, although they had been unofficially circulated before these dates. Shakespeare died in 1616. Rudolf Steiner has indicated that both Shakespeare and Francis Bacon were 'overlit' by Christian Rosenkreutz.[14] The Rosicrucians were fostering the new form of human consciousness on many different levels; the ancient mystery teachings were given to the uninitiated in the form of legends. Clément Wertheim Aymès explains this in his book *The Pictorial Language of Hieronymus Bosch*:

> They taught by means of pictures and symbols, appealing to imagination rather than intellect. They can only be understood if the student himself is able to develop imaginative faculties. The Rosicrucians tried to evoke imaginative effort and ability in all sorts of ways, not only through pictures, but through a wealth of fairy tales, legends, proverbs and songs—even to children's games and acrobatic feats. By all these means, they were able to bring the content of esoteric wisdom to the people in the form of picture and parable, and at the same time to educate in the people the faculties needed to understand them.[15]

It was with this aim that Shakespeare's plays were written, plays whose appeal and effect have continued to foster the development of the consciousness soul age throughout the world ever since.

The teachings resulting from the Council of 869, that man 'consists only of a body and soul, had by the time of Christian Rosenkreutz become elevated to the status of a dogma'.[16] As a result, the wine had been withdrawn from the sacraments. 'Against this dogma the Rosicrucians taught that man not only has a body and a soul, but also a spirit.'[17] As the consciousness soul age dawned 'men ... became less and less bound to that religious order of life which had prevailed throughout the Middle Ages. Similarly, the old social order no longer sufficed to contain the new dynamic brought into society by new outer experiences of the world, and the new quality of self-consciousness in individual men.'[18]

The essence of Rosicrucian teaching was that as people began to develop this self-consciousness, accompanied by sharper observation of the surrounding world, the newly perceived 'outer world' should not only be perceived as a physical fact but also the spiritual source of nature should be seen working through its outward manifestation. Quoting Steiner, Wertheim Aymès adds:

> The true Rosicrucian belongs to the spiritual stream of esoteric Christianity, which adapts and transforms the way of its teaching according to the needs of new historical circumstances. Its message remains the same in spiritual essence, but its form must always be appropriate to the historical circumstances.[19]

It can be said that Rudolf Steiner's activities at the turn of the twentieth century constitute another transformation of the way in which these essential spiritual teachings are given out. In briefly tracing the spiritual stream of esoteric Christianity through the centuries, we arrive at a transformation fit for the circumstances in which we now find ourselves. On Tuesday, 25 December 1923, at Dornach in Switzerland, Rudolf Steiner laid the Foundation Stone for the Anthroposophical Society in the form of a mantra spoken to the assembled members.

> From the way Rudolf Steiner delivered the opening address, beginning by making a special sign, it was immediately apparent that a deed would be performed which would introduce a new phase in the development of the Mysteries of mankind.[20]

During the speaking of the Foundation Stone Meditation it has been related that some of those present supersensibly perceived Christian Rosenkreutz and his host entering the hall to join the anthroposophists gathered there. At that moment the secret stream of esoteric Christianity that had passed down from the ancient mysteries, through the Gnostics, Manichaeans, Cathars, Templars and Rosicrucians, now re-emerged in the twentieth and twenty-first centuries as anthroposophy or 'spiritual science'.

When Rudolf Steiner founded the 'New Mysteries', the underground stream resurfaced once again. This new form of esoteric Christianity is based on an understanding that the advance of modern civilization demands that all the phenomena available to human experience are explained from a scientific and rational point of view. Calls to simple faith and passive belief are no longer apt for a humanity that has come of age.

The New Mysteries

Steiner spoke about how at the turn of the twentieth to the twenty-first century a natural transformation of human spiritual faculties will increasingly be experienced. A symptom of this has been that, at the eleventh hour, a new reverence for life has prompted increasing numbers of people to turn to holistic medicines and therapies. The desire to find alternatives to the materialistic medicine and science of our age has also been driven by the widespread pollution and degra-dation of our living environment. At the same time the scientists are pulling back the familiar boundaries of reality and the ground is almost literally being whipped away from beneath their feet. As a result of this transformation in consciousness, conventional science is now standing on the edge of a threshold which it is not equipped to cross unless a new understanding is developed. It is unprepared to cope with the next frontier. The enigma ahead is the mystery of *life* itself.

Eric Bailey, reviewing *The Arrow of Time* by Roger Highfield and Dr Peter Coveney (August 1990) in the *Weekend Telegraph*, stated that the book offered 'a view of science which suggests that a change in direction and attitude is imminent, drawing away from the obsessive delving into atoms and molecules of the last 40 years, and adopting a broader perspective.'[21] Later on in the review Bailey, referring to the second law of thermodynamics and entropy, asks: 'If the universe amounts to a progressive cosmic degradation, how do we explain the formation of life, which represents a formidable process of organization, evolution and improvement?'[22] Elsewhere Bailey describes how, while the authors were 'studying the behaviour of chemicals mixed together', they

> found that the molecules formed transient symmetrical patterns. The patterns were apparently spontaneous and disappeared as the chemicals moved towards the complete mix—its state of equilibrium and maximum entropy. The patterns suggest that the molecules 'knew' where to go and create the brief semblance of order. Could it be that the beginnings of life were self-organized in the primeval soup?[23]

If there is a simple notion that links the diversity of unorthodox research it is perhaps the idea that as well as the laws of material nature there is a *complementary* life force or principle, which is as real, if not more so, than the realm of pure matter. Those who have become champions of this idea have arrived at it from many different directions, often after long and rigorous scientific journeys. This is the knowledge that was forced underground long ago before humanity was ready to understand it consciously. By the nineteenth century the mechanistic view had completely taken over in science and medicine. In 1905 Rudolf Steiner made the following comments:

> Physical, chemical and mineral laws hold sway in man's physical body. Yet even as far as his spiritual nature is concerned he belongs to the mineral kingdom since he understands through his intellect only what is mineral. Life, as such, he is only gradually learning to comprehend. Precisely for this reason, official science disowns life, being still at the stage of development in which it can only grasp the dead, the mineral. It is in the process of trying to understand this in very intricate detail.[24]

Rudolf Steiner made it clear that:

Life is not to be understood here on earth. Occultism alone can give knowledge of life; external science can never fathom it. It would be the wildest fantasy to believe that one could ever penetrate the laws of life as one can physical or chemical laws. To do so remains an ideal; it can never be reached. On the physical plane there is never any possibility of giving knowledge of life. This knowledge of life must remain the preserve of supersensible knowledge.[25]

This is a metamorphosis of the original mystery wisdom that was concealed in the knowledge passed from Plato to Aristotle, in danger of premature exposure at the Academy of Ghondi Shapur, and which began to lose its spiritual content when Aristotle was translated into Arabic at the court of Baghdad. Then, with the birth of the consciousness soul, mankind began to be increasingly aware of the physical environment; the Rosicrucian influence was lost as the march of scientific progress took man's curiosity into realms of materialism where the infinitesimal was investigated and the unity of creation separated into ever-multiplying isolated subdivisions.

Rudolf Steiner once more turned to the mystery knowledge and adapted it for twentieth-century consciousness. He showed how the realm from which the life-force streams can be thought of as a vast cosmic ocean that stretches to the zodiac, controlling and harmonizing the planetary movements while also imbuing the tiniest living creatures with life and motion. In this context his early meeting with the scientific work of the German literary genius J.W. Goethe was very opportune. At the Vienna Polytechnic Steiner discovered the scientific works of Goethe, and later, at the recommendation of his teacher, Karl Julius Schröer, he went to work at the Goethe and Schiller Archives in Weimar. Here he had the task of editing Goethe's copious scientific papers.

The meeting with Goethe's ideas could be seen to mark Steiner's outward connection with the stream of Rosicrucian knowledge. Goethe's work was imbued with the Rosicrucian thought that was still active at the end of the eighteenth century. It was during this period, one of an ever-deepening involvement with Goethe's work, that Steiner wrote his first major work. This was *Goethes Weltanschauung*

(Goethe's World View), later published in English as *A Theory of Knowledge Implicit in Goethe's World Conception*.

Goethe (1749–1832) wished to remain steadfastly true to his actual experience of the world. He began with the rational assumption that, if attentively studied, through time phenomena would reveal their secrets to human consciousness. Close and intensive study of plant and animal morphology led him to a basic yet revolutionary conception. He realized that the organic and biological form unfolded according to *laws of metamorphosis* in which the later development was a transformation of the earlier form. From this phenomenological approach evolved a non-reductionist scientific theory and evolutionary biology.

In his classic work on plant morphology[26] Goethe describes how the individual plant unfolds its being according to a rhythmical principle of expansion and contraction, through a modulated interweaving between polarities. Goethe discovered the workings of life in the plant. Organic forms unfold, according to Goethe's observations, through a formative process involving metamorphosis and polarity. These ideas were derived through disciplined observation of organic forms and their development. Whilst Goethe's work has been derided as 'pseudo-science' by the establishment, the mathematical underpinnings to support his views were already in existence.

It was also during the time that Steiner was working on Goethe's scientific ideas that he wrote *Die Philosophie der Freiheit*, which was published in 1894. (In English, *The Philosophy of Freedom*.) He once said that if all the rest of his writings and the content of his lectures disappeared, this book alone held the most important information for humanity at the present time. In it he gives a descriptive account of human cognition, stating that intuitive thinking is central to any understanding of the human being.

> In thinking we take hold of a corner of the world process where we must be present if anything is to come about . . . it is just because we ourselves bring [thinking] forth that we can know the characteristic features of its course. What in all other spheres of observation can only be discovered indirectly is, in the case of thinking, known to us quite directly.[27]

The conventional theory of human cognition states that all human brain activity is the result of other, invisible, unknowable forces; atoms, chemical forces, the unconscious. Steiner's main point is that, whilst this could be the case with some phenomena, it cannot be the case with thinking as defined above. It is self-generated, self-sustained, and has to be taken as the starting point for all knowledge, both of the human being and of the world. Without this self-sustaining activity we could know nothing about the world. All knowledge begins with the elaboration of thoughts about our perceptions.

According to Steiner, where thinking occurs, the material aspects of the brain withdraw, they make room for the activity of thinking and allow that activity to be impressed upon the material substance. Thinking produces activity in the material substance of the brain, rather than activity in the tissues of the brain resulting in the production of thinking. Steiner points out that the nervous system (the basis of human cognition) is composed of hardened matter—matter that is less alive than that of the tissues or the blood. This is because the 'life' or 'etheric' force working into the structures of the nervous system has been liberated to form the substance of cognition.

In founding anthroposophy, Rudolf Steiner outlined a new path of spiritual development that aimed to reintegrate the *thinking process into the living world*. Awakening the inner potentialities of human cognition, the individual finds higher states of consciousness already present in a seed form within daily consciousness. As humans evolve and perfect their moral and cognitive faculties, the realities of the *world of life-processes—the etheric realm*—are made more directly available to them. This gives access to the 'Grail castle' and then lays firm foundations for what could be described as a 'Science of the Grail'.

3.
Science of the Grail

The four ethers

The Holy Blood and the Holy Grail was concerned with a connection between the Holy Grail of legend, the Cup of the Last Supper and the mystery surrounding Rennes-le-Château. This connection was developed in various ways by the books that followed, culminating in *The Da Vinci Code*. At the heart of the mystery of Rennes-le-Château, it is claimed, is the forbidden knowledge of Jesus Christ's marriage to Mary Magdalene, which resulted in a bloodline stretching down through the ages to the modern royal houses of Europe. This bloodline passed through leading families connected with the area around Rennes, who in turn were connected with the enigmatic Priory of Sion. There is always a grain of truth in any mystery or hypothesis so, at this point, I would like to begin to steer the mystery of Rennes through phenomena which are also recognized as being connected with the area and which are also related to the etheric science that we are beginning to investigate in more detail.

The dramatic countryside surrounding Rennes-le-Château appears to affect many people through more than the accepted five senses. I was once at a lecture on Rennes-le-Château at the Research Into Lost Knowledge Organization (RILKO) in London when a member of the audience jumped to his feet in question time and declared: 'I challenge anyone in this room to go and sit on any of the mountain tops surrounding Rennes and not to feel that they are individually affected by something powerful and intangible in the countryside around!' It is this 'something' that I would like to investigate in relation to the legend of the Holy Grail and its connection to the Rennes mystery.

Throughout the ages saints and mystics have described an experience of attunement with nature, a fusing together of individual consciousness with the source of life in all organic forms. When we walk through a wood or in open countryside, even if we are not able to say that we share the vision of the seers and initiates, we can still sense a connection with the life force and, at the same time, feel recharged and uplifted when surrounded by all that is constantly coming into being, growing, and then passing out of existence again.

The etheric realm is connected with rhythm and with all that lives in time.[1] If the same walk is taken every day throughout the year, awareness of the working of the etheric in nature becomes evident. One is then able to observe each bud and blade of grass as living in time rather than space. The physical body is also constantly growing, developing and decaying, following a similar cycle to the other rhythms of nature around us. If left to itself, it would follow purely chemical and mineral laws. It is the etheric body, or organism, which maintains the principle of life within the physical body.

Rudolf Steiner has stated that man, at his present stage of scientific understanding, is only gradually learning to comprehend life. 'Precisely for this reason, official science disowns life, being still at the stage of development in which it can only grasp the dead, the mineral.'[2] On a later occasion he stated that: 'Life is not to be understood here on earth. Occultism alone can give knowledge of life; external science can never fathom it.'[3] And in another lecture Steiner asks:

> What then is the Holy Grail? For those who understand this legend correctly, it signifies—as can even be proved by literary means—the following. Till now, man has only mastered the inanimate in nature. The transformation of the living forces, the transformation of what sprouts and grows in the plants and of what manifests itself in animal [and human] reproduction—that is beyond his power. Man has to leave these mysterious powers of nature untouched. There he cannot encroach. What results from these forces cannot be fully comprehended by him.[4]

Rudolf Steiner described the life force, the etheric realm, in four divisions which operate as higher octaves of the four elements. The element of fire or heat manifests as the *warmth ether*, which creates a link between the physical elements and this higher octave. Gas and air descend towards matter in physical terms, but their correlative, the *light ether*, has a higher spiritual status than the warmth ether. When we reach the fluid element we are entering the realm of the 'higher ethers', which Steiner described as the Holy Grail. The higher octave of the element water is described as the *Chemical-tone-sound* or *number ether*. Finally, the element earth relates to the very highest of the ethers, the *life ether*, which works down from the greatest spiritual heights into the densest of the elements. These four ethers work in concert through materially manifest creation.

Rudolf Steiner describes how the interrelationship between the etheric body, the astral body and the physical body can be illustrated by means of a geometrical figure: 'If we ponder deeply this figure we find that it contains—like an occult sign on which we can meditate—all the proportions of the size and strength of the forces of physical, etheric and astral bodies respectively. You see that what I am drawing is a pentagram.'[5]

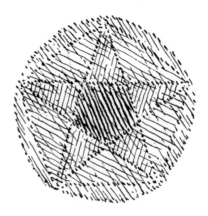

Steiner describes how the pentagram can be seen as a symbol for the etheric body, but because the etheric body is the centre from which the maintaining forces for the other two bodies originate, it is possible to show '... in this sign and seal of the ether body, what in the human body is the ratio between the strength of the forces of the physical body, the strength of the etheric body, and the strength of the forces of the astral body respectively.'[6]

The pentagram is the archetypal form of the Golden Section. This forms an important bridge for studying how the etheric forces bring into matter information that qualifies and differentiates. The pentagram makes an early appearance in *The Da Vinci Code*, when a body lying in this shape, with arms and legs outstretched, is found in the Louvre Museum in Paris.

In *An Outline of Esoteric Science*, Rudolf Steiner explores the origins of the warmth, light, chemical and life ethers in the process of evolutionary metamorphosis. He describes there how our world has gone through three previous stages of planetary transformation. Adopting the names of planets to designate these evolutionary phases he describes them in order as: Ancient Saturn, Ancient Sun and Ancient Moon. The process of evolution described here is not caused by chance but through the continuous work of spiritual beings known within the Grail tradition as the Spiritual Hierarchies.[7]

At the stage of Ancient Saturn, an all-permeating *warmth* became the basis for a future physical world. Steiner asks us to imagine this warmth as a *qualitative* substance, not reducible to the quantitative and hypothetical activity of atomic particles but, in the full Goethean sense, as a living reality. This state of warmth was the element for certain beings, much as the earth is the element for human beings, animals and plants now.

During this planetary state, some of these beings were going through their human or ego stage of evolution. Steiner called these particular beings 'Archai' or 'Spirits of Personality'. These beings: 'caused their own being to be rayed back to them from the Saturn bodies, and this very process bestows upon the Saturn bodies the fine substantiality which was described above as warmth.'[8]

This development took place towards the middle of the Saturn evolutionary period. At this time the warmth ether, relating to the element of fire, became active. Within evolution its function is to bring about at the upper border of physical nature the chaos which allows the material to be opened up to impression by the life forces. We see this in the fertilization of the egg in conception. The sperm introduces chaos into the previously quiescent egg, and the etheric forces flow into the material form, enlivening it and unfolding its latent potential.

Commenting on Saturn evolution in the series of lectures published as *Man as Symphony of the Creative Word*, Rudolf Steiner states that:

This Saturn-condition must be thought of as already containing within itself everything belonging to our planetary system. The separate planets of our planetary system, from Saturn onwards to the moon, were at that time still within Old Saturn—which as you know consisted only of warmth ether, as undifferentiated world-bodies. Saturn, which had not even attained to the density of air, merely warmth ether, contained in an undifferentiated etheric condition everything which later took on independent form, becoming individualized in the separate planets.[9]

The temperature of human blood was first established on Ancient Saturn. Blood during this present Earth evolution becomes the mediator between the highest principle in man—the ego—and the physical body, which was emerging as a *pattern of warmth* on Ancient Saturn. Steiner mentioned this in a lecture given in Stuttgart in 1907:

> It will be interesting to mention here a parallelism about which ordinary science has little to say. What does the man of today have in him of Saturn's warmth? His blood heat. What at that time was distributed over the whole of Saturn has in a measure freed itself and today forms the warm blood of man and animal. When you investigate the temperature of a beehive, you find it to be about the same temperature as that of human blood because, in accordance with the nature of its being, it goes back to the same source as does the human blood.[10]

Having reached this point of evolution, it happened that not all the members of the Archai were able to progress to the next planetary incarnation. During Saturn evolution warmth came into being, but there was no light. Those Archai who were unable to progress to the next stage of evolution remained behind as beings who had only progressed to a state where darkness prevailed. They remained beings of darkness. However, these beings are described by Steiner as still having a vital role to play in evolution:

> ... the retarded Archai ... those Spirits of Personality who manifest not through light but through darkness, are made use of so that the whole course of earth's becoming should progress with well-ordered harmony. They are allotted their right place so that they may make their proper contribution to the regular development of

our existence ... The activity on Saturn with regard to the physical body had to be a constructive one, and that was what was being taken care of on Saturn. The destructive processes in our body take place particularly in the daytime, under the influence of the light, but there was as yet no light during ancient Saturn. This is why the work of Saturn on our physical body was an up-building one.[11]

At the end of this first stage of creation the whole of Saturn evolution enters a state of cosmic sleep that gives way to the next planetary epoch which Steiner called Ancient Sun. Light and space come into being now, and the light ether begins to operate. Air is the element that comes into existence for the first time on Old Sun. Space is that which creates an interval between things and thus a connection can be formed with light, which separates and forms around each object a coloured border. Light separates objects by making them distinguishable from each other.

The germs of the human physical body and of the future mineral kingdom were laid down on Old Saturn along with the activity of the warmth ether. On Old Sun, with the appearance of the light ether, comes the germ of mankind's etheric organism and of the future plant kingdom. Old Sun is also the realm where those beings known to us as the Archangels go through their human, ego-conscious stage.

When this Sun epoch comes to an end, it emerges again, after a period of cosmic rest, as the Ancient Moon epoch. To the germs of the physical and etheric organisms, which have undergone further evolution by this time, are added the astral body, the bearer of sentience and desire. To the mineral and plant kingdoms the animal kingdom is added on Old Moon, and the element of water. The *chemical or tone* ether emerges and becomes active.

We have seen that the astral body is added to the twofold man on Ancient Moon. The astral brings form to the physical through the medium of the etheric body. Through the astral organism the feeling and desire nature of the individual arises, both in the animal and the human kingdoms. Through the variation of tone the human being can convey a multitude of subtle or dramatic differentiations of feeling in music or in the human voice. In the animal world this is at a rudimentary stage where, for example, the tones of a dog's bark can begin to indicate whether the animal is feeling desperate or showing defiance.

In the visual arts the tones of colour and spacial relationships between the objects represented in the picture convey feelings between artist and observer. In sculpture and architecture an experience of mood is conveyed by the relationships of heights, proportions and surfaces.

All that has to do with differentiation and relationship between separate parts is created by the influence of the chemical ether. The present moon still fulfils this formative activity each time a new physical creation enters into being.

Also during the Moon phase of cosmogenesis, the planetary body separated into two members for the first time, namely, a sun, which is neither Ancient Sun or our present sun, and a moon. Steiner explains this as follows:

> ... along with the sun the higher beings and finer substances withdrew from the whole stellar mass as sun, while the coarser substances and the lower beings remained with the Moon. So during the evolution of the Old Moon we have two heavenly bodies instead of one: a sun body harbouring the higher beings, and a Moon body, the dwelling place of the lower beings. Had the whole remained united, with no separation occurring, certain beings who developed on the sundered Moon could not have kept pace with the sun beings: they were not sufficiently mature and therefore had to segregate, cast out, the coarser substances and build themselves a sphere of action apart. Nor could the higher beings have remained united with these coarser substances, for it would have obstructed their more rapid progress. They, too, required a special field for their development and that was the Sun.[12]

The beings of the sun were of a more developed spirituality; those on the moon lagged behind at a coarser stage of development.

Those beings who are known to Christian esotericism as the Angels experienced their human stage of evolution upon Ancient Moon. It was here that they received into themselves from higher powers the self-conscious ego.

After a duration in which the substance and experiences of this evolutionary epoch are absorbed back into the spiritual world, the evolutionary process begins anew. The present evolutionary epoch commences as the one in which the future Spirits of Freedom experience their human phase, that is, our current earth phase. To the warmth, light and chemical ethers is added the life ether. The life ether is connected both with the highest spiritual powers and with the lowest of the elements, earth. The life ether's activity can be found before the coming into being of matter and at its dissolution. If the life ether, then, is to do with the coming into being of matter, it could also be described as 'the coming into matter of being'.

To the threefold human organism that has passed over to the Earth phase from the three previous epochs is added, in this fourth evolutionary period, the individual human ego. The ego, like the life ether, has the task of working down into and transforming matter. Whilst all the evolving spiritual beings have had an ego phase, the conditions in which this phase has occurred has never been as dense, dangerous and difficult as the Earth phase. Because of this, for the present-day human being the greatest possibilities and the most profound dangers open up. Whilst those beings who experienced their ego-development on Ancient Saturn, Sun and Moon have developed self-conscious ego awareness, the environment in which that awareness was gained presented them with less challenge than the present state does to modern man. Therefore the heights to which the ego could be evolved, the capacity for free will and independence were not available to the degree that they are now. It is this crucial development, the consciousness soul development, which, as we have seen, is still in progress today.

With the Earth epoch the individual human ego enters into the process of reincarnation. The ego incarnates into an organism built up of three sheaths—the astral, etheric and physical bodies—and has the task of permeating and transforming them. The great task, laid as a seed within the human soul, is the attainment of free will and independence.

With the separation of the planetary system into two members during Ancient Moon evolution, when two groups of beings were separated out, there was a pre-enactment of the event known as the Fall which happened during Earth evolution. This is when other elements began to enter into human evolution. In preparation for this it might be helpful to quote from a passage from Steiner's *Genesis* lectures:

> ...we have to realize that whether beings attain their goal or whether they stop at an earlier stage of evolution, all these things happen from out of cosmic wisdom, and that whenever beings remain behind at a particular stage, it means something. It means just as much to evolution as a whole whether beings remain behind or whether they attain their goal; in other words, there are certain functions which cannot be carried out at all by the progressive beings, and for these functions beings are needed who remain behind at an earlier stage. Their backwardness puts them in exactly the right place.[13]

Each time our planet goes into a new phase, it passes first through a re-staging of the previous evolutionary phases. When the present earth reached its recapitulation of the Ancient Sun stage a time was reached which legends refer to as Paradise.[14]

> It is really not easy to portray the splendour of the earth at that time. We must perceive it as a light-filled globe, shone round by light-bearing clouds and generating wonderful phenomena of light and colour. Had one been able to feel the earth with one's hands one would have perceived warmth-phenomena. The luminous masses surged back and forth. Within them were all of the human beings of today, woven through by all the spiritual beings, who rayed forth light in manifold grandeur and beauty. Outside was the earth-cosmos in its great variety; inside with the light flowing about him was man, in close connection with the divine-spiritual beings, raying streams of light into the outer light-sphere... From the beginning the earth was not only glowing and shining but was also resounding.[15]

This passage illustrates how, at the beginning of the present stage, sun, moon, earth and the other heavenly bodies interpenetrated one another with the four ethers working together in balance.

In the Grail legend this stage is represented as the 'Grail castle'. It is a region that still exists but is outside the three-dimensional continuum of measure, number and weight. This region is the etheric realm, *the realm from which the life force streams and can be thought of as a vast cosmic ocean which stretches to the zodiac and controls and qualifies the planetary movements while also imbuing the tiniest living creatures with life and motion.*

In Parzival's search for the Holy Grail he enters the Grail castle, and witnesses there the mystery of man and the cosmos out of which he has been created, but does not yet understand the living relationship between the celestial hierarchies who weave creation from beyond the world of senses.[16]

Rudolf Steiner has described the Holy Grail as living forces. These living forces are the etheric forces which we share with the earth and the organic kingdoms of nature. In Wolfram von Eschenbach's *Parzival* we read that:

> The Gral was the very fruit of bliss, a cornucopia of the sweets of this world and such that it scarcely fell short of what they tell us of the Heavenly Kingdom ... For whichever liquor a man held out in his cup, whatever drink a man could name ... by virtue of the Gral he could see it there in his cup.[17]

Here in the Grail legend the Holy Grail is described as having the power to bring new creation into being in matter. This is the particular function of the two higher ethers. The marvellous properties of the Grail demonstrate the activity of the chemical and life ethers as they work into matter, causing all of the diverse forms of nature to come into being.

The Holy Grail is described here as a *cornucopia*. If we look at a picture of a cornucopia (see over) and then observe the phenomena of nature we find its form again in the shape that water manifests in the formation of a vortex. We now know that the similarity is not only visual, for the vortex in water is an organ which links the etheric world to the physical and is the conduit along which information for creation is funnelled into matter.

The vortex as it channels information from the etheric dimension into the physical through the medium of the chemical ether is representing the harmonic interaction of the planetary bodies.

In addition to its connection with the water out of which a vortex is

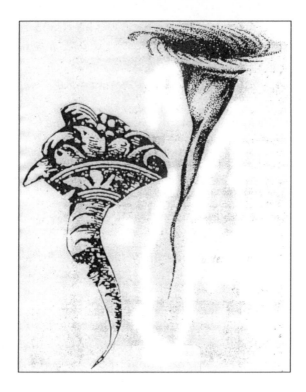

formed, the chemical ether is also manifest in sound. Steiner, when describing 'Paradise', states: 'From the beginning the earth was not only glowing and shining but was also resounding.'[18]

We are now reminded of the opening words of St John's Gospel: 'In the beginning was the Word and the Word was with God and the Word was God.'[19]

The laws governing the possibility of abundance in nature, represented by the cornucopia as Holy Grail in Wolfram von Eschenbach's description of the Grail castle, are mysteriously but realistically connected with sound, with the Cosmic Word, the LOGOS of which we hear at the beginning of St John's Gospel. If mankind knew the secret of these laws, he would receive not only whatever his heart desired from creation, but also perfect health in body, soul and spirit. The Grail legend gives a realistic description of the early paradise time of the earth, and it is at the same time describing the etheric realm which forms an interface with that time in evolution.

In addition to describing the two higher ethers as the Grail, Rudolf

Steiner also calls them the Tree of Life. The two lower ethers are the Tree of Knowledge.

The Fall

After a certain duration the original blissful paradise state was interrupted by the event of which we learn in many of the religious books that has been described as the Fall. We have seen that certain beings can lag behind the normal course of evolution. In his book *Man or Matter* Ernst Lehrs describes Steiner's view that these fallen beings have an essential role in bringing about the development of a higher consciousness in man. By opposing him they strengthen him. Through them man may 'experience those forms of opposition which he needs in order to gain the forces without which he could not reach the goal of his evolution. By the same token, every step man makes towards this goal becomes at the same time a step towards the redemption of those beings.'[20]

Elsewhere Rudolf Steiner describes the luciferic rebellion against the progressive stream of evolution that resulted in the Fall:

> An impulse arose in a number of the Third Hierarchy to develop an inner life of their own. Everything else was simply the result, the consequence of this impulse. What then was this result? It was in fact a terrible one, namely, the betrayal of their own nature; untruth, falsehood... You should understand that the spirits of the Third Hierarchy that had this impulse did not do what they did for the sake of lying, but in order to develop an independent life of their own; but in so doing they had to take the consequence, they had to become Spirits of Untruth—spirits that betrayed their own being—in other words, Spirits of Lies... Now all the spiritual beings which in this way, through betraying their own nature, arose as a second category besides the spirits of the Third Hierarchy are called in occultism luciferic spirits. These beings whom we may call the rebels of the Third Hierarchy had brought about nothing less than the actual independence of man—making it possible for him to develop an independent life of his own.[21]

The Fall as described by Steiner caused a split in the ethers as far as man's ability to control them was concerned. This meant that they did not work through mankind (and the animal kingdom) in a uniform way. Several effects were simultaneously caused by this. One of them was that procreation, which should have come about autonomously, was divided between *two kinds of being: male and female*.

> Now if we compare the etheric body of a human being incarnated in a male organism with one incarnated in a female, we see that the different formative forces [ethers] have been diverted ... by the two sexes into [opposite poles] of the body and, for this reason, have assumed quite different functions in the psychical and physical organism ...
>
> If we assign to the human being an upper, spiritually creative pole and a lower physical pole, we may say:
>
> The male organism is so constructed that,
>> warmth and light ether prevail at the physically creative pole.
>> chemical and life ether prevail at the spiritually creative pole.
>
> The female organism is so constructed that,
>> chemical and life ether prevail at the physically creative pole.
>> warmth and light ether prevail at the spiritually creative pole.
>
> Or, to state it otherwise, in the male being a female ether body is active in the spiritual and psychic domain, and in the female being a male ether body is active in the spiritual and psychic domain.[22]

To create harmony, a fusion of both male and female is necessary so that all four ethers can combine. When we investigate this spiritual-scientific fact, a beginning can be made towards solving the gender problems that we face today. It also provides us with a background to the mystery of a possible union between Jesus and Mary Magdalene and an explanation of the feminine appearance of the 'John' figure in Leonardo da Vinci's *The Last Supper* (although this cannot be described in detail here).

Rudolf Steiner has not only described the two higher ethers as the 'Grail' but also points out that they are referred to in the Book of Genesis as the 'Tree of Life' and the two lower ethers, the warmth and light ethers, as the 'Tree of Knowledge'. The story of Adam and Eve eating the apple from the Tree of Knowledge is a realistic pictorial illustration of the second effect caused by the split in the ethers at the Fall.

> [When] light ether permeated the organism of man to excess, this led to a cleavage in the use of the formative forces in man's organism, thereby differentiating male and female physically as well as spiritually ... this process was connected with an enlightenment of the consciousness in relation to its environment.[23]

This meant that the faculty of *thinking* came into being for mankind as a direct result of his newly acquired control over the warmth and light ethers. This is illustrated in the Book of Genesis as Adam and Eve eating the apple from the Tree of Knowledge.

> The permeation of warmth and life ether, the lucifer forces into the earth-sphere signified for the human organism acceptance of the forces of the 'Tree of Knowledge' ... This event shown in the Old Testament as the 'Temptation', the eating of the fruit of the 'Tree of Knowledge', indicates that man has accepted the forces surging in upon him which he was unable to resist.[24]

Following this event it was necessary that a greater danger should be avoided. If the luciferic influences had been allowed to penetrate the astral body at that time the two higher ethers—chemical and life ethers—would also have been affected by the Fall. This would have happened because the astral makes contact with the etheric body via the chemical ether and therefore the luciferic contamination of the astral body would have had a detrimental effect on the two higher ethers, the chemical and life ethers. Just as the Fall had given man control over the warmth and light ethers, permeation of the chemical and life ethers would have eventually given mankind *conscious control* of the life processes.

> Man could not remain as he was after he had taken the luciferic influences into himself, he must be protected from the luciferic influences in his astral body. This was achieved by making the man of that time incapable of using the whole of his etheric body, part of the etheric body was withdrawn from man's jurisdiction. If this

beneficial action had not taken place, if he had retained power over the whole of his etheric body, he would never have been able to find his way rightly through earth evolution... That is the inner meaning of the teaching that when Man had attained the distinction between good and evil ... then partaking of the Tree of Life was also withdrawn from him. That is to say, man retained absolute power over the forces of warmth and light ether only; power over the formative forces of sound and life ether were withdrawn from him.[25]

As a direct result of this loss of the Tree of Life man's physical body, which hitherto had been composed of warmth, light and air, contracted, condensed and formed a body that was first of all fluid and later solid:

And it is not at all a figure of speech, but fairly literally describes the situation when I say that, because of the contraction of the human body brought about by the luciferic influence, the human being became heavier and descended out of the periphery onto the surface of the earth. That was the withdrawal from paradise as described in picture form. Not until now did man acquire so to speak the force of gravity to sink down from the periphery onto the earth's surface. This is the descent of man onto the physical earth, what brought him right down to earth, whereas he had hitherto dwelt in its periphery. Therefore the luciferic influence has to be reckoned among the actual formative forces which have fashioned man.[26]

As the condensation and solidification of the earth intensified, certain beings concerned with the forces of the life ether and with the future 'ego-consciousness' of humanity could no longer endure matter which had condensed as far as the watery state. These beings are described by Steiner as the 'Six Sun Elohim'.

Out of the whole earth-mass they separate the substances which alone are suited to their use, and take their departure to make themselves a new dwelling place in the Sun. Henceforth they work onto the earth from without, from the Sun. Man, on the other hand, needs for his further evolution a scene of action where matter will condense still more.[27] Six [of the Elohim] made the sun their dwelling place and what streams down to us in the physical light of the sun contains within it the spiritual force of love from these six spirits of light . . . One separated from the others and took a different path for the salvation of humanity. He did not choose the sun but the moon for his abode. And this spirit of light who voluntarily renounced life upon the sun and chose the moon instead is none other than the one whom the Old Testament calls 'Yahweh' or 'Jehovah'.[28]

Because of the very immature condition of humanity at that time, it was vital for the Higher Hierarchies guiding evolution to remove the two higher ethers (the Grail, the Tree of Life) to create new sun and moon spheres outside the earth. In the case of the removal of the sun the Book of Genesis describes what happened very accurately. After God 'drove out the man, he placed at the East side of the Garden of Eden Cherubims and a flaming sword which turned every way to keep the way of the tree of life.'[29] This might be compared with a description of the surface of the sun as seen through a modern telescope. Here we might bear in mind that the activity of the life ether is known to modern science as 'Zero-point-energy' or 'Anti-matter'. In his book *The Sun*, Georg Blattmann, a priest and scientist, describes the surface of the sun.

> The surface, which appears so smooth and shining to the naked eye, appears through the telescope as a bubbling, boiling cauldron and very grainy . . . A mighty seething of currents, a conglomeration of furnaces, a clashing together of darkness and light, a collision of foaming tidal waves, towering up one moment and thrusting down the next, a wild ebullience of thunder and lightning; all of which must be accompanied by the sound of a roaring hurricane in terms of terrestrial experience. That is what is shown us in the boundary zone where opposing worlds of matter and antimatter rub against one another, collide and separate in eternal, incompatible turbulence.[30]

Modern science has recently corroborated a fact that Steiner many times pointed to, namely, that the interior of the sun is cool, a realm of the etheric world, of 'anti-matter'. The passage from the Book of

Genesis quoted above precisely describes the Cherubim's 'flaming sword'; this could be seen as the outer surface of the sun which conceals the Tree of Life, the region of the pure life ether that was removed to 'East of Eden' at the Fall. The comparison is reinforced by the ancient Persians' understanding of the nature of the sun.

> When the Persian looked up to heaven, then he knew that behind the surface of the sky, hidden by the darkness of the heavens, shines the Spiritual Sun. At one spot it becomes visible, where the Sun's disc appears. Out of this wonderful radiant background of gold appear the coloured forms of the Gods seen in imagination. This experience is reflected in Persian art ... for example in the Persian mosaics, where the most beautifully coloured pictures appear on a golden background. The sun is the door, but is also the Guardian before the door, for in looking up to this Guardian the earthly glance perishes. He who later spoke the words: 'I am the door' and 'No man comes to the golden radiance of the world foundation (to the Father) but by Me', He was still experienced in cosmic space as the Sun Spirit in the most ancient Persian time.[31]

The physical sun that is dangerous to perceive with the naked eye stands as both the marker and protector of the point where matter ends and spirit begins. Steiner mentions that, after the departure of the sun, the moon was moved to its present position by the Seventh Elohim, Yahweh. Steiner tells us that the subtle, spiritual counterparts of the other planets of the solar system, *excluding Uranus and Neptune*, also left the original paradise state and, following the Fall, became points of matter in space. After the Fall, the sun's rays channelled the life ether, which is experienced during the daytime when it affects the earth from a *vertical* direction. The effect of the chemical ether is received by night when the moon works upon the earth from a *horizontal* position. Together with the light ether the chemical and life ethers have left a 'fallen' residue within the earth when they were removed to the spiritual spheres of sun and moon.

When one considers this description of the Fall, the Manichaean and Gnostic idea of the earth as a 'secondary' and not original creation, involving the activity of the 'Demiurge', becomes understandable. The *original creation* proceeded from the Godhead. The *creation in matter* is a direct result of the Fall, which was instigated by Lucifer and compounded by the other adversary Ahriman, the Zoroastrian god of darkness.

Luciferic powers took hold of human nature in an attempt to accelerate human evolution, breaking humanity free from the holistic grip of the spiritual world in order to set mankind upon the path to individuality. Since that time Lucifer has manifest as a power calling mankind onwards, back towards the spiritual world. Ahrimanic forces incorporated themselves into the human being for a different reason. They wished to bind man to the material earth for all eternity, and also wished, through mankind, to mechanize the universe into their own image. Luciferic illusion, manifesting as a weightless spirituality, became one of the balancing poles of human nature. At the other extreme, the forces of soulless death, void of any redeeming spirituality, worked towards creating a counterbalance.

4.
The Triple Goddess

At the Fall many things were sundered. Our original spiritual home, the paradise state of the earth, faded as a new and unfamiliar physical world solidified. The creation of the Gnostic Demiurge, earth, moon, planets and the directions of the zodiac became points of matter in a dark and empty space from which the music of the spheres could no longer be heard. As the consciousness soul age was beginning, its guiding figures were aware of this; Shakespeare was one of them:

> Sit Jessica: look, how the floor of heaven
> Is thick inlaid with patines of bright gold:
> There's not the smallest orb which thou behold'st
> But in his motion like an angel sings,
> Still quiring to the young-eyed cherubins;
> Such harmony is in immortal souls;
> But, whilst this muddy vesture of decay
> Doth grossly close it in, we cannot hear it.[1]

Humanity was split in two—male and female. The highest power of the life force, the Tree of Life, was hidden behind the flaming sword of the Cherubim—the towering leaping flames on the surface of the sun. Mankind was left with the increasingly limited power of the Tree of Knowledge to guide him through the thousands of years that followed. The remaining subtle energy of the earth and its creatures had been thrust down to a realm below matter to become electricity, magnetism and the 'terrible force of destruction', which Steiner referred to as the 'Third Force' and said of it that 'it can only be hoped that before some discoverer gives this force into the hands of humankind men will no longer have anything unmoral left in them'.[2]

Over the last three or four decades there has been much interest in 'earth energy' at sacred sites. As the New Age has progressed, interest in this manifestation has become increasingly connected with a rediscovery of the Goddess in her various aspects and the pagan religions have been turned to for a spiritual backdrop to the many new discoveries of measurable energy in ancient sacred places. In numerous cases these energies have been described by new fringe science as electromagnetic. It seems increasingly possible that these places also manifest the qualitative, negative space of the etheric realm, which cannot be monitored by electronic equipment, together with its fallen, measurable electromagnetic counterpart.

In a lecture titled 'The Interrelation of Man and Cosmos', given on 1 February 1947, Walter Johannes Stein correlated electricity, magnetism and the Third Force with the three concentric layers within the earth, realms described as the domain of the Mothers in Goethe's *Faust*. According to a report of this lecture:

> Dr Stein said that these three layers are the earth's past, the relic of its past evolution still buried within it. 'At the central core lies Old Saturn, above it the stratum which is Old Sun and the outermost layer, coming beneath the mineral earthly surface, is the relic of Old Moon evolution ... Mephistopheles spoke of the Mothers with the greatest awe as goddesses unknown to men, and told Faust that he "must burrow to the uttermost Profound" if he would find them in the 'ever-empty Far'".[3]

Many years earlier in a lecture on Goethe's *Faust*, Rudolf Steiner had described how the Mothers represented the stages of planetary metamorphosis prior to Earth evolution. He connected Demeter to Moon evolution, Persephone to Sun evolution, and Rea to Saturn evolution.

The Mothers of Ancient Greek tradition represent the fallen counterpart of the ethers. They also can be seen as representative of the *potential for transformation* into the pure etheric condition as it was before the Fall.

In the *Faust* lecture Rudolf Steiner described the Mothers as personifications of the pure life force in its different aspects as it originated on Ancient Saturn, Ancient Sun and Ancient Moon respectively:

> Let us ask ourselves what the Greeks looked for in their three Mothers, Rea, Demeter and Persephone. In these three Mothers they saw a picture of those forces that, working down out of the cosmos, prepare the human cell. These forces however do not come

from the part of the cosmos that belongs to the physical but to the supersensible. The Mothers, Demeter, Rea and Persephone, belong to the supersensible world. No wonder then that Faust has the feeling that an unknown Kingdom is making its presence felt when the word 'Mothers' is spoken . . . For all the forces that are in Saturn, Sun and Moon are still working—working on into our own time.[4]

The Goddess is the creative impulse behind the coming into being of creation. In the Three Mothers we have the Triple Goddess evolving in creative strength from Persephone to Demeter—Spring forces to Summer forces—to the Crone when the laws of matter release their hold and the spiritual forms return to their source, as summer turns to autumn and then comes winter. This power moves from spiritual cause to material manifestation, but it can also be an ominous destructive force in its fallen aspect. The Hindu goddess Kali demonstrates this.

A connection can also be made between the Mothers and their Christian counterparts: the Virgin Mary, Mary Magdalene and the enigmatic figure behind the Black Madonna. The identity of the latter is hard to establish. She could be Anne, traditional mother of the Virgin, a position which echoes the relationship between Demeter and Persephone. But she also possesses an ancient quality which identifies her with Rea, namely, her *blackness* which is reminiscent of the darkness of Ancient Saturn, the primal origins of matter.

Both Cathars and Templars settled in locations where the Goddess is variously manifest in the energies that rise up from the fallen etheric domain beneath their feet. The energy that is experienced at Rennes-le-Château, particularly within the church, seems to be a definite example of the deepest of the fallen ethers which we have related to Kali. The Egyptian version of the same archetype is Nepthys, the consort of Set, who can be considered as belonging to the same archetype as the backward Archai on Ancient Saturn, Time Spirits who, it will be remembered, are involved in the building of matter in the darkness of night, echoing the darkness of Ancient Saturn. Another author involved in the Rennes mystery, David Wood, also found evidence of a connection with Set together with Isis in the landscape at Rennes. As the three layers of the earth also correspond to the fallen energies and their indwelling beings, we can begin to understand why the Triple Goddess has been so vilified by the Church and changed to St Anne, the Mother of the Virgin Mary, the Virgin Mary, and Mary Magdalene.

If Rea, Persephone, Demeter/Anne, the Virgin Mary and Mary Magdalene relate to the Ancient Saturn, Sun and Moon evolutions, to the physical, etheric and astral principles in turn, then who personifies this Earth evolution for which the Goddesses have prepared? Later in this book we will see that it is the Christ Being, recognized by the Gnostics, who becomes the Higher Ego of all of mankind and who rescues the lower ego from the Fall at a time when it was not yet strong enough to withstand the intervention of first luciferic and then later ahrimanic beings. Our earth occupies the central position in a progression of seven planetary incarnations; it is the turning-point in evolution.

Through the Goddess, whose face has constantly changed, the development towards physical incarnation is achieved. Once this descent into matter has been reached, the way back again can begin as an inner process through the activity of the human ego which, as we have seen, makes its first appearance during Earth evolution. The centre of the labyrinth has been reached. If the thread which has been brought to this point in time by the Goddess is once more traced outwards, the whole of creation can be taken forward to a completely new, gradually spiritualizing state through the next three incarnations of the earth. The Goddess has given birth to matter. She has borne humanity into Earth evolution. Now, during the remaining half of earth's incarnations, human beings must work towards the increasing transformation of their latent spiritual faculties in cooperation with the Goddess. This gradually happens as work on the astral body progresses from the stage of the sentient soul, through the intellectual soul stage to the consciousness soul, which finally transforms the astral body into Spirit Self. These three soul stages are, in turn, represented by Mary Magdalene, Mary Cleophas and, finally, the 'Mother of Christ' or the 'Divine Sophia',[5] the last being representative of the fully developed consciousness soul.

Since the consciousness soul is the principle in which the Spirit Self has evolved, we call it the 'Mother of Christ' or, in the esoteric schools, the 'Virgin Sophia'. Through fecundation of the Virgin Sophia, the Christ could be born in Jesus of Nazareth. In the esoteric schools of Dionysius, the intellectual and sentient souls were called respectively 'Mary' and 'Mary Magdalene'.[6]

When the astral body has been transformed into Spirit Self, it is then able to return to the etheric body the full power of its 'Paradise' condition, reincorporating the Tree of Life. In the future, this transformed etheric body becomes Life Spirit, which is then capable of transforming the physical body into Spirit Man.

This goal has been the aim of the underground stream that ran through the mysteries, the old esoteric schools, Cathars, Templars, Rosicrucians, who all understood the central importance of the Goddess, both in her ancient and future significance.

5.

Christ Energy: The Power of Transformation

The significance of the incarnation

At the Council of Nicaea in AD 325, the dispute as to whether Christ, the Son, was of the same essence as the Father or only of like essence to that of the Father put a seal on the fate of the following centuries of Christianity. The Gnostic interpretation of Christ was an echo of the ancient mystery wisdom that combined a vision of Christ (still in spiritual spheres) with wisdom relating to the universe. Rudolf Steiner has described how modern Christianity can have very little knowledge or understanding of the deep discussions that took place among the Church Fathers during the early centuries over the way in which the two natures—the divine and the human—had been combined in the personality of Jesus of Nazareth. In this chapter we will see how this lost understanding of the dual nature of Jesus Christ has been restored by Rudolf Steiner's spiritual research.

> Where there is an understanding of Jesus only, the Christian sacrament perishes, and with it both Christian knowledge and Christian life. Then all that is left is only human thought, human words, human morality. Only when a new understanding of Christ is achieved can sacrament, word and life be again filled with higher forces.[1]

In the paradise state we were not separate from the Divinity. We are derived from the same source as the Divinity. Then, at the Fall, the Six Sun Elohim removed the highest ether, the life ether, to form a new sun sphere. As a result this previous close connection was interrupted and changed into a new relationship between the Six Elohim in the sun sphere and humanity remaining on earth. After the Fall these Six Sun Elohim, who manifest the Christ, begin to work on the prototype for a human individuality from the spiritual sphere of the sun

It is inspiring if we remember that the emblem for Celtic Christianity is a sun-cross and then connect this continued activity of the

Elohim from the sun sphere with the following statement of Rudolf
Steiner's: 'Only towards the end of the Atlantean period, *approximately
in the region of modern Ireland*, does man begin to manifest ego-
consciousness and become able to think clearly and logically.'[2]

This new development takes place together with the parallel
development of human conscience.

> From an esoteric standpoint the arising of conscience is associated
> principally with the working of the ego-impulse within the sentient
> soul, which calls forth within man a kind of dim memory of his
> paradisaical condition *before* the Fall and at the same time enables
> him to be inwardly aware of the voice of that part of his soul—a
> kind of 'inner Ireland'—where divine forces untouched by any-
> thing earthly are still preserved.[3]

The Celtic sun-cross is a visual reminder that the Six Sun Elohim,
representing the highest ether, the life ether, the Christ, was worshipped in the sun sphere as a Sun Being by many pagan peoples
through those thousands of years between the Fall and the Incarnation.

Hymn to the Sun Being

The mighty one, bearing the royal promise
The sun–ether–aura, created by God,
We worship in prayer
That will be transferred to the most victorious of redeemers

And the others, his apostles,
Who further the world,
That enables them to overcome age and death,
Decay and putrefaction
That helps them to eternal life,
To thrive eternally,

To free will.
When the dead rise again,
When the living conquerer of death comes
And through his will the world will be advanced
Further.[4]

This hymn from the Zoroastrian book the Avesta was written six hundred years before the incarnation of Christ in Jesus at the Baptism in the Jordan in his thirtieth year.

As time passed the effect of the Tree of Life energy would have become weaker in all the life-systems of the earth, significantly in human blood in which the Tree of Life energy no longer pulsed with the primal power of chemical and life ethers. One human individual had remained in the spiritual world who did not incarnate after the Fall and therefore retained the possibility of possessing the full force of all four ethers in his bloodstream. This was the Jesus individual we hear of in Luke's Gospel. Rudolf Steiner explains that this is why his genealogy is traced back beyond Adam to God.

At the incarnation of Christ in the Luke Jesus' body, the Sun Logos is returned to the earth with the potential of becoming the highest principle in all individual human beings in the future. This would renew the activity of the Tree of Life within the human bloodstream.

Whence came the Christ? He came from those very regions that have been closed to man by the temptation of Lucifer, from the region of the Music of the Spheres, from the region of the cosmic life. With his soul man really belongs to the region of the living cosmic ether. But he was driven out from it. And so it is given to him again, so that by degrees he may once more be able to imbue himself with that which he had forfeited.[5]

The writers of *The Holy Blood and the Holy Grail* construed the Holy Grail to be a bloodline reaching back from Jesus, through Solomon to King David. The authors find an enigma in the Bible which they themselves point to but which they cannot explain. This enigma leads us directly to the answer coming from Rudolf Steiner's research regarding *two Jesus Children*. In this answer one finds not only evidence that negates the possibility of an external bloodline passing through Jesus as bearer of the Christ; it also indicates the real and *esoteric reality* of the Grail. Here is this enigma as described in the *Holy Blood and the Holy Grail* by Baigent, Lee and Lincoln:

Only two of the Gospels—Matthew and Luke—say anything at all about Jesus' origins and birth; and they are flagrantly at odds with each other. According to Matthew, for example, Jesus was an aristocrat, if not a rightful and legitimate king—descended from David via Solomon. According to Luke, on the other hand, Jesus' family, though descended from the house of David, was of somewhat less exalted stock... The two genealogies, in short, are so strikingly discordant that they might well be referring to two quite different individuals.

The discrepancies between the Gospels are not confined to the question of Jesus' ancestry and genealogy. According to Luke, Jesus on his birth was visited by shepherds. According to Matthew, he was visited by kings.[6]

Their interest in this discrepancy may also have been highlighted by the fact that behind the altar in the church at Rennes are *two* Jesus children, one held by Joseph, the other by Mary.

A plaque on the wall explains:

The Two Statues of Baby Jesus

Mary, Mother of God is always shown with her Son, the Virgin of Apparition and the Woman of the Apocalypse are shown without a child. The other infant in Joseph's arms symbolizes paternity.

Rudolf Steiner many times described how *two human beings* prepared the body into which the incarnation of Christ took place in the thirtieth year of Jesus' life. Steiner's words on the subject remained uncorroborated for nearly half a century until the discoveries at Nag Hammadi and Qumran. From Qumran in the *Testaments* it is said: 'For the Lord will raise up from Levi a High Priest, and from Judah a King, who will save all the Gentiles and the tribe of Israel.'[7] Andrew Welburn has written extensively on these findings. In his *The Beginnings of Christianity* he tells us that

The Essene evaluation is confirmed by the Qumran Scrolls... The kingly Messiah is again 'the shoot of David', and pre-eminently 'the Messiah of Israel' who will bring death to the ungodly and establish 'the kingdom of his people'. More important, however, is the priestly Messiah; he and the 'Messiah of Aaron'—Aaron having been a priest and companion of Moses—and thus 'the Priest', and 'the Interpreter of the Law' . . . The kingly Messiah is to defer to his judgment . . . in all matters of the Law . . . Startling as it may at first seem, the religious groups who like the Essenes created and guarded the traditions about the coming of a Messianic Priest and a King Messiah expected them to be fulfilled by separate individuals. Before the discovery of the Dead Sea Scrolls, the only clear statement of this double expectation was in the writings and lectures based on Rudolf Steiner's researches.[8]

'The Kingly Messiah' is the Jesus whose lineage is described in Matthew's Gospel, an individual who has been incarnated many times, gradually gaining in experience and wisdom and so overcoming the effects of the Fall of man as it has been described in the Book of Genesis.

Twelve years after the Nativity this individual of the kingly line merged with the child of the priestly line referred to in Luke's Gospel. This happened in a manner which has been described with great care and detail by Rudolf Steiner in his many books and lectures, particularly those on the Gospels. This mysterious happening took place shortly before Jesus was found by his family in learned discussion with the doctors in the temple at Jerusalem. The innocent, loving child seemed to have become a wise young boy, gifted with great knowledge, in the space of a few days.

From twelve years onwards the individual described at the beginning of Matthew's Gospel developed within the physical body and life-processes of the human being described in Luke's Gospel, until he, in turn surrendered that body with its particular life-processes to the incarnating Christ at the Baptism in the thirtieth year. The *body* of Jesus described in Matthew's Gospel, who was visited by Kings, and in which hereditary blood could be traced back through Solomon to David, was not that into which Christ *incarnated*. This means that claims of a hereditary bloodline connected with Jesus Christ are void.

The human being described in Luke's Gospel, who was visited by shepherds, was the 'Priestly Messiah' referred to in the Qumran texts. He developed a body already carrying blood which was of a different quality from the blood of the rest of mankind, a quality which would have been present in all of humanity if the Fall had not occurred. This body carried *the original prototype of the blood of all humanity*.

Thus after the Fall certain forces were no longer in 'Adam', and still the *guiltless* part of his being was nurtured and fostered in the great Mother Lodge of humanity. This was, so to speak, the Adam Soul as yet untouched by human guilt, not yet entangled in what had actually caused the 'Fall' of man. These pristine forces of the Adam-individuality were preserved; they were there and were then led as a *provisional* 'Ego' to the child born to Joseph and Mary . . .

Who, then, was the Being in the child born to Joseph and Mary of the Nathan line? The progenitor of humanity, the 'old Adam' as a 'new Adam'! This secret was known to St Paul and lies behind his words. And St Luke, the writer of the Gospel—who was a pupil of St Paul—knew it too. For this reason he speaks of it in a special way. He knew that a very definite process was necessary in order that this spiritual substance might be let down to humanity; he knew that a blood relationship reaching back to 'Adam' was necessary. Hence for Joseph he shows a lineage reaching back to Adam who issued directly from the spiritual world and in the word of the Gospel was a 'son of God'.[9] The sequence of generations is traced back to God himself.

The Luke Jesus is therefore an individual who is descended from no 'royal bloodline', but the mystery of his incarnation and of the special quality of his blood is the *esoteric mystery of the Holy Grail*.

At the Baptism in the Jordan the Sun Spirit descended into the man Jesus, who received him as the final stage in a process that had taken two human individuals long ages to prepare. The Matthew Jesus individual, incarnate in the Luke body, then become the first bearer of the Higher Ego, prepared by the Six Sun Elohim, within the astral, etheric and physical sheaths.

Zechariah, the father of John the Baptist, had prophesied the imminent appearance upon earth of the Sun Spirit: '. . . because of the tender mercy of our God, by which the rising sun will come to us from heaven to shine on those living in darkness.'[10]

At this point the effect of the Fall begins to be reversed. The only way for the Logos[11] to re-enter evolution was to descend into matter and enter into such an intimate relationship with humanity that the individual ego could be transformed by a free, subjective recognition of the divine essence within itself and other human beings.

> The pre-human event—the Fall of Man—needed a counterpoise, but this again was not a concern of human beings, but of the Gods among themselves. And we shall see that this action had to take its course as deeply into matter as the first action had taken place above it. The God had to descend as deeply into matter as He had allowed man to sink into matter.[12]

Central to the spiritual research of Rudolf Steiner and to all of the practical activities arising from this research, central to anthroposophy, which reopens the ancient mysteries as a twenty-first century continuation of esoteric Christianity, is the event which Rudolf Steiner referred to as the Mystery of Golgotha. Rudolf Steiner describes how at the Mystery of Golgotha 'In majestic seclusion the Divine Power poured from this deed into the whole subsequent evolution of mankind.'[13] This event took place 'in a remote corner of the earth for the sake of no particular race or denomination'.[14]

We can now begin to understand the significance of the shedding of Jesus Christ's blood on Golgotha. When the blood flowed from the cross two events of immense evolutionary importance occurred. First of all the influence of Lucifer and Ahriman was cast out from the human sheaths so that the Tree of Life forces could be safely returned to the human blood. Secondly, the power of the four ethers was returned to the earth. At the climax of the Crucifixion the Logos passed into the earth.

> ... as the blood flowed from the wounds on Golgotha there occurred a corresponding spiritual event: at this moment it happened for the first time that rays streamed forth from the earth into cosmic space, where formerly there had been none ... Darker and darker had the earth become with the passing of time up to the event on Golgotha. Now the blood flows on Golgotha—and the earth begins to radiate light.[15]

At the event of Golgotha the Sun Spirit became the Spirit of the Earth so that, just as the human ego works through the bodily sheaths to transform them, so it will eventually work together with Christ to transform the earth's sheaths in the same way. At the Last Supper the Christ had already directed the attention of the disciples to the new condition of the earth when he spoke of the *bread* and *wine* as *body* and *blood*, also implying the body and blood of the earth itself. At first this began within the astral sheath of the earth, where Christ could be perceived clairvoyantly as he permeated the earth with the power of a sun, which it will one day become.

Resurrection and transubstantiation

Rudolf Steiner has described how the intervention of Christ in evolution gives the immature human ego the chance to reverse the effect of the Fall within all three of the human sheaths or members, the physical, the etheric and the astral. During the three years of the incarnation of Christ within the body of a human being this process was carried out as a prototype for the future activity of the individual human ego; this future activity is the aim of present Earth evolution.

The oldest and most highly developed of the three sheaths is the physical body, which has now been perfected through the three previous incarnations and during the present incarnation of the earth. The second oldest is the life or etheric body, which passed through two previous stages before it reached this earth state. The third oldest is the astral body, which was prepared on Old Moon. The youngest and most fragile of all is the ego of each individual human being, the spiritual and eternal part which began a separate existence during this present earth state. The Fall separated us from the guidance of the higher beings, leaving this fourth member with almost total responsibility for the direction of the astral sheath which was also very immature. As we have already seen, part of the etheric sheath was also affected by the Fall, while the physical body became subject to both of the traumatic experiences of birth and death.

During the three years this process began with the transformation of the astral body. This takes place as a re-enactment of the original temptation by Lucifer. Jesus was approached by Lucifer in the wilderness where, by withstanding Lucifer's repeated attacks there, he was able to reverse the effect that Lucifer had on the human astral body. The astral body in its transformed state was given the name Spirit Self by Rudolf Steiner, who stated that just as the astral body was prepared during Old Moon evolution so will the Spirit Self become fully developed in a future evolutionary condition—referred to by Steiner as the Jupiter Epoch. Later we will see that this is what John called the New Jerusalem.

Next the event known in the Gospels as the Transfiguration occurred when the Christ Ego fully permeated the etheric body of Jesus. This etheric body was then changed into a 'sun' radiating its own light: 'There he was transfigured before them. His face shone like the sun, and his clothes became as white as the light.'[16]

Only three of the apostles can accompany Christ this far into the macrocosm, into the sphere of the sun itself. Christ's etheric body shines with all the elementary power of the light that was one of the evolutionary goals of Old Sun. This Christ-permeated etheric body was named Life Spirit by Steiner and will only become fully developed in an evolutionary period that will follow the Jupiter phase; this is known as the Venus Epoch of human evolution.

Once the transformation of Jesus' astral and etheric bodies by the Christ energy into the Spirit Self and Life Spirit had been completed it was possible for the transubstantiation of matter in the physical body to be achieved in only three days. During the three days that his body lay in the grave, the final phase of the complete transformation of matter into spirit took place.

Finally in that sublime event of death the Being of Christ fully permeated the disturbed relationship between the etheric and physical bodies. Rudolf Steiner says this re-establishment of harmony 'could take place not as a miracle but as the result of the three years of gradual, progressive re-establishment'[17] of the balance that existed between the members of the human being in the paradise state.

Only one of the apostles can accompany Christ this far. This is the disciple John. He alone of the twelve stands before the cross on Golgotha, participating in Christ's permeation of the physical body. Just as the secrets of Sun and Moon evolution are unveiled to the ego as it penetrates into the etheric and astral sheaths, so does the physical body yield up full knowledge of events on Old Saturn. The fully spiritualized physical body is known as Spirit Man and its attainment by humanity will only occur in the most distant reaches of cosmic evolution, an evolutionary epoch that Steiner named Vulcan. This future planetary incarnation will carry human evolution to its completion, after which humanity will join the Cosmic Hierarchies as a new member: the Hierarchy of 'Freedom'.

During the three days following the event on Golgotha, Christ descended to the centre of the earth. As a result of the Fall a residue of the life ether and of the chemical ether, which had later been removed to create the new moon sphere, were driven down to a realm below matter, a realm which Steiner has described as the 'Realm of the Centric Forces' whose region of activity is related to the earth's centre. The Realm of the Centric Forces is also indwelt by a number of the backward beings that were left in a retrogressive state as the previous incarnations of the earth progressed. There the Christ, incarnate in a human physical body where the laws of matter were at that very moment in the process of reversal, confronted these fallen beings. In his new position as Spirit of the Earth he confronted those beings who had gained in strength there since the Fall. It needed the combination of two different natures that had come together in Jesus of Nazareth to achieve dominion over these spiritual beings, 'the old *Chela* nature deeply connected with the physical plane which could also work effectively on the physical plane and through its power could hold it in balance; on the other hand there was Christ himself who was a purely spiritual being.'[18]

In *The Fifth Gospel* Rudolf Steiner describes how an earthquake followed the darkening of the sun when Jesus' body had been laid in the grave:

> It shook the grave in which the body of Jesus had been laid and the stone covering it was wrenched away; a fissure was rent in the Earth and the corpse was received into it. Another tremor caused the fissure to close again over the corpse. And when the people came in the morning the grave was empty, for the dead body of Jesus had been received into the Earth.[19]

The physical body of Jesus descended into the earth and the transformation of the physical substance took place in those regions where the centric forces predominate, laying the foundation for the future transformation of all physical earthly conditions. The power of those beings particularly concerned with fallen matter was thus held in check and an impulse was then given to the whole of fallen creation by the body of Jesus Christ as it was transformed within the earth. After this the way lay open towards the metamorphosis of the earth into the next planetary incarnation, the Jupiter evolution, the New Jerusalem. Steiner comments:

> The physical body which was laid in the grave was dematerialized to such an extent that it was spread over the whole world, and that is why no body could be found when it was looked for. The Resurrection Body was the ether body which was so densified by the Christ that Thomas was able to touch it, which is as we all know impossible with a usual ether body. It was indicated that it was a different body from the physical one hinted at in the Gospel by the fact that Mary Magdalene and the others did not at first recognize him again.[20]

On Easter Sunday, when the tomb was found empty, the risen figure of Christ was *first* seen by Mary Magdalene—as a fully perfected etheric body, which has total control over the physical realm. If we remember that the human etheric body was split by the effect of the Fall, causing two different types of human being to exist after that time, male and female, then this meeting between Christ and Mary Magdalene just after the completion of Christ's perfected etheric body takes on a new and profound significance. This is not a physical connection in the old sense from this time onwards but a new reality which will apply to everything that was previously governed by the laws of fallen matter. We might take this into consideration when we try to understand the true relationship between Jesus Christ and Mary Magdalene.

When Christ *transformed* his physical body at the Resurrection he also empowered the human ego existing within all of mankind to begin a *similar* process within the various bodies of the human being. Man is now able to join forces with Christ in transubstantiating matter into this new substance that is physical—but a physicality not subject to the effect of the Fall.

The full reality of the Resurrection as an impulse working through human evolution in a *continually* transformative way cannot be grasped unless we pause here to reconsider the work of the ahrimanic beings within the human organism. For Ahriman has brought into evolution the power of the human intellect. This intellect is a *death* force. With its destructive analytic process, it kills the intimate warmth of the soul's life. Essentially, the intellect is to do with what has died, which belongs to the past as opposed to the living immediacy of the life of body and soul. When we were looking at the New Mysteries earlier we considered the need for a *new type of thinking,* a *living* thinking that is holistic and fully self-conscious right down into the depths of its soul-filled activity. The capacity for this thinking came through the Mystery of Golgotha. It is the working of Christ within the sphere of the heart that creates the possibility that thinking can become a spiritual force within human evolution. The Fall had created an inner chasm in humanity, an almost unnegotiable abyss between the human soul and its higher self. The new freedom-filled thinking is the Christ-capacity that will heal the chasm introduced into human consciousness by the Fall.

This understanding can also be found as central to the original, uncorrupted teachings of St Paul. In his letters and teachings Paul outlined the renewed nature of human consciousness, which will be attained when each of us absorbs into ourselves the 'over-lighting' Ego of Christ. The result of this will be a new faculty of cognition, one that has already begun to manifest in its primal radiance in the works of Goethe and Rudolf Steiner. If we think of the many selfless hours spent by Goethe studying the sense-perceptible process of plant formation, we can understand the cognitive dimensions of Paul's teachings on the nature of love: 'Love is patient. Love is kind. It does not envy, it does not boast, it is not proud. It is not rude, it is not self-seeking, it is not easily angered, it keeps no record of wrongs. Love does not delight in evil but rejoices with the truth. It always protects, always trusts, always hopes, always preserves.'[21] This love is the Christ-cognition, which will renew all of human knowledge as it works in transformation right down into the human physical body, reversing the effects of the Fall which subjected the body to the effects of centralization and calcification.

The mission of the earth is thus redirected by combating the cal-

. cifying effect of the centric forces and restoring the original goal of Earth evolution—a state into which the newly created ego of man can work without the danger of being dragged down into a lower sphere. Then the Cosmic Word will once more sound into all the life forms of creation. The three days in the Underworld marked a turning point; seeds have been planted for a process that will gradually increase but which can only be accomplished with the cooperation of human individuals working freely out of their own conviction of the necessity and urgency of the task. The intervention of fallen beings in evolution has made it possible for us to act in freedom, but a heavy price has had to be paid for this. All of the entanglements and complications of materialistic civilization, the horror and perversion that faces us daily in the media, where the truth is distorted to goad humanity into further desperation, is the result of our relationship with the same beings who have made it possible for us to become responsible co-workers with the nine Hierarchies above and Christ beside us. Without the intervention of the fallen beings this possibility would not be there. But as a result the responsibility for mankind is twofold: the transformation of evil and the transubstantiation of fallen matter.

In his short book *Radiant Matter,* Christian Community priest Georg Blattman beautifully explains this rather difficult concept of transubstantiation, in which substance is ' "transported" into another world':

Here we are concerned with the inmost secrets of matter and its transformation, for bread and wine become body and blood. But what is it that makes matter capable of being 'body' in the first place? In our bodies, for example, there are a number of different substances that go into making up our flesh, blood, bones, and so on, all of which can be chemically analysed. But this is not a unique feature, for these substances can be found outside us too. And when we are dead and buried and our body begins to decay, these substances will all be somewhere in the earth, where the rain can come and wash them away. They then belong to the earth. So what is it that makes these substances our bodies? They are our bodies because, in a word, we are inside them. This 'piece of the world' is our tool, but it is much more than a hammer or a pair of pliers, for we are completely inside it, we identify with it. We have slipped into it right down to the individual molecules, so to speak. This is what makes 'matter' into 'body'.

In similar fashion, bread and wine become the body and blood of a divine spiritual being who slips into them, as we have slipped into the various parts of our bodies. When the bread is brought in at the beginning of the service, it is not yet body, but merely a piece of bread. It becomes body when Christ 'incarnates'—becomes flesh— in it.

And now we must perform the final act of uniting the bread and wine—the body and blood—that are already present, but still separate as a true polarity. It is essential that these two opposites be united—and here, man is necessary, for this process can take place only in the person who receives 'Communion' (which means 'becoming one'). The transubstantiated elements merge with man's own substance, but at the same time, bread and wine also become one. Thus those who question the need of giving the Communion in two forms ('Surely bread alone would be sufficient, Christ's blood is "included" in it as body') are only playing with words. For the goal of the whole process up until now has been that this polarity must finally be resolved. And through its resolution, primal unity is achieved on a new level—the counterpart of the origin of the first elements.

Every service at the altar gives the world a 'working model' of the way future evolution will renew the dying earth.[22]

6.

Knights Templar: Guardians of the Grail

Maintaining the higher ethers within the earth

In Wolfram von Eschenbach's *Parzival*, the Templars are described as 'Guardians of the Grail'; in the context of this book, the Grail represents the higher ethers creating the energy of the terrestrial locations over which the Templars chose to settle. The Templars carried on the mission of those who had worked from very early times to purify and raise the energy which had been subject to the dynamic of the Fall as it manifests within the earth. The ancient peoples of north-western Europe built dolmens and stone circles over the energy points, thus directly connecting them with the approaching Christ, the Sun Being who was descending to bring back the higher vibration, the pure life and chemical ethers to the earth.

We know that cathedrals, abbeys and churches have been built over areas of concentrated etheric activity ever since the time that Christianity took over their stewardship. The energies of these places were often transformed by pagan acts of worship long before they were rededicated to Christian saints. Their original fallen quality was gradually raised by constant religious practices, so that one could describe them as having been changed back to the pure etheric state. One might also conjecture that they had never lost that state since paradise had faded at the beginning of Earth evolution. Rudolf Steiner has related:

> Such places were ... sought after by the Druids—places where imaginations lingered long in the atmosphere, and where the influences of nature on human beings was stronger, owing to archaic layers coming to the surface.[1]

In Druid times the sacred grove would have been composed of several varieties of trees, each of them corresponding to a different planet. The grove itself would be imbued with the harmony of the spheres which was merged with the upward rising earth energy over which the grove was positioned. Much later the sacred geometry of the religious buildings covering these same holy places brought in the Cosmic Word in another way. The soaring arches and fan vaulting of the sublime Gothic cathedrals, built with Templar knowledge, subtly echoed a distant memory of the sacred grove. In a lecture entitled 'The Sacred Geometry of Canterbury Cathedral', Colin Dudley remarked how sacred geometry was 'so easy for these architects that they had no need of complicated mathematical head work'.[2] Most of the Templar sacred buildings are dedicated to the Christian form of the Goddess, the Virgin Mary or Mary Magdalene. In *Paths of the Christian Mysteries*, Manfred Schmidt-Brabant refers to Rudolf Steiner's words in this context:

> Thus he says, 'at the centre' of the Templars' teaching stood 'something feminine ... the divine Sophia, the divine wisdom'. This is a key phrase for everything the Templars do. The Templars saw the Mystery of Isis Sophia as a great world-ether Mystery, now become essentially goddess-like ... They venerated Mary Magdalene as the earthly, human reflection of this being.[3]

The 'mystery of man and the cosmos out of which he has been created'[4] is the mystery which the Templars were materializing by incorporating cosmic and human dimensions into the buildings they created: 'As above, so below.'

This endeavour was inspired by their connection with the tradition from which the dimensions of the Temple of Solomon arose. Rudolf Steiner describes this connection in his lecture series *The Temple Legend*: 'And now an outward symbol had to be erected, as man is God's temple. The Temple had to be a symbol, illustrating man's own body'.[5] We might say that, following these indications of Rudolf Steiner, the temple in Jerusalem was a prototype for the transformation that we have to carry out on ourselves to create the New Jerusalem.

> Later, in the Middle Ages, the idea of Solomon's Temple was revived again in the Knights Templar, who sought to introduce the Temple thinking in the west.[6]

The dimensions of Solomon's Temple, when realized in physical form, represent the whole physical organization of man in the future.

It is said of Solomon that 'he carried within him all the cosmic wisdom of the previous mysteries. He could conceive the true temple—he knew the cosmic secrets of the physical body—and he knew the divine measure and secrets of the Ark of the Covenant, which was also a symbol for the mathematical secret of the physical body.'[7]

In *The Mysteries of Chartres Cathedral,* Louis Charpentier describes how the nine knights were originally sent to the Holy Land for a particular purpose by Bernard of Clairvaux, head of the Cistercian Order. He suggests that the Ark of the Covenant containing the Tables of the Law may have been the object of their mission in the Holy Land. He also says of the Tables of the Law:

> In the language of today we should call the Tables of the Law the tables of the Cosmic Equation. To possess the tables then is to have the possibility of access to the great law of unity that rules the worlds, of relating effects with their causes and, consequently, of acting on the phenomena that causes produce as they diversify into plurality.[8]

Charpentier continues by saying that a man would:

> ...be unable to make use of the Tables unless he had been initiated into the secret of reading them. Moses gave such an initiation in a commentary on the Semitic language and in a writing that he perhaps devised; a cryptic writing in a numerical system that was later called the Cabbala. The secret was well sealed up. More so even than it seems.[9]

Moses was initiated into the mysteries of Egypt. Here we need to pause in order to refer to information which Rudolf Steiner gives us in Lecture 3 of his lecture cycle *The Gospel of St Matthew.* There we find a detailed description of the initiation knowledge which Moses gained in Egypt and passed on to the Hebrew peoples. We are told how there was a 'deeply significant interaction between Hermes and Moses, the two great pupils of Zarathustra'. The knowledge in which they were instructed was of the Harmony of the Spheres. In this lecture Steiner refers to the 'paradise situation' and emphasizes that it was not an exact repetition of the conditions of Ancient Sun evolution where only the warmth and light ether manifest.

During the Old Moon stage not only was there light but also the *sound ether* or *chemical ether*. What is here called sound ether is not to be identified with what we call physical sound or tone. The latter is only a reflection of what is experienced by clairvoyant conscious-ness as the 'Harmony of the Spheres', as etheric sound or tone weaving as a living power through the Universe. In speaking of this ether and of this sound we are therefore speaking of something far more spiritual, far more ethereal than ordinary sound.[10]

Steiner describes how, although the sound and life ethers were withdrawn from our direct perception at the Fall, they continue to work into our astral body during sleep.

At the moment of going to sleep, the inner forces in the astral body and in the Ego actually begin to expand over the whole solar sys-tem, to become part of it. From every direction man draws into his astral body and into his Ego forces which strengthen his life during sleep, and on waking he contracts into the narrower confines within his skin and pours into these what he has absorbed during the night from the whole solar system. That is why medieval occultists too called this spiritual body of man the 'astral' body, because it is united with the world of the stars and draws its forces from them ... What is it that permeates the astral body during sleep when it is outside the physical and etheric bodies? It is the weaving life of the harmonies of the spheres, forces that can otherwise operate only in the sound ether. Just as when a violin bow is drawn across the edge of a metal disc strewn with sand the vibrations pulsing through the air also pulsate through the sand and produce the well-known Chladni sound-figures, so do the harmonies of the spheres vibrate through the human being during sleep and bring order again into what has been cast into disorder during the day through his sense-perceptions.[11]

In a lecture given in 1997 Manfred Schmidt-Brabant explained that many of the Templars had been 'incarnated in the Pythagorean school, either directly as pupils or within its sphere of influence' ... where 'the way the harmony of the world was taught demonstrated that access to it arises out of what takes place between music and mathematics'.[12] In

Lecture 3 in the cycle on Matthew's Gospel quoted above, Steiner had also said that: 'In the Pythagorean schools the power to become aware of the Harmony of the Spheres was understood to be the reopening of man's being to the sound ether and to the divine life ether.'[13] When we consider this *karmic* connection between the Knights Templar and the Pythagorean school we can understand that knowledge of the Harmony of the Spheres and mathematics which they might have experienced there laid a very broad basis for their building work. The most lasting remnant that we have of this work survives in the sublime architecture of the Gothic cathedrals. The dimensions of these buildings conform to the same laws as the Harmony of the Spheres. Through the experience of these dimensions, the nature of the plain chant sounding through them and the accumulative power of their many coloured windows, the effect on the astral body of the worshipper was of a similar nature to its night-time experience in the great cosmos.

The Knights Templar were very much in evidence at Chartres. An effigy of the Black Virgin was venerated at Chartres in pre-Christian times and was later kept in the chamber under the cathedral until it was destroyed in one of the many fires which it has suffered in its long history.

There are clues to be found at Chartres which lead one to believe that in the early traditions of its founders, both pre-Christian and Christian, there was knowledge of the life force and of its connection with the Christ Being. The relic around which the cathedral is built— the veil supposedly worn by the Virgin Mary when she gave birth to Jesus—is refreshingly unusual, being a symbol of life instead of death. There are strange stories of how all efforts to bury the dead there were thwarted; the cathedral itself rejected the bodies while strange rumbling noises were heard when the attempt was made.

Chartres is located over granite. Granite manifests the effect of the life ether as it is thrust up from the deepest rock layers of the earth, which as we have seen is the realm in the interior of the earth where it manifests powerfully. Pierre Morizot writes about Chartres from this point of view in his *The School at Chartres*:

Again we may ask: why were those places chosen? The study of etheric forces has provided Rudolf Steiner with the answer. In some regions of the globe the crust of the earth has subsided to a marked degree, while the emergence of powerful chains of mountains has distributed the concentric layers of the etheric forces which, from the core of our planet, rise up to the highest reaches of our atmosphere. Thus gigantic fissures have enabled man to come into close contact with etheric influences differing from those of his natural surroundings. Such are the deep valleys which form the bed of the River Jordan, the Dead Sea, the lakes of the upper Engadine, and the clefts where are to be found the caves of Chartres, Lourdes and Delphi. Our physical frame has lost its elasticity and become rigid, but, in the distant past, man was highly sensitive to these differences in etheric activity... Where there is a cavity of characteristic form and geological nature, the forces issuing from the earth escape from the ground and enable the inhabitants to put into use faculties which, normally, are dormant in man.[14]

Ancient Saturn gave birth to Ancient Sun, where the etheric realm had its point of origin. Anne bore the Virgin Mary who can be related to the etheric. This progression from Ancient Saturn to Ancient Sun, Anne to the Virgin Mary, is acknowledged both in the presence of the Black Virgin in the crypt of Chartres Cathedral and in the beautiful stained glass windows there.

At the beginning of this chapter I have quoted Rudolf Steiner when he spoke, on a rare occasion, of earth energy and sacred places. He added that: 'Wherever there is or has been a Black Madonna, etheric forces have issued from deeper levels, making a region quite special for connection with the elements and through them for communion with the cosmos.'[15]

In Chartres, as is often the case, the Black Virgin is found represented in the same building as the Green Man—another personification of the concentrated life forces. In *The Green Man,* William Anderson and Clive Hicks unknowingly give a living picture of the quality of original Ancient Saturn evolution and its subsequent repetitions in the later planetary states when they describe the Black Virgin of Notre-Dame d'Espoir in Dijon:

There is another link between the Black Virgins and many representations of the Green Man in this period [eleventh and twelfth centuries]. All the ancient Black Virgins I have seen have a numinous and hierarchic calm, as with the Virgin of Notre-Dame d'Espoir in Dijon. She is a manifestation of a level of being and experience infinitely beyond human failings and sufferings and it is, perhaps, precisely because she possesses this freedom from misery that she is able to comfort and to bless through her presence. The atmosphere she generates is the evidence that there is, in truth, a level of peace that is attainable and is full of succour for human griefs and hopes. Many of the Green Men possess something of her calm and independence of the vicissitudes of ordinary mortals.[16]

Here surely is the description of a time before even the most potent 'backward' being had fallen, long before unwitting humanity had been caught up in the 'wars amongst the gods'. In her archetypal beauty the Black Virgin persists in a time before evil began.

The Green Man, a pagan figure, strangely appears in most of the churches built on ancient sacred locations, and therefore one can find a direct connection between him and the Templars. The early stonemasons still had an awareness of the etheric world, which breathed freely through the countryside before the city encroached too densely around sacred buildings. The further one goes back the more one finds that the forest covered a very large area of western Europe. People in the early settlements will have held the depth of their surrounding forests in awe, as places one would enter with great trepidation and respect. The forest, representing the etheric world manifest in nature, is a place of renewal, entry into which could be compared to our experience of the night, when the conscious daytime world fades and our dimmed comprehension is filled with beings of other dimensions who bring us refreshing new energy to help in facing a new day of immersion in the physical world.

William Shakespeare recognized the forest in this way, using it as a location where things get 'sorted out' when there is no answer to a problem in the outside world. The lovers rush into the woods around Athens on Midsummer's Night, when the overbearing older generation and misaligned relationships threaten to thwart their hopes of happiness. They emerge in the morning, their problems solved, having been incorporated into the doings of the elemental beings during the night. The Merry Wives of Windsor teach Falstaff his lesson in Windsor Forest at night, representing elemental beings with their accomplices and dressing Falstaff as Herne the Hunter.

In the areas where the energy has been guarded from the times of ancient peoples one feels that one is walking into the etheric world as it was in the paradise-time before the Fall. However, these earth chakras can still manifest at both ends of the spectrum. The Virgin Mary and Christ have been experienced in many places such as Mejegure and Lourdes, but at Mellory Grotto in Ireland the Devil also appeared. At Shipley in Sussex the energy outside the Templar church there was discovered to be very turbulent. Inside the church is an atmosphere that gives one a sense of profound stillness, where the surroundings are holding their breath. When this was remarked upon, the vicar affirmed: 'The Templars prayed this into these walls.' How did they achieve this?

In studying two different passages, a lecture given by Rudolf Steiner and then an article written by Gunther Wachsmuth, we gain insight into how the transformation of the fallen-earth energy might have been achieved by the Templars. In his lecture, given in Dornach on 2 October 1916, Steiner speaks with great emphasis.

> We find that this order of the Knights Templar, inwardly considered, expresses a specially deep approach to the Mystery of Golgotha on the part of modern humanity... The blood of the Templars belonged to Christ Jesus. Each one of them knew this—their blood belonged to nothing else on earth but Christ Jesus. Every moment of their life was to be filled with the perpetual consciousness of how in their soul there dwelt 'Not I, but Christ in Me'.[17]

Then, in his lecture cycle *An Occult Physiology*, given in Prague in 1911, Rudolf Steiner describes how an intense contemplative preoccupation with high ideals, inwardly maintained as a free act of the spirit, causes the nerves to withdraw from the blood:

> In ordinary life the process that takes place is such that each influence transmitted by means of the nerves inscribes itself in the blood as on a tablet, and in doing so records itself in the instrument of the

ego ... But let us suppose that in spite of the interrupting of the connection between the nerve and the blood a certain impression is made upon the nerve. This can be brought to pass through an external experiment by stimulating the nerve by means of an electric current ... But there is still another way of affecting the nerve under conditions in which it cannot act upon the course of the blood normally connected with it.

It is possible to bring about such a condition of the human organism; and this is done in a particular way, by means of certain representations, emotions and feelings which the human being has experienced and made a part of himself, and which, if this inner experiment is to be truly successful, ought, properly speaking, to be really lofty, moral or intellectual ideas. When a man practises a rigorous inner concentration of the soul on such imaginative representations, and if he does this in a state of waking conscious-ness, forming these into symbols let us say, it then happens that he takes complete control of the nerve and, as a result of this inner concentration, draws it back to a certain extent from the course of the blood.[18]

This transformation could have been achieved by the Templars as a result of the fact that 'every moment of their life was ... filled with the perpetual consciousness of how in their soul there dwelt "Not I, but Christ in me".'[19] Then, when each individual ego was replaced by the Christ Ego, a further effect may have become possible, that of expanding this personal indwelling of Christ to resonate into the body of the earth itself.

In this way the power of the Tree of Life that had been returned to earth by the Christ and brought to perfection within the body of Jesus could have become available to the Templars. With this personal initiation might have come the possibility of facilitating the influence of the individual human bloodstream to influence the eventual transformation of the earth itself. In his essay 'The Face of the Earth and the Destiny of Mankind', Gunther Wachsmuth gives us an insight into how such a process could have occurred:

We have seen that certain forces mould the body of the earth and of man in accordance with uniform, harmonious laws. In conclusion, we will consider yet another deeply illuminating phenomenon that can tell us how and why the destiny of man is bound up with the earth; why, in effect, the face of the earth becomes part of the destiny of man . . .

A study of the etheric formative forces which on the one hand are responsible for the formation of the interior body of the earth, and on the other for the structure of the human blood corpuscle, will reveal the fact that the solid earth is ruled by the life ether, the fluid elements by the chemical ether, the airy elements by the light ether, and the warmth process by the warmth ether. We find exactly the same thing in the corpuscle of human blood! Thus, we can study the configuration of the etheric body of the earth which is a reflection of our own inner being and we must realize that the etheric forces moulding the body of the earth are the same as those in our blood corpuscles . . . Furthermore, it now also becomes clear that if new etheric forces arise within the earth in the course of cosmic 'becoming' this reflects itself right into the corpuscles of the human blood; on the other hand, when a change takes place in the etheric structure of human blood, this will be reflected into the etheric sphere of the earth, because, in effect, the earth and the blood corpuscles are formed according to the same laws . . . We are thus led into a quite different relationship with the earth, a truly Christian knowledge of the spirituality of the earth, to a Gaia-Sophia.[20]

The fallen energy of the ethers can be transubstantiated into its higher counterpart, but this would entail engaging with the fallen beings residing within the earth. This process began when Christ 'descended into the forecourts of hell'.[21] There these potentially destructive beings were 'chained' and held down by the power of the Christ who simultaneously began to effect the transformation of physical substance. The centre of the earth, which had been their sphere of action, from then on began to radiate the 'Christ Sun'. But responsibility for the remaining work of transformation now lies with the remainder of humanity. Maybe this points to the significance of the statement made by Christ Jesus: 'He that believeth on me, the works that I do shall he do also; and greater *works* than these shall he do.'[22]

Within the etheric our familiar experience of distance and separation vanish. The concept of *kinship* replaces the concept of *spacial distance*. Those things which are *akin* are joined in unity in the etheric, *irrespective of the distance between their physical manifestations*. This explains how if there is a kinship between the blood cell and the earth organism changes in the one will reflect in the other.

We now reach a point where we ask: if the Knights Templar were performing work of such importance to the earth and humanity, how could the tragedy of their fate have been allowed to take place? Pierre Morizot throws light on this question:

> In the year 1307 the Knights Templar were arrested on the order of the French king Philippe the Fair. This began the wave of torturing and burning of Templars that would continue during the years which followed. The personality of Philippe, as Rudolf Steiner saw it, was that of an extremely gifted man, cunning, resourceful and wise, with an unconquerable and even pathological passion for gold and silver. This was directed less to the economical value than to the metallic quality of those elements.
>
> With every material substance, in particular with every metal, are connected spiritual forces responsible for its structure and formation. In the case of precious metals like gold and silver these forces are specially powerful. A man permeated by them is extremely lucid and has penetrating powers of the brain.[23]

This passage continues by explaining how Philip the Fair had

> ...to an unusual degree, fallen prey to ahrimanic beings who developed and intensified in him the forces arising from gold and silver... Thus Philip had become the subject and lieutenant of Ahriman. From him he had received his cold calculating mind, which was never troubled by sentiment but made straight for its goal, crushing all resistance to its will. The supersensible forces connected with gold and silver added to its sharpness. It can even be said that the king throve on them. He took special delight in handling gold and silver coins, in experiencing their physical nature and, when there was enough bullion in the royal treasury, he would walk into it, stirring it up with his hands and feet ... it was as if [he]

was meant to occupy this high position in order to oppose the Templars and crush their spiritual impulse.[24]

Steiner connects the demise of the Templars with the work of Sorat, the Sun Demon, who, in his cycle of 666 years, came to influence the earth again in 1332. He also says that the Templars, in their work to establish an understanding of the Christ energy as a Sun Being, were also approaching an understanding of the work of the Sun Demon, 'a view that knew about the mighty oppositions that are brought about by such obstinate beings as Sorat'.[25] In the rise and fall of the Knights Templar can be seen the balancing of opposing forces played out in the arena of worldly affairs.

7.
The Rosicrucian Impulse

The Grail as Living Forces

Just a century after the arrest of the Templars in 1307, the birth of the consciousness soul in 1413 gradually brought the mission of the Rosicrucians to focus in western Europe. On many occasions Rudolf Steiner described John the Divine's connection with the esoteric Christian stream and Rosicrucian stream of initiation knowledge. In all of his incarnations the 'John individual' is connected with this stream of knowledge which was particularly directed towards an understanding of how the creation in matter has directly proceeded from the form principle that exists in the purely spiritual world.

We have been attempting to study how spirit becomes matter, and matter transforms again into spirit from various perspectives through the previous chapters of this book. 'The Secret Book of John', one of the texts found at Nag Hammadi is described by Andrew Welburn as 'a primary Gnostic cosmological treatise giving an account of the earliest, purely spiritual phases of world evolution, followed by the origin of the material world and the moulding of man's physical body'.[1] One of the earliest incarnations of John the Divine referred to by Steiner was as Hiram Abiff, builder of Solomon's Temple.[2]

> The best known Rosicrucian incarnation in antiquity is that of Hiram Abiff, the master builder of the Temple of Solomon. Solomon had the ability, within his spiritual vision, to determine the measures and proportions of the Temple. He could observe the way the spiritual powers required the Temple to look. But he could not make the specific, precise calculations for the construction. He needed an architect for that who could handle earthly matter, who could build something which in the sphere of the earth would not remain a vision but a lasting reality.[3]

There were two incarnations of Christian Rosenkreutz himself, one in the thirteenth century and the second not long after, in the fifteenth century. These followed the incarnations as Hiram and St John. After the Rosenkreutz incarnations it is described how he appears as the Comte de Saint Germaine in the eighteenth century.

Rudolf Steiner has often indicated that the fostering of this new stage of the soul's development, the consciousness soul age, was the special responsibility of Britain. If we look back to the time of Atlantis, we find there the origins of the earliest mysteries of all. These were the Hibernian Mysteries which originated from the 'High Sun Oracle' of Atlantis, whose aim had been to further the work of the Six Sun Elohim, manifesting the Christ and establishing the prototype for the human ego, human individuality. The Hibernian Mystery centre was originally situated slightly above and to the west of Ireland, before the waters of the Atlantic obliterated its traces.

Before the destruction of Atlantis the highest initiates of the Hibernian Mysteries, Skythianos and Manu, left this centre and together with their people moved eastwards across Europe, returning to western Europe after the beginnings of recorded history as the Celts. It is described how, when the Celtic people died out, they were absorbed into various nationalities and the Hibernian Mysteries were withdrawn into the spiritual world. Thus the British Isles were imbued with these mysteries from very early times.

Steiner explains what he discovered when researching these mysteries by consulting the Akashic Chronicle, a record of all past events which exists in the etheric world:

When one approaches the pictures of the Hibernian Mysteries ... one finds that something is repelling one. It is as though some force were holding one back, as though one's soul could not reach them. The nearer one approaches the more one's goal seems to be eclipsed, and a kind of stupefaction comes over one's soul. One has to work one's way through this stupefaction, and the only possible way of doing so is to kindle ones' own independently acquired knowledge of similar matters.

And then one understands why it is so difficult to approach the Hibernian Mysteries. It becomes evident that they were the final echo of an age-old gift to humanity from the divine-spiritual powers, but that when these mysteries withdrew into a shadowy existence they were at the same time surrounded by a stout defence so that human beings cannot find their way to them if they maintain a passive attitude of soul. They can approach these mysteries only by kindling their own spiritual activity—in other words, by becoming modern human beings in the true sense. Access to the Hibernian Mysteries was barred so that people could not approach them in that way, but are compelled to experience with the full activity of consciousness that which must be discovered *inwardly* in this age of freedom. Neither by a scrutiny of history nor by clairvoyant vision of great and wonderful ancient secrets can these mysteries be discovered but only by the exercise of a human being's own conscious inner activity.[4]

In this description we find the essence of the consciousness soul's particular characteristic: the fact that these mysteries can only be found 'by the exercise of a human being's own conscious inner activity', which highlights the necessity to develop the strength of the ego in order to transform the original human members into their eventual higher counterparts. This is the characteristic that the Rosicrucians were beginning to foster in Europe through all the influences that they filtered into the consciousness of society in every possible way. As we have seen, they used the media of art, fairy tales, legends, proverbs and songs.

When the Celts died out as an individual race their guiding spirit, the Celtic archangel, became the guardian of esoteric Christianity. 'All the underlying teachings and impulses of esoteric Christianity, especially the real, true esoteric Christianity, have their source in his inspirations . . . Esoteric Christianity . . . was destined to live on further in the mysteries of the Holy Grail, in Rosicrucianism.'[5]

It is not surprising that Shakespeare's plays were written in the spirit which the Hibernian Mysteries were directing towards the establishment of the consciousness soul age, developing the activity of the human ego for our own times and on into the future. The composition of Shakespeare's plays was a very important part of the Rosicrucian programme. Their content was a continuation of the aims of the Hibernian Mysteries and later Grail Christianity. This is more important than the authorship controversy. According to Rudolf Steiner

...at the time when Bacon, Shakespeare, Jacob Boehme, and a fourth were working on the earth there was one Initiate who really spoke through all four ... This Initiate—like many a modern initiate—is described to us as a rather intolerable fellow. But he was not merely so... He was an individuality from whom immense forces proceeded, and through whom were really due Bacon's philosophic work as well as Shakespeare's dramas and the works of Jacob Boehme, and also the works of the Jesuit, Jacob Balde.[6]

Whether or not the identity of the individual to whom Steiner refers is ever established, the important thing to remember is that ultimately it is Rosenkreutz who stands behind whoever was exoterically involved in sending out the impulse given to the world by Shakespeare's writings.

It is known that the initiation of the first incarnation as Christian Rosenkreutz happened in 'the place in Europe which cannot be named yet' in 1250, six years after the Siege of Montségur. For various reasons it is therefore possible that the Cathar treasure of Montségur was the young Rosenkreutz in his thirteenth-century incarnation.[7]

Christian Rosenkreutz (1378–1484), in his second long incarnation, was 35 years old when the consciousness soul age began. His mission, and that of his fellow Rosicrucians, was to foster the development of the human individuality in the physical world without losing the spiritual substance which is the human being's birthright—to teach the finding of spirit through the senses. He returned to Europe from his travels with all the star knowledge and wisdom of the ancients. He then founded the first Rosicrucian community. The movement gradually grew from four original members until in 1489 it was very large. Christian Rosenkreutz was fully initiated at the age of 81, and died when he was 106. In 1604 his tomb was discovered and opened. His body had not decayed, seeming as though he had only just died. In his hands he held a tiny book. On its cover were written the words: 'A seed buried within the heart of Jesus. Lieber M. The book of the world.'[8]

In 1612 in Europe, with the marriage of Catholic James I's daughter Elizabeth to Frederick V, Elector Palatinate of the Rhine, leader of the German Protestants, it would have seemed that outer historical currents were beginning to run together with the underground stream. Frederick's court was in Heidelberg, one of the towns in Europe in which Rosicrucian influence had permeated the new climate of thought brought about by the consciousness soul age.

> Earlier patterns, the patterns of the old Queen's times, were indeed implicit in this happy event. The old Elizabeth had been the support of Europe against Hapsburg aggression, allied to Catholic reaction... There was a certain piquancy in the fact that the young Elizabeth ... was to cement these sacred policies through her marriage... But would that promise be allowed to develop peacefully or would disasters intervene? The auguries were not good... Most informed people believed that war was inevitable and that it would break out in Germany. There were thus dark shadows behind the splendours of this wedding, and these rather charming and innocent young people, Frederick and Elizabeth, would in a few years' time find themselves at the very heart of the whirlwind.[9]

Bohemia had been a haven of 'exoteric' Rosicrucian culture, fostered by the maverick Habsburg King Rudolph II who died in 1612. In 1617, the fanatical Catholic-Habsburg Archduke Ferdinand of Styria became King of Bohemia:

> ...a pupil of the Jesuits, determined to stamp out heresy ... Ferdinand immediately put an end to Rudolph's policy of religious toleration by revoking the Letter of Majesty and beginning to set about the suppression of the Bohemian Church. Some people have said that the true beginning of the Thirty Years War lay in the beginning of the application of intolerant policies in Bohemia.[10]

The Bohemians rebelled 'and at a stormy meeting in Prague two Catholic leaders were thrown out of a window'.[11] On 26 August 1619 the Bohemians offered the crown of Bohemia to Frederick, Elector Palatinate.

Confident in the support of his powerful allies, the German and French Protestants, together with the Dutch and the King of Great Britain whose daughter he had married, Frederick made the difficult and dangerous decision to accept, and began the journey from

Heidelberg to Prague on 27 September. Prince Frederick 'wrote to his uncle, the Duke of Bouillon, "It is a divine calling which I must not disobey ... my only end is to serve God and his Church." '[12] Public support in Britain had been ecstatic; the Archbishop of Canterbury wrote to Frederick 'advising the acceptance of the Bohemian crown as a religious duty'.[13] But King James refused to help them, exercising his 'divine right' against the decision of parliament. When the backlash came from the infuriated Habsburg armies the other allies also let Frederick down, so that the glorious reign of the 'Winter King and Queen of Bohemia' only lasted during the Winter of 1619–20. Frederick, Elizabeth and their family were banished and the Bohemian Church brutally suppressed. These tragic events and the outcome of the Thirty Years War once more drove the stream of esoteric Christianity underground.

★

New information on the history of the Rosicrucians began to emerge after a group of Manchester plumbers on a January day in the early 1960s made a discovery which led to a quiet and steady line of research that increasingly reveals that there was a strong link between Hermeticism, Cabbalism, Templars, Rosicrucians, and even the Hibernian Mysteries.

Vast cavities behind the chimney flues and a secret chamber with a flight of stone steps disappearing into a brick wall were found in a house that appeared to have been built in the 1920s. The owner of the house, Joy Hancox, an Associate of the Royal College of Music, gave up her work in education to research the vistas of hitherto unknown information which opened in front of her when she began delving into the history of the house and of a former tenant, Thomas Siddal.

His story, steeped in the events of the eighteenth-century Jacobite risings, led her to John Byrom (1691–1763), an enigmatic Manchester citizen who spent much of his time in London, rubbing shoulders with people who stood at the crossroads between ancient knowledge and the birth of modern science. Byrom had invented the first phonetic system of shorthand from which Pitman's shorthand was developed. His journals, originally written in shorthand, had been transcribed and published in a heavily edited form. Joy was given access to another shorthand manuscript in private ownership. She learned the shorthand and, as a result, uncovered facts that would otherwise have never been discovered. In these journals Joy found two references which led to Byrom's connections with arcane activities in eighteenth-century London. One of these referred to the Sun Club, where meetings were held under the room where the Lodge of Antiquity met. This was one of four founder-lodges of the Grand Lodge of Freemasonry in England. Some members of the Sun Club also belonged to this lodge, and in addition were members of the Royal Society. All were leading figures in the emerging scientific establishment of the time. In the other reference Byrom mentions a Cabala Club which he himself established. There is no other mention of this Cabala Club in his journal after the one entry.

Joy's continuing investigation into John Byrom's enigmatic activities eventually led to her receipt of and the loan of two large envelopes containing a collection of cards and paper which were in private ownership. The collection, which includes 686 diagrams on 516 pieces of card and paper, extends from 1570 to the 1730s.

> Most significantly the drawings include plans for the original Globe Theatre, the Rose and five other Elizabethan playhouses [the Theatre, the Swan, the Hope, the Fortune and the Bear Garden].
>
> There are also designs for medieval Templar churches, early precision instruments and even a hidden mystical numerology in the layout of Westminster abbey. Linking cabalistic philosophy, mysticism, Freemasonry, cosmology and navigation.[14]

In *Kingdom for a Stage* Joy outlines her reasons for thinking that John Dee together with Theodore de Bry, a Hugenot engraver originally from Liège, were the most likely candidates for originating the theatre designs.

> Dee had precisely the kind of knowledge that made him pre-eminently capable of the grand vision of the Elizabethan playhouse. In this he was helped by Theodore de Bry who translated that concept into ideal representations as well as more practical patterns for the builders.[15]

The Theatre was built in 1576. 'That same year' de Bry 'was employed in making a detailed engraving of the installation of the Knights of the Garter at Windsor'.[16]

Joy had been researching the background to some of the engravings in the collection in Frances Yates's 'Theatre of the World' when she came across a reference to Elizabethan playhouse architecture which was based on Vitruvius' plans for the Roman theatre. Joy had immediately recognized these from the Byrom drawings. In the course of her meticulous examination of the dimensions marked out on the theatre drawings Joy made this discovery:

> It seems that in at least three of the Elizabethan playhouses there was one common feature, one uniform measurement. This did not mean that the theatres were identical, but it did point to an interesting possibility that there was a purpose in this uniformity. The use of the dimension of 72 in each of the theatres appeared to be part of the overall structural constraints. The Theatre, the Rose and the Globe were polygonal, although the Globe had a different number of sides from the Rose. Nevertheless, both had been built to a design where the principal frame number was 72. The archaeology showed this; the Byrom drawings showed it. The more I pondered this fact in relation to the Vitruvian influences in the concept, the more the measurement of 72 seemed to be essential— and not simply to ensure structural stability. It looked more like the evidence of another dimension purposely invoked in the concept of the Elizabethan playhouse. I came to call this 'the missing dimension', because it comes from a tradition that for the most part has long since been replaced in modern architecture and has no place in the reconstructed Globe on Bankside.[17]

Elsewhere Joy points out other significant instances of this number, culminating in the fact that with the precession of the equinoxes 'the terrestrial globe moves approximately one degree every 72 years'.

In his essay on 'Microcosm and Macrocosm', in *Rhythmic Formative Forces of Music*, Michael Theroux of the Borderland Research Foundation, relating the earth and man to 'a greater cosmic connection', describes how there is a definite relationship between the breathing rhythm of the earth organism and the breathing rhythm of the human being.

The earth organism's breathing process is observed in the alternating barometric pressure of day and night; exhaling at sunrise, and inhaling at sunset. The average person inhales and exhales approximately 18 times a minute, or 1080 times an hour, 1080 itself is a most prominent number in ancient geometrical cosmology, and is also the radius in miles to the moon, or 25,920 times a day (24 hours equalling one earth breath). The number of human breaths in one day corresponds to the number of years (revolutions of the earth around the sun) it takes the sun to pass through each of the twelve signs of the circle of the Zodiac, called the precession of the vernal equinox. This duration of time (25,920 years) is also called the Platonic Year.

The rhythmic perceptions of the body are not only confined to the function of breathing but through the propagation of blood from the heart to the limbs (a likening of our circulatory system can be observed in the earth as well: i.e. the alternating temperature differences in night/winter and day/summer). Now if we take the average pulse rate which is 72 beats a minute and compare it to the average breaths in one minute (180), we will find precisely the same relationship in the astronomical sphere between the procession of the vernal equinox and the nutation of the moon (the period during which the axis of the earth, under the influence of the moon, describes a small cone around the axis of the earth) is a period of about 18 years. Thus we have a ratio of 72:18, or 4:1. All of this should lead us to the conclusion that the human organism is completely immersed in rhythmic formative force [*originating in the surrounding cosmos*].[18]

In the light of all of this it is fascinating to observe that Dan Brown has chosen the number 72 for a chapter in the *Da Vinci Code* where he brings up the subject of iambic pentameter!

For centuries, iambic pentameter had been a preferred poetic meter of outstanding literati across the globe, from the ancient Greek writer Archilochus to Shakespeare, Milton, Chaucer and Voltaire—bold souls who chose to write their social commentaries in a metre that many of the day believed had mystical qualities.[19]

Joy Hancox's ongoing work increasingly brings more evidence to light which shows how the Hermetic and Cabbalistic knowledge of number and sound holding the secrets of cosmic and earthly relationships was integrated into the building of the Elizabethan playhouses. Whoever wrote the lines of Shakespeare's plays, there was surely the input of more than one man in the total experience that accompanied a performance inside buildings built to those dimensions. John Dee masterminded the building of these theatres which was based on Hermetic Tradition:

> This tradition was carried on in the building of the great cathedrals of Europe. Tools and techniques predominated in the medieval guilds, but behind these was the figure of the Sage with his sacred knowledge. John Dee was part of that tradition, using his knowledge in the service of his patrons ... Dee strove to achieve the philosophical power exemplified by Moses in the Monas Hieroglyphica, as well as in his angel-magic. Similarly, he attempted to endow the Elizabethan playhouse with something of that power.[20]

*

The scientific work of the great German poet Wolfgang von Goethe created Rudolf Steiner's exoteric connection with Rosicrucian knowledge. Steiner's extensive development of Goethe's ideas was in turn taken up by his pupil George Adams Kaufmann. The unity between Goethe's scientific world-conception and the new forms of projective geometry was explored in depth by Adams who was educated at Cambridge. There he was inspired by the works of A.N. Whitehead and gained valuable help in his mathematical pursuits from such notables as Bertrand Russell and G.H. Hardy.

At this time Adams began to be fascinated with the ideas of projective geometry. In his scientific research he wished to bring together a factual account of outer reality with the deep poetry of an intensely lived subjective experience. To him modern science, with its material monism, did not seem true to the world that it was attempting to describe.

In contrast to the rigid geometry of Euclid, with its description of fixed and static forms, the thought forms of projective geometry were mobile and living. Adams saw this geometry as the bridge to an understanding of a type of counter-space that underlies the space of the physical/material world. Projective geometry describes the process of space-in-creation, the creation of form out of living formative processes. Goethe had described these laws of polarity and meta-morphosis, and now Adams was explicating the mathematical underpinnings. Like his great predecessor, Adams turned to the study of plant life. In his book *The Plant Between Sun and Earth* (co-authored with Olive Whicher) Adams states:

> The new geometry has a close relationship to the quality of thinking of the great artist-scientist Goethe. It cultivates a qualitative, pic-ture-forming aspect of mathematics, which approaches closely the Goethean experience of nature. Not only in the method but in the content of the new geometry we find significant possibilities of bridging the gulf between Goethe's qualitative and completely phenomenological way of approach to nature and the natural science of our time, permeated as it is with mathematical thought.[21]

The prime, indivisible entity of projective geometry is not, as in Euclidean geometry, the point, but the plane. The plane is the fun-damental etheric unit, and flows in from the periphery of the universe. Whereas material forces are point-centred, radiating out from fixed points, the formative forces, or counter-space, are planar. These planes are organic and holistic. Between the celestial plane and the material point weaves the rich tapestry of phenomenal existence. The term etheric or ethereal is used to denote these planar forces. Adams continues:

> The ethereal forces ... are the peripheral cosmic forces ... With the ideas of projective geometry we have transcended the one-sidedly centric approach to form and are capable of becoming spiritually perceptive towards the signature of the peripheral forces and the planar space-formation of natural phenomena. The concept of ethereal space enables the Earth-planet as a whole to be regarded as a living entity—not in a vaguely philosophic sense, but in a way that lends itself to detailed investigation.[22]

As an example of how this works we can consider the potentization process utilized in the production of many homoeopathic and Weleda medicines. Potentization requires that some original substance, say a medicinal plant, be radically diluted in some pure medium—water or milk, for instance. The dilutions continue to the point where any trace of the original substance has completely vanished. The process of dilution is dynamic, involving a rhythmic shaking process. According to Theodor Schwenk in his book *The Basis of Potentization Research*:

> Obviously the measurable sense-perceptible remedial substance disappears to an ever greater extent as potentization proceeds. This means that observation focused exclusively on matter sees only a stepwise dilution in progress, one which permeates all of nature: every natural happening is accompanied by a complementing visible or invisible process. For example, a *diluting* of earthly substances (comparable to a withdrawal from the terrestrial) is balanced by a *condensation* process of etheric universal forces running parallel to it (in other words, the inflowing of cosmic elements).[23]

When a material substance is rhythmically diluted, the loosening and dissipation of the material substance allows its corresponding etheric forces to stream more forcefully into the medium in which the material is being diluted. The etheric forces work into matter by taking up material substance. The process of dilution and hence potentization takes place constantly within the human body, and also throughout nature. Schwenk continues: 'The forces inhering in plants, minerals and so on ray into a potentizing medium such as water and bind themselves to it.'[24]

In his book *Sensitive Chaos* Schwenk describes how, as water flows through intercrossing rivers or as currents intercross deep within the oceans, subtle inner organs are created within the body of water. In the potentization process planar surfaces are created between streams of fluid slipping past one another at varying speeds. The etheric forces have a natural affinity for 'plane' surfaces in material nature. They work into nature more powerfully the more they encounter extended plane surfaces. The large inner surfaces generated by rhythmic movements of the fluid are ideal. As the material substance is liberated, the etheric forces ray into the dynamic medium with ever greater potency. Schwenk comments that these inflowing planar forces 'imprint themselves on these surfaces like a seal impressing its form into a mass of softened sealing wax'.[25]

The usual view of this is of atoms being transferred from the remedial substance to the medium. But considering all that has been said above, there is no need to attribute the imprinting of the medium to material transference of elements of the remedy, as point-orientated atomistic thinking has the habit of doing. Indeed the fewer the atoms or molecules in the imprinting by the seal, the purer is the resulting picture.

The Virbela Flowforms are one of the most popular applications of etheric ideas in the realm of practical technology. These sculpted forms, developed by John Wilkes, allow water to flow through them in a pulsing figure-of-eight movement. The problem they were designed to solve was the reversal of water pollution via some means of water purification. The lemniscatory movement pursued by the water allows etheric forces to work powerfully into the medium. The Flowforms are also of great aesthetic and therapeutic value and are used as much for the purposes of landscape enhancement as they are for scientific purposes. However, within the realms of etheric science and technology, these are not functions that can be separated. The Flowforms combine visual and musical aesthetics with scientific methods to create a device that heals both the human and natural world at the same time.

If we visualize a sphere we can see that it exists between the two polar distances of point and plane. Shrink the sphere down to its smallest imaginable size and it vanishes into a point. Now inflate it again, but take it to the other extreme. Inflate the sphere out to infinity and eventually it becomes a plane, a plane at infinity. We experience this plane at infinity as an encompassing sphere, the sphere of the starry heavens.

In connecting the influences of the cosmos in relation to the etheric forces we learn: 'From all sides they work, these forces, as if striving towards the central point of the earth. They would tear asunder the material nature of the earthly realm, dissolve it into complete form-lessness, were it not for the heavenly bodies beyond earth which mingle their influences in the field of these forces and modify the dissolving process.'[26]

In Chapter 3 we read Rudolf Steiner's statement about the Grail representing the 'living forces', which, as we have already seen, 'can be thought of as a vast cosmic ocean that stretches to the zodiac, controls and qualifies the planetary movements while also imbuing the tiniest living creatures with life and motion'.[5] This realm has been compared to the 'Grail castle', a realm that exists outside time and space. It encompasses the spiritual regions of the planets and the zodiacal stars.

In a lecture given at the 1984 Conference of the Anthroposophical Society at Michael Hall School in Sussex, Lawrence Edwards, a mathematician following Rudolf Steiner's indications, described how he had taken thousands of photographs of the leaf buds of beech trees, whose buds for the new year are already formed in September, where they hang on the branches until they open in the spring. Lawrence's photographs show that the buds were delicately changing all through the winter, turning in their sleep in accordance with the great celestial movements of the moon and Saturn. Whenever the moon drew into a straight line with Saturn the sleeping bud gave a little 'wave' as if to acknowledge Saturn as the ruling planet of the tree. Edwards suggested that the buds of all trees ruled by Saturn could be measured for related movements. The same experiments have also been carried out by connecting other plants and trees to other planets.

The planets and fixed stars are recognized as much more than material realities. They have an etheric dimension too and it is these potencies, flowing down to the earth from the zodiac, the constellations and the planets, carried by the planar forces, that give life its varied and complex characteristics. Not only the forms of all living things but also the colours and scents are differentiated and qualified by these 'formative forces', which come to us from the spiritual regions of the planets and zodiacal stars. The threshold of the Grail castle and all the wonders of the Grail procession lie ahead of us if we are worthy to enter.

8.
Mary Magdalene, the Great Work, Venus and the Pentagram

The story of *The Da Vinci Code* begins with a murder. The victim, curator of the Louvre in Paris, had used the last agonized minutes of his life to write the numbers of the Fibonacci sequence[1] on the floor of the gallery with a felt-tip marker pen only visible in black light. He had then inscribed a pentacle on his stomach in his own blood before positioning his dying body in the form of a human pentacle resembling Leonardo da Vinci's Vitruvian figure. These clues point to the secret of the victim who Dan Brown has named 'Saunière' after the priest in the story of Rennes-le-Château. The original Saunière had supposedly visited the Louvre to buy copies of the paintings that allegedly hold secrets to the mystery of Rennes-le-Château, upon which the plot of *The Da Vinci Code* is based. Sophie, the heroine of Dan Brown's story, is the niece of the victim; she helps the hero, Robert Langdon, unravel clues that point to her uncle's membership of the Priory of Sion and therefore also to both of their positions in the supposed bloodline.

It is indicative of the stage we have now reached in the consciousness soul age that only a story served up with extreme violence, bloodshed and intrigue should be capable of catching the attention of such a wide readership. Yet possibly it creates resonance at a deeper level. *The Da Vinci Code* claims to expose the secrets of the underground stream of knowledge but is only capable of presenting a materialistic interpretation of it. The quest follows a convoluted trail where, as with today's world, nothing and no one are what they first appear to be. It finally leads to a 'Holy Grail' which has now been presented to the public for more than three decades as the womb of Mary Magdalene. Even so, something has resonated with millions of people who may, as a result, now search elsewhere to rediscover the half-remembered story of their origin.

The pentacle and the Fibonacci series represent life, not death. We have seen how the pentagram is a very real symbol for the inter-connection between the subtle bodies and the physical body of man; their interaction maintains life and form in matter. The Fibonacci series is also to do with the form principle working into matter, and is in turn linked to pentagonal geometry. Therefore the latter holds the secret of the interaction of cosmic and earthly forces.

In addition to man and other forms of life, the earth also has a subtle body which manifests at various 'chakra points'. These are sometimes linked across its surface by ancient sacred routes, which became pilgrim routes in Christian times. Understanding this relationship between the subtle body of man and that of the earth is central to the next stage in linking the mystery of Mary Magdalene to the possible activities of Bérenger Saunière. These forces are also interconnected with traces of the earth's previous incarnations in the form of the Goddess and the Green Man. Most of these locations have been sacred to the Goddess and the Green Man for thousands of years and are stretched in formation over great distances as earth chakra systems. These chakra points in the earth were the Grail that the Knights Templar were guarding. It will be remembered that there was a strong Templar presence around Rennes-le-Château. Also we have seen that the Templars worshipped the Goddess and named their churches after her Christian counterpart, Mary.

Where ancient earth-chakra systems have been recognized since early times there is a direct correlation between spiritual reality and legend. Rennes-le-Château has been recognized as the sacral chakra in two of these ancient systems. Rennes is a place where our etheric nature is merged with the power of the etheric earth and so fuses with it. There are many legends and topographical connections with Mary Magdalene in the area around Rennes.

It is possible that the human Mary Magdalene could have travelled to France from the Holy Land as both locations were part of the Roman world. Also the direct family and disciples of Jesus were fugitives in the early years after the crucifixion. Les Saintes Maries-de-la-Mer on the south coast of France is the location where tradition relates how Mary Magdalene came ashore in a boat with no oars, together with the two other Marys, the Virgin Mary and Mary (the sister of Jesus' mother and the wife of Cleophas), as mentioned in John

19:25, their servant, Sarah, and St John. In his book *Zoence*, Peter Dawkins describes Les Saintes Maries-de-la-Mer as the base chakra of a system which stretches across France, through Rosslyn south of Edinburgh, ending on the north coast of Scotland. The complete chakra system is as follows: Les Saintes Maries-de-la-Mer, the base chakra; Rennes-le-Château, sacral chakra; Chartres, solar-plexis chakra; London, heart chakra; York, throat chakra; Edinburgh (Rosslyn Chapel), the Third Eye; and the crown chakra, a location that is shrouded in mystery on the north coast of Scotland. Mary Magdalene was also connected with a second pilgrimage route which culminated at Rosslyn. This route is known as 'the Camino'; it runs from Santiago de Compostella on the north-west coast of Spain, then through Toulouse, Orléans, Chartres, Paris, Amiens and Rosslyn.

The seven sites of this system were also the sites of seven ancient mystery centres, earth chakras corresponding to the human chakras, each dedicated to the planetary mysteries of the moon, Mercury, Venus, the sun, Mars, Jupiter and Saturn. On the outside wall of the Villa Bethania at Rennes there was once a small plaque with the Shell of St Jacques, showing that the pilgrim route from Santiago de Compostella passed by Saunière's very door!

Mary Magdalene is connected with the sentient soul. At the sentient soul stage of development mankind felt at one with nature; it was then still possible to experience a fusing of the human etheric body with the etheric counterpart of the natural world. Therefore the experience of the Magdalene in this area of France could be described as a real meeting with her on the sentient soul level.

Mary Magdalene and James were the two leaders of esoteric Christianity at the time when the Camino, the pilgrimage to Santiago de Compostela, first began. In *Paths of the Christian Mysteries*, Manfred Schmidt-Brabant[2] describes how the pilgrimage route started here, then progressed northwards through each of the sites in turn before culminating at Rosslyn, which in this system of chakras represents the crown chakra. Mary Magdalene is esoterically connected with the sacral chakra in the Toulouse area, which relates to Mercury. Tim Wallace Murphy and Marilyn Hopkins describe this stage in the Camino in their book *Rosslyn Guardians of the Secrets of the Holy Grail*. In Toulouse the novice would arrive at 'the church built on the site of the Mercury Oracle... At Toulouse he would be introduced to the mysteries of the second degree with the opening of the sacral or abdominal chakra, which lies between the base and solar plexus centres and works closely with them.'[3]

When one considers the ancient connection with sacral energy in this region, Mary Magdalene's rightful place there can be fully recognized. She then becomes a realistic archetype rather than a historical figure whose physiological womb has been turned into a diminished symbol of the Holy Grail. Manfred Schmidt-Brabant also describes the Magdalene's connection with the Camino; here the archetypal figure interconnects with the pilgrims on an inner level.

> Many knowledgeable individuals from esoteric schools travelled the Camino; they were fully aware that human beings accompanied Mary Magdalene through the world of elements into the interior, to James, the brother of our Lord. These paths were not accidental: they were ancient star paths, star routes. What we mean by this is the following. Although the earth rotates, every place on the earth corresponds to a part of the firmament of the fixed stars. It is as if the phantom of the physical earth contains the reflection of the starry heavens.[4]

Mary Magdalene's association with the sacral chakra in the Toulouse area, which is connected with Mercury, can also be seen as a connection with Venus. Mercury has been described in esoteric circles as 'Occult Venus'.

The pentagram around Rennes was recognized long before *The Da Vinci Code* was written. 'The Pentagram of the Mountains' had previously been referred to in the last of Henry Lincoln's original television documentaries, but there was no mention of it in *The Holy Blood and the Holy Grail*. The whole question of the validity of Henry Lincoln's research into the Pentagram of the Mountains will be investigated in Chapter 10.

In *Genisis*, published in 1985, David Wood, an experienced surveyor and cartographer, followed Lincoln's research by referring again to significant relationships to be found in the landscape around Rennes-le-Château. In *Genisis* the central point of diagram 105 is surrounded by a circle and then two triangles that he represents as a five-pointed star. Further out in the diagram there are two crescents, while the entire figure is enclosed by a huge square. In Wachsmuth's continuation of scientific research into the ethers, each of the four ethers is represented by a geometric symbol. The exact nature of this representation is still controversial, but at the very least one might find a symbolic correlation between the circle, the triangle, the crescent, the square, and the warmth, light, chemical and life ethers. These could mark the development of creation from Ancient Saturn to the present earth, which sequence is repeated in the development of the human foetus from conception to birth. The seeming representation of the ethers spread over the terrain surrounding Rennes-le-Château could be seen to recreate the birth of matter from the point of its inception in the spirit.

In the beginning of this chapter we saw that the sacral energy in the Toulouse area was concentrated at Rennes. From the earlier Triple Goddess chapter we remember that Demeter/Mary Magdalene manifests as magnetic energy funnelled up through the fault systems of the earth. We can also verify both from a geological map of the area directly around Rennes and from people's personal experience that this place is a source of powerful earth energy which we can now identify as 'Magdalene energy' where the chemical ether/magnetism can be experienced together with a deeper energy, the life ether and its fallen counterpart.

The pentagram is also connected with the formation of a rose, which is a flower connected to Mary Magdalene:

> The combined pentagon-pentagram figure may recall a five-petalled rose about to open. This beautiful figure is a spiritual reality. As its rhythms evolve the patterns in time, they reveal the harmonious relations and proportions recognized on earth in many spatial and organic forms as those of the Golden Mean. In old days this invisible star of Venus was more important than the visible planet in its orbit.[5]

The rose was also a symbol used frequently by the troubadours and was then taken up by the Rosicrucians both for the name of their order and for the name of its founder—Christian Rosenkreutz. Both of these groups, as we have seen, continued the impulse of Manichaeism, whose greatest aim was the transformation of evil and

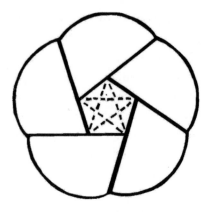

the transubstantiation of matter. It is not surprising therefore that the Magdalene should be so closely connected with this region of France that bears the image of the pentagram and lies within the sacral chakra area of the pilgrim route from Compostela to Rosslyn, and from Les Saintes Maries-de-la-Mer to Rosslyn. The Rennes area, which sheltered Cathars and Templars, still today manifests the deepest energy—energy before matter. We will later see that this is the same raw energy that manifests in certain places, e.g. Sicily. The mysteries of matter were known in the esoteric stream of knowledge to which the Cathars and Templars belonged. Both they and the Rosicrucians guarded the secrets of the life and chemical ethers, the mysteries of physical female energy. This was experienced in the energy of the terrain populated by both of these groups, who were prevalent in the Languedoc in the twelfth and thirteenth centuries, and later by those concerned with the secrets of the Rosicrucians. The pentagram connects in a realistic way to the planet Venus, as will be seen in the following passage:

> If the positions of Venus in the zodiac at the times of conjunction are observed and recorded, it can be realized how, by the interacting rhythms, particular patterns are constantly created in the cosmos in the course of time. One such pattern is of vital significance for our Earth evolution. We find it if we imagine (or draw) a path, not following the orbit, but in straight lines, between the points where meetings of a similar kind occur—namely, the points of five inferior and five superior conjunctions. This path traces five diagonals across

the Zodiac, inscribing there over a period of eight years an almost, but not quite exact, five-pointed star—a pentagram. The difference between the position of one conjunction and the following one eight years later is very small but very important. The first point of the new pentagram cycle, after eight years, is a few degrees distant from the first. And in this way the pentagram-star as a *whole* makes a continued cyclic journey round the Zodiac—as if rotating upon the sun at its centre. To follow one single revolution of this pentagram round the whole Zodiac, we may join the points in an enclosing figure—a pentagon. Twelve hundred years must pass before the pentagon performs one complete rotation through the Zodiac. The meetings between Venus and earth continue for about a century in each constellation; the period varies according to the direction of the Zodiac in which they are taking place.[6]

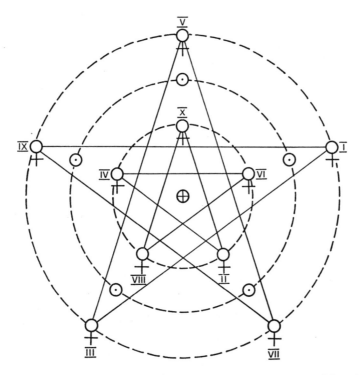

Conjunctions of Venus with the Sun. Inner circle: inferior conjunctions. Middle circle: path of the sun. Outer circle: superior conjunctions. Numbers refer to conjunctions in sequence, in the course of eight years. Between two conjunctions, from inferior to superior or vice versa, elapse c. 290 days. (Willi Sucher.)

The formation of a rose is based upon the form of a pentagram, and the rose is connected to Mary Magdalene. The path of Venus in the heavens is reflected around Rennes, which in turn lies within the region governed by Mercury or Occult Venus, the sacral chakra of the two pilgrim routes.

In Day Five of *The Chymical Wedding of Christian Rosenkreutz*, the Rosicrucian publication that was issued in 1616 and was attributed to Valentin Andrea, the Magdalene could be substituted for the Lady Venus discovered lying naked in a deep sepulchre. An inscription on the copper door leading to her announces:

Here lies buried
Venus
that beauty which hath undone
many a great man
Both in fortune, honour, blessing
and prosperity.[7]

The Tree of Life is mentioned in connection with Venus who symbolizes the challenge of those deep forces connected with her archetype; etheric forces which have become entangled in matter and are waiting for redemption.

When the fruit of my
tree shall be quite melted down
then shall I awake and
be the mother of a
King.[8]

When the Tree of Life, the chemical and life ethers, in its fallen state has been transformed then the lower nature of man will realize its true goal and give birth to the higher ego, the Christ. Here the fallen forces of the ethers could be indicated, lying waiting for redemption in the depths of the earth and in the fallen nature of the human being. The Magdalene in her role as the sentient soul of humanity suffers with all of us as we pay the great price involved in the attainment of individual maturity and consciousness.

Lucifer and his host were responsible for the scenario of the Fall. If we consider the rose and pentagram as symbols of emerging individuality in human nature, we can tie up all of the strands that have been followed in connection with Mary Magdalene and relate them to Lucifer's intervention at the Fall through a statement of Rudolf Steiner's.

> Within the spiritual evolution of the Earth are mighty, highly significant Beings, with their leader, who, because they had ... [to be involved with the] earth without having reached their full development, really feel this yearning for a star outside in the cosmos which they regard as their true home, but to which they cannot attain. These hosts are the hosts of Lucifer. Lucifer himself takes part in Earth evolution with the perpetual longing for his true home, for the star Venus outside in the cosmos.[9]

The pentagram bears within it a beautiful form-principle, the Golden Section or the Golden Mean. This demonstrates a proportion found in nature, in the human being and in traditional art. Leonardo da Vinci's Vitruvian figure demonstrates this same proportion. 'The mathematician Filius Bonacci (called Fibonacci) wrote a treatise on the number series related to the Golden Mean ... Pythagorus claimed that its proportions were musical, and it is true that the harmonious blending of musical intervals is governed by the series.'[10]

The rose incorporating the form of a pentagram was a Rosicrucian symbol that reflected the mission of this group, which, as we have seen, was aimed towards fostering the newly emerging consciousness soul which is concerned with emerging individuality, where the human ego begins to assert itself. One could connect the pentagram with present Earth evolution in which, through the Fall, this independent ego first comes into being. Earth evolution is spoken of by Steiner as 'The Cosmos of Love'. Steiner has elsewhere illustrated how the five-pointed star, the pentagram, is a fitting symbol for the activity of the ego working through matter. The relationship of Venus to the sun could also be seen as an illustration of the relationship that the human ego has to Christ. Here we could also include a parallel with Mary Magdalene, the representative of humanity, joined with the path of Venus in relationship with Christ and the sun.

When the ego begins to transform the damaged relationship between the sheaths then the influence of the Tree of Life, the healing power of the Cosmic Word, the Christ, can bring in the cosmic forces introducing form and differentiation to the activity of the life ether as it creates into matter. When one is suffering from a serious illness, as for example in the case of cancer, it is the action of the ego within the sheaths that brings healing to the physical body through introducing the forces of the cosmos in the same way that the pentagonal geometry evident in the Fibonacci series brings the form principle into all manifestations of nature. This correlation between the Venus penta-gram in the zodiac and the human ego helps one to understand how it was long ago recognized as the 'healing' planet. We have already seen how in ancient times Venus, as understood by modern astronomy, was called Mercury, the planet traditionally connected with healing.

Mary Magdalene was a historical figure in the Gospels, but 'we must never forget that the Gospels are initiation writings and not journal-ism'.[11] Elaine Pagels, an authority on the Gnostics, states:

> According to the *Dialogue of the Saviour*, Jesus warns his disciples to 'pray in a place where there is no woman', and to 'destroy the works of femaleness' . . . Yet in each of these cases the target is not women, but the power of sexuality. In *The Dialogue of the Saviour*, for example, Mary Magdalene, praised as 'the woman who knew the All', stands among the three disciples who receive Jesus' commands: he, along with Judas and Matthew, rejects the 'works of female-ness'—that is, apparently, the activities of intercourse and pro-creation.[12]

The physical world in which we exist between birth and death came about as a result of the Fall, the event through which we gained our freedom. The 'works of femaleness' as quoted above were unavoidably caused by the fact that the human race was physically divided into two separate beings each using a different combination of their subtle energy fields. The sacrament of marriage is the first stage in bringing this discrepancy of the energy fields into a preliminary form of alignment. Rudolf Steiner has referred to sexual union amongst ancient peoples as the beginning of a long process in the transfor-mation of physical love into its future spiritual counterpart. When the polarity of male and female is eventually brought together in such a way that the problems caused by immersion in matter are finally overcome, the final goal of the alchemists, the 'Great Work', will have been achieved.

In line with Christ's commandment 'Be you whole', this is also the essential Christian mystery of the esoteric schools. It is the most secret sacrament of the Bridal Chamber, as depicted in the Gnostic Gospel of Philip: 'Great is the mystery of marriage! For without it the world would not have existed. Now the existence of the world depends on man, and the existence of man upon marriage. Think of the undefiled relationship for it possesses a great power.'[13]

Here we are a long way ahead of 'Hieros Gammos', Sacred Marriage, the physical, sexual ritual which takes place at the end of *The Da Vinci Code*. This ritual that Sophie sees happening between her grandparents, while hooded members of a secret society watch, is but a poor reflection of the sacred responsibility of bringing children into this world. In very early times physical love between the sexes took place within specific parameters sanctioned by the spiritual worlds and presided over by their representatives in the community. An example of this is described by Rudolf Steiner in relation to North European tribes in the third millennium BC:

From those places of the Mysteries on the peninsula of Jutland, among the tribes which at that time called themselves the Ingaevones, or were so called by the Romans—by Tacitus—the Temple-Priest gave the sign for sexual union to take place at a definite time during the first quarter of the year. Any sexual union outside the period ordained by this Mystery centre was taboo; and in this tribe of the Ingaevones a man who was not born in the period of the darkest nights, at the time of greatest cold, towards our New Year, was regarded as an inferior being. For the impulse went out from that mystery centre at the time of the first full moon after the vernal equinox. Only then, among those who might believe themselves united with the spiritual world as became the dignity of man, was sexual union permitted. The characteristic virility—even in its aftermath—marvelled at by Tacitus, writing a century after the Mystery of Golgotha, was due to the fact that the forces which enter into such sexual union were preserved through the whole of the rest of the year.[14]

Elsewhere Rudolf Steiner clarifies the deeper implications involved with the debasement of the sexual act:

> In itself, the reproductive force is the most holy thing we have because it is immediately divine. The more divine the thing we drag into the mire, the greater the sin. Our reproductive organs will become our heart and larynx. As the word became flesh in Christ, so must the flesh become the word 'in the future'. That is the Mystery of the Holy Grail, the holy lance of love, the fructifying light of the sun, which will once again unite with Eve.[15]

In his commentary on the Gospel of Philip, Andrew Welburn describes how the Christian 'mystery' of marriage 'is not the sexual act (the "defilement of the appearance") but the inner wholeness which is the reattaining of Paradisaical unity.'[16]

'When Eve was still in Adam, death did not exist. When she was separated from him, death came into a being. If he again becomes complete and attains his former self, death will be no more.'[17]

The work of the Bridal Chamber is, then, the Great Work, the quest for the Grail and the end goal of the researches of the alchemists, the achievement of conscious immortality.

The final plate in the *Codex Rosae Crucis*, reprinted with a commentary by Manly Hall, shows the highest aim of the alchemists, the Magnum Opus or Great Work, in diagrammatic form, headed with the phrase:

SUM TOTAL AND THE FINAL CONCLUSION[18]

This is is a statement of consummation and perfection. The left side of the plate represents the divine nature, and the right side the earthly nature. These opposites are combined in a circle entitled 'By this sign thou shalt conquer.'[19] Within this quartered circle are the symbols of the elements, the colours and the numbers that point towards the completion and the consummation of all things. The divine and earthly nature reconciled and equilibrated 'on the scales of R. C.'[20] result in the perfected adept, a son of light, an embodiment of the Christos. The perfected man reveals the purpose of the Great Work: the achievement of conscious immortality. The inscription 'By this sign thou shalt conquer' appears twice amongst

SUM TOTAL
AND THE FINAL CONCLUSION

AND AT LAST: THE TWO PROVERBS CONTAIN EVERYTHING THAT IS HIDDEN IN THE HEAVENLY AND NA-
TURAL LIGHT. HE WHO RIGHTLY UNDERSTANDS AND KNOWS THESE TWO PROVERBS ACCORDING TO ETER-
NITY AND TIME, IS A RIGHT AND TRUE THEOSOPHER, CABALIST, MAGUS, AND PHILOSOPHER, AND HE WHO
CAN CORRECTLY INTERPRET THESE TWO PROVERBS ACCORDING TO THE *Alpha* AND *Omega* YOU MAY SURE-
LY AND WELL TRUST, AND THEREBY YOU CAN ALSO TEST ANYONE JUSTLY AND RIGHTLY AND WEIGH HIM
ON THE SCALES OF R. C.

MARK THIS WELL:

1.

IN CHRIST, THE VISIBLE AND
COMPREHENSIBLE GOD AND
MAN DWELLETH THE ENTIRE
INVISIBLE DIVINE NATURE: THE
HOLY TRINITY, GOD, FATHER,
SON, AND HOLY SPIRIT.

BODILY

2.

IN THE VISIBLE, COMPREHENSI-
BLE AND BEAUTIFUL GOLD,
DWELLETH THE CREATED NA-
TURE: THE INVISIBLE, ALL-PER-
FECT NATURE: THE NATURAL
EARTHLY THINGS: THAT IS:
MERCURY, SULPHUR, SALT.

BODILY

F
E
R
T
O
I
L

OF THE PHILOSOPHERS
THE GOLDEN AND SILVERY RIVER.

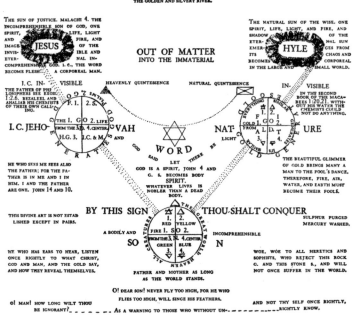

the Rennes clues. It is inscribed in Latin on the pedestal of a statue of the Virgin and Child along with the inscription 'To the master who shows the way'. It is one of the signposts to a tomb in Rennes-le-Bains churchyard, which offers more clues to the mystery of Rennes. The other version is written in French amongst a group of alchemical figures in the church at Rennes, but here an extra word has been added: 'By this sign ye shall conquer him.'[21] What might Saunière have had in mind here when he was decorating the church? It is important to keep the aim of the Great Work in mind when approaching the question of what Bérenger Saunière's secret might have been at Rennes-le-Château.

The quartered circle referred to above could be interpreted as a symbol for the four ethers when they have been united at both the physical and spiritual poles. This unification may either be brought about by the overcoming of gender as already described by Wachsmuth above or by the overcoming of the lower nature in man through rigorous spiritual work. We are, by now, aware that the fruit of the Tree of Life can eventually be given back to mankind as we become increasingly worthy to guard its potency. The figure also closely resembles the Resurrection Flag, a symbol used in medieval and Renaissance art to represent the triumph over death. The circle is quartered; in the first quarter is inscribed 'Fire' and the colour red. The elements are not further described in the remaining three quarters but the colours yellow, green and blue are. Through the action of the etheric formative forces in the earth organism the different variations in the world of colour arise in the following fashion:

When there is predominantly active in the illuminated world of substance of the earth organism:

Warmth ether, then appears the colour red;

Light ether, then appears the colour yellow;

Chemical ether, then appears the colour blue;

Life ether, then appears the colour violet.[22]

We have already noted that the main goal of this 'Sum Total and Final Conclusion'—the unification of the sexes—is conscious immortality, the final goal of both alchemist and Rosicrucian in the past. This goal is expressed in the diagram in bold letters, and stands both as an emblem and a high and exacting ideal for students of esoteric Christianity.

OUT OF MATTER
INTO THE IMMATERIAL[23]

Here we may begin to understand that Mary Magdalene and Jesus Christ may be seen to have achieved the Great Work through the purity of their relationship. This involved reversing the effect of the Fall by bringing the two human poles together once more, thereby overcoming death. There is a further possible explanation in the fact that the Church has often been referred to as the 'Bride of Christ'. The deeper meaning of this could be what Steiner was referring to when he spoke of Mary Magdalene as the sentient soul of humanity, therefore our representative.[24] Human beings were of one substance with the Creative Word, before the Fall. If we understand the Creative Word to be Christ, then at the Fall we were sundered from that union. If both humanity and the Magdalene have been described as fallen then we might deduce that, where Mary Magdalene is named as the sentient soul of humanity, then the concept of a marriage between Christ and Mary Magdalene can also apply to a marriage between Christ and mankind, or the Church. Those people on earth who begin to move forward to a new relationship with Paradise, the eternal, spiritual ground of existence, do so through their relationship to Christ.

9.
Opposing Forces and the Double

At this point it seems necessary to access knowledge held in esoteric Christianity and concealed in the Grail tradition as a preparation for deeper understanding of the mystery of Rennes-le-Château. The most uncomfortable and, at the same time, the most liberating aspect of these traditions for us today is the Manichaean notion that evil is not only necessary in human evolution, but that we all share in its essential nature. The idea that evil is an external force, located in other people, in other races or nations, but never within ourselves or the groups we belong to is a common one. Rudolf Steiner has brought the Manichaean interpretation into the twentieth century in his statements on the human 'double', sometimes referred to in literature as the *Doppelgänger*:

> It may shock you to hear of another spiritual being inhabiting the human body, concerning that entity known to spiritual science as the double or *Dopplegänger*, but in biology lessons we are not shocked to learn how many other inhabitants from the animal, plant and mineral kingdoms also cohabit our physical bodies. Just as we have discovered the bacteria and fungi rather recently, so we have rediscovered the *Doppelgänger* ... It is part of the physiological behaviour of these beings to move into the human body shortly before we are born and to accompany us from then on beneath the threshold of consciousness with their cleverness and their strong nature-bound will.[1]

Later in this passage, it is related how Rudolf Steiner described the fairy-tale character Rumpelstiltskin as an imaginative picture of the working of the double. He then described how Rumpelstiltskin is found in that part of the forest where 'the fox bids the hare goodnight'. The hare is a well-known symbol of the etheric world. Pictures of the cat as a symbol for Lucifer and the fox as a symbol for Ahriman can be found throughout folk tales. In bidding the hare 'goodnight' Ahriman is rendering the etheric body of man unconscious in that region of the etheric body where the double—Rumpelstiltskin—dwells, so that in this part of the etheric body electrical and electromagnetic impulses predominate over pure etheric activity.

Feeding off the degenerated etheric force, the double can be monitored by standard electrical devices. Wherever currents of electricity are running in the electromagnetic phenomena of the body there is the activity of the ahrimanic beings. For this reason it will be impossible for science to eventually claim that electrical devices are able to detect finer manifestations of the etheric as these would only be finer echoes of the activity of the double. The etheric body, which is free of its influence, lies outside the range of all physical investigations. Rudolf Steiner explains further:

> The *Doppelgänger* cannot bear death, wants to survive death and have a human body at the disposal of its intelligence and will-power; but it has to leave when the human ego is about to pass over the Threshold.[2]

The double cannot go through the death process when the time comes for the host to depart this world. The double leaves a few days before death, and the sick person appears to get better, to be much calmer and happier, only to die later.

The ahrimanic beings have worked tirelessly in evolution, influencing the course of history. Their aim is to separate humanity from its spiritual origin by binding man to matter and material values in every possible way. One example of this is in the manner in which many inventions have come about. Some of the ideas that have inspired our mechanistically oriented science have come to the inventor when he was in a state of suppressed consciousness:

> Between 1858 and 1865, Kekulé founded modern structural chemistry, thus making a significant contribution to research in the field of the new dyes. The following incident illustrates the part destiny played here. Kekulé fell asleep while riding on the upper deck of a London bus and missed his stop. This was compensated for by a dream in which carbon atoms joined hands and danced around him in a circle. This dream inspired the creation of his structural chemistry.[3]

The powers of opposition are able to manipulate the course of human evolution through the double in each individual, while the overall effect of many people succumbing to the forces of the double is caused by the opposing forces' widespread subversion and re-routing of human history. One interesting, and relevant, example of this can be found in the history of sugar consumption. There has been a gradual descent from sweeteners derived from the flower of the plant (honey) to the stem (cane sugar), and finally to the root (beet sugar). A materialistic knowledge of diet would find no difference in the effect of sweeteners derived from these three sources. But according to spiritual science the plant is inverted in its effect upon the human body so that the root effects the head forces of the human being. If the intellect is not carefully balanced with the heart, a cold, calculating 'ahrimanic' attitude will develop.

It is to the great advantage of ahrimanic beings to bring materialism deeper into human life and at the same time to increase their domination over each individual that they inhabit. One very effective way of doing this is by encouraging human beings to eat substances such as refined sugar which bring the *Doppelgänger* into dominance over the ego. An example of this can be seen in the case of some hyperactive children. In certain cases, chemicals in food have been shown to have a powerful role in suppressing the child's normal nature and exchanging it for the ravings and wilful demands of a different being. Why does it take very little to lure even the most carefully trained young appetite away from foods that are beneficial to those that are full of synthetic sweetners and chemicals? Could it not be the *Doppelgänger* whispering to the child to take in as much as possible of a diet on which the latter will thrive?

What happened after Kekulé's 'inspired' dream, mentioned above?

> It was soon discovered that substances of this group, produced at intermediate stages of dye manufacture, react on the human organism. They ushered in the era of synthetic drugs ... This was the start of chemical therapy, which sought to exploit the discoveries of the dye chemists ... No one can dispute that this expansion of coal tar chemistry is a triumph of the human mind. But what spiritually was behind it and how are these substances related to the cosmic whole?[4]

Chemically derived substances are like a 'synthetic mirror image'[5] of their naturally occurring counterparts. Their origin lies in the physical world with no relationship to the realm of life forces. This synthetic world creates the 'foodstuff' for the double, a source of nourishment that is entirely cut off from any cosmic, spiritual or living influences. Is it surprising, therefore, that a society increasingly supplied with this 'shadow food' should be unwittingly providing opportunity for those beings who are entirely without soul, who work with enormous strength and Mephistophelian cleverness to gain an increasing foothold in all the affairs of human beings? One way of entry for ahrimanic beings can therefore be through reduced consciousness and faulty diet.

One of our main concerns here is to investigate the connection that the human double has with what has been identified as electromagnetic energy or earth-energy, where, since the Fall, ahrimanic beings have been working in the unredeemed regions deep in the earth. When humans are positioned over these powerful areas a way of entry is made for the double to affect the individual human being's consciousness and resulting behaviour through the etheric geography of the earth itself.

After the paradise state ended as a result of the Fall, the etheric state of the earth also became subject to its degenerating dynamic. The light ether, chemical ether and life ethers were thrust down into a *subphysical world,* a realm below matter, from which they now manifest as the 'centric forces'. In this way these three ethers then become: electricity, indwelt by luciferic beings; magnetism, indwelt by ahrimanic beings; and the Third Force indwelt by the Asuras, manifesting 'terrible forces of destruction'.[6]

Rudolf Steiner often spoke of how the earth was a living being coursed through by the same subtle energy as the kingdoms of nature, including our own. It has generally been identified as electromagnetic energy, but in some locations the energy manifests in a form so powerful that it seems to interact with the psyche of those living over it. Here Rudolf Steiner's statements about the 'human double' or *Doppelgänger* are helpful.

In the various regions of the earth different forces are radiated upwards. There are magnetic forces and electrical forces, but also forces which come up out of the earth and which influence man in different ways according to the geological formation ... man's *Doppleganger* has a direct relationship to these forces which emanate from the earth in differentiated ways.[7]

Sicily is an island which produces enough evidence of the double's activity to fuel several conferences! This may well be because of its location in relation to the divide between the south European and north African tectonic plates. The terrain of Sicily also includes two volcanoes—Mount Etna near the east coast, and Stromboli on an island between the north coast and the Italian mainland. In a series of eight lectures given in Paris between 25 May and 14 June 1906 Rudolf Steiner spoke of volcanic activity in relationship to the human will:

Underneath the solid earth there are a large number of sub-terranean spaces which communicate to the sixth layer, that of fire. [Steiner was speaking of nine concentric layers within the earth.] This element of the fire-earth is intimately connected with the human will. It is this element which has produced the tremendous eruptions that brought the Lemurian epoch to an end... And yet they [volcanic eruptions] are still produced as a result of the human will which, when it is evil and chaotic, mag-netically acts on this layer and disrupts it. Nevertheless, when the human will is devoid of egoism, it is able to appease this fire. Materialistic periods are mostly accompanied and followed by natural cataclysms, earthquakes, etc. Growing powers of evolu-tion are the only alchemy capable of transforming, little by little, the organism and the soul of the earth.[8]

In a series of four lectures given in Berlin, 3–7 February 1913, Rudolf Steiner speaks of how the powerful etheric forces emanating in Sicily were misused in the past causing 'double' activity to flow in the opposite direction to the norm—from man to earth. Access to the interior of the earth caused by the geological conditions in Sicily also gave rise to exactly the right conditions to empower the activities of the double. 'At one time evil arts were practised in that place, arts which penetrated right into physical life and thence launched their assaults on the part of the human soul that had become unconscious and on the portion of the human organism that had become dead' [in other words the region of the double].[9]

In relation to the Grail legend, the evil figure of Klingsor, who was based on the historical figure of the Duke of Terra de Labur, united with Iblis, who was in her turn connected with Lucifer. Between them they conjured up great hostility to the Grail. All this took place in Kalot Bobot, which is located in Sicily.

> Even as today, if we tread Sicilian soil and have occult sight, we are aware of the Akashic after-effects of the great Empedocles still present in the atmosphere, so we can still perceive there the evil after-effects of Klingsor, who allied himself from his Duchy of Terra de Labur, across the straits of Messina, with those enemies of the Grail who occupied the fastness known in occultism and legend as Calot Bobot.[10]

In a biography of Cardinal Newman, *The Pillar of Cloud*, Meriol Trevor describes how on a tour of Italy Newman was suddenly compelled to return to Sicily after an initial visit there. His fellow travellers decided to journey home but Newman organized servants to accompany him there alone, and then suffered experiences that affected him so dramatically that he fell seriously ill and nearly died.[11]

As he lay ill in Sicily Newman wrote that he felt 'God was fighting against me—and felt at last I knew *why*—it was for self-will. I felt I had been very self-willed.'[12] The biographer also describes Newman descending to the crater of Vesuvius on the mainland then comments: '. . . it was a suitable beginning to his classical expedition to make a descent into the underworld, especially as he was about to make a similar descent spiritually'.[13] Later the biographer comments: 'Having the fever and going through a crisis were all part of the same experience; it deeply affected the whole of his being and his life. Prompted into an encounter with the Double, Newman was able to use the experience to intensify his personal evolution.'[14] The secret of this is to be found in the Gospel of Philip: the archons (the fallen powers) thought that they do what they do by their power and will. But the Holy Spirit secretly brought about everything through them as he wished.[15] The activities of the double, horrendous as the outcome may be to the individual host, remain under the ultimate control of a higher power.

When we further investigate these geological connections with the etheric earth, a regular pattern emerges. Box Hill in Surrey has been described as one of the most powerful energy points in the south of England, and two geological strata meet there. It has been reported from independent witnesses that living on the hill has a polarizing effect on relationships. It is interesting to note that the village which lies below Box Hill was named Mickleham, maybe at a time when there was still an awareness that 'where the dragon lies, so Michael can also be found'. St Michael traditionally fights the dragon as he is interchangeable with St George. It is also fascinating that there is a small area named Dragon's Green close to the tiny hamlet of Shipley in Sussex. Shipley is also a very powerful centre of earth-energy. (There was a large Templar settlement there during the Crusades.) This illustrates how the energy emanating out of the ground is untamed, and needs to be properly directed if it is to be used for good. It can equally be directed to the opposite pole and be manifested as wrongdoing. Newman battled with his double and triumphed over it.

These are locations where subjective and objective merge, creating experiences of a different reality. Rennes-le-Château is a location where experience is very dramatically polarized. In Rennes-le-Château varied anecdotal experience has led me to believe that the individual human double reacts to its counterpart in the complex geological strata below. In a sense Rennes is like a magic mirror, where subjective experiences turn to face one as objective fact. This is a symptom of what happens when the etheric world mixes strongly with physical existence. It is a place where potential violence in a simmering relationship will explode. A detailed geological map of Rennes corroborates the visible faults in the landscape while the edges of two different rock strata meet under the village itself.

Over the entrance to the church at Rennes are inscribed the words: 'Terribilis Iste Locus este', 'This Place is Terrible'—not necessarily terrible in the usual understanding of the world, but 'awesome'. This inscription was usually displayed where the construction of a new, sacred building had been completed over a powerful place on the earth. In the entrance to the church at Rennes the garish figure of a demon, Asmodeus, holds the water stoup at the base of a group of alchemical figures. As we now move forward in our investigation of the mystery of Rennes-le-Château we will begin to realize that an understanding of the double is also helpful in understanding Saunière's secret.

10.

Saunière's Secret and the Priory of Sion

Part One: The Philosopher's Stone and Knowing the Pentagram

The story of *The Da Vinci Code* was mainly based on information from *The Holy Blood and the Holy Grail*, which in turn took its inspiration from a book by Gérard de Sède[1] (later translated in English under the title *The Accursed Treasure of Rennes-le-Château*).

The now familiar theme of Rennes-le-Château, which was originally introduced to the English-speaking world in *The Holy Blood and the Holy Grail*, all began with the story of the sudden mysterious wealth acquired by the parish priest of Rennes-le-Château.

> We did not discount the argument that Saunière discovered treasure. At the same time it seemed clear to us that, whatever else he discovered, he also discovered a secret—an historical secret of immense import to his own time and perhaps to our own as well. Mere money, gold or jewels would not, in themselves, explain a number of facets to his story ... we grew increasingly convinced that Saunière's story involved more than riches, and that it involved a secret of some kind, one that was almost certainly controversial.[2]

At this point Baigent, Leigh and Lincoln began to unfold their interpretation, that the mystery of Rennes-le-Château, the knowledge of a very significant royal bloodline, lies behind Saunière's sudden rise to wealth—not worldly treasure, but something which nonetheless gives its owner great power. As we have seen, this thesis, which has since been taken up by other writers, turned the mystery of Rennes into an industry which has recently developed into the meteoric success of *The Da Vinci Code*. The treasure of Rennes-le-Château was originally reported as gold and was then represented as the result of a physical union between Christ Jesus and Mary Magdelane and its fulfilment in a dynastic bloodline.

This was the impression that *The Holy Blood and the Holy Grail* continued to leave with its huge readership for over 20 years until *The Da Vinci Code* picked up the baton and continued to run with it to the horizon. This impression has successfully planted large question marks for people whose Christianity was reasonably secure but whose knowledge of mystery language was non-existent, while it has possibly completely wiped the board for the many thousands who hovered in the outer reaches of faith.

Once this initial impression had successfully taken root, the voice of reason began to be heard from various quarters pointing out flaws in the original story, in some cases indicating a hidden and purposeful intention, which is quietly carried on behind the scenes by someone who changes the details that are put out in order to steer the course of their agenda—a gourmet feast for the conspiracy theorist! It seemed that many of the clues that had enticed researchers further into the mystery over the years had been put in their path for the purpose of encouraging potential readers to give their interpretations to these clues, thus gleaning necessary information from groups or individuals—rather like a skilled card player in search of the ace.

It has increasingly been pointed out in recent years that the basic facts upon which the authors of *The Holy Blood and the Holy Grail* based their research was a fabrication put forward by imposters posing as a supposed 'Priory of Sion'. In *The Treasure of Rennes-le-Château, A Mystery Solved*, Bill Putnam and John Edwin Wood say that 'in England there has been no book written with the aim of critically examining the source of the mystery and asking what facts are supported by hard evidence and what is supposition'.[3]

In an earlier publication from America, *The Unknown Treasure: The Priory of Sion Fraud*, Robert Richardson states: 'While Rennes-le-Château has genuine spiritual importance, the information forming the core publicity about it was fabricated in the last several decades for deliberate ends.'[4] He describes how the Priory of Sion was founded upon another organization, which in turn was founded and run in the 1920s by a George Monti: 'This group behind the Priory of Sion had limited factual information about the actual events at Rennes-le-Château and does not actively comprehend the information which it does possess.'[5]

Lynn Picknett and Clive Prince corroborate this further in their recent publication *The Sion Revelation* where they state that one thing that had become very clear to them was that the Priory's motivating ambition is not purely the political power which Baigent, Leigh and Lincoln have claimed for it. The dossiers constantly name people who are not politicians but *occultists*. They maintain that in their own experience the individuals concerned with the modern Priory also fall into the same category.

These points of view corroborate thoughts which had been building in my mind for several years before the first version of this book was published in 1996. At that time there was not enough evidence to confidently state the hypothesis that I nevertheless put forward then, but now reinforce it in this new edition. It appears indeed that 'the history of the false Priory of Sion has been constructed to build upon the histories and traditions of esoteric, initiatic, and Masonic Groups'.[7] The original Priory of Sion is described by Richardson as 'a small—but genuine—Catholic monastic order ... Sion is the ancient name for Jerusalem, where the mother house of the order was located at the monastery of Our Lady of Mt Sion.'[8] We shall now first of all ask what might be the cause of this gradual slide into decadence and, secondly, what was the information on the events at Rennes-le-Château for which the Priory of Sion were searching.

Modern occult groups no longer have knowledge of spiritual realities, which in ancient times came to people quite naturally. As time passed this spiritual perception gradually disappeared, the intellect sharpened and ancient mystery practices became decadent. Thus various levels of interpretation emerged. The natural human yearning for a spiritual birthright remained but was eventually fostered on the one hand by orthodox religion, on the other by mystery centres and later by esoteric groups. The remnants of ancient knowledge were no longer understood without the backdrop of spiritual insight which was maintained within these centres and groups. Those who belonged to them underwent a strict programme of preparation to discover truths which were once more perceived. By the nineteenth century, occult groups who still followed the ancient esoteric traditions may have found that certain vital information was missing. This meant that the original meaning behind the ceremonies, which had been handed down from the most ancient times, was also lost as materialism advanced. For example, the Hieros Gammos as reported in *The Da Vinci Code* was not originally to do with physical union between the sexes, but with a union bringing the male and female energies together at a higher level and, in so doing, restoring the original balance between the ethers that existed before the Fall, i.e. before death was experienced. As awareness of our spiritual origin faded, the natural human yearning for this birthright sent some seekers after truth down paths which led towards magical practices. One might deduce, however, that what remained of this secret relating to immortality held in the ancient ceremonies became information that eventually belonged to the highest degrees of Freemasonry. In the ninth lecture of the series *The Temple Legend*, given by Rudolf Steiner in Berlin on 16 December 1904, the following statement is made:

> It is important that we should speak about the higher degrees of Freemasonry, because this manner of instruction sets itself special tasks, certain aspects of which will be discussed in the near future. We are dealing, in the main, with a special rite that is called the combined rite of Memphis and Misraim. I have already mentioned that the Memphis and Misraim rite possesses a great number of degrees, that ninety-five degrees must be undertaken, and that usually the Supreme Leaders of the Grand Orients—i.e. those of Germany, Great Britain and America—possess the ninety-sixth degree. These degrees are so arranged that up to the end of about the eightieth to eighty-ninth degree they are divided up in the way I shall presently describe to you.
>
> From about the eighty-seventh degree onwards start the real occult degrees into which no one can be initiated who has not made a thorough study of the subject. I always make the reservation that in Europe there is nobody who has undertaken all these degrees or who has really undergone an occult Freemasonry training.[9]

Steiner would appear to be describing a situation where the higher degrees of Freemasonary have been lost. Furthermore, in his opinion, there is no one who is sufficiently trained to advance to the higher degrees which he describes as 'the real occult degrees'. One would assume that there are certain individuals who want to achieve the knowledge held by these lost degrees without the necessary training.

And so they lay bait to catch the knowledge by publishing a kaleidoscope of genuine information mixed with fiction to see if anyone out there will respond.

Steiner continues:

> First of all, it is to be borne in mind that the whole of the Masonic higher degrees trace back to a personality often spoken about but equally very much misunderstood. He was particularly misunderstood by nineteenth-century historians, who have no idea of the difficult situations an occultist can meet in life. This personality is the ill-famed and little understood Cagliostro. The so-called Count Cagliostro, in whom an individuality concealed itself which was recognized in its true nature only by the highest initiates, attempted originally to bring Freemasonry in London to a higher stage . . . He did not succeed in London at that time. He then tried in Russia and also at the Hague. Everywhere he was unsuccessful, for very definite reasons.
>
> Then, however, he was successful in Lyons, forming an occult Masonic lodge of the Philalethes [Searchers after Truth] out of a group of local Masons, which was called the Lodge of Triumphing Wisdom.[10]

Cagliostro is a fascinating character who has been the subject of a smear campaign in that his reputation has been made out to be a good deal worse that it should have been. He was famous in his time, being like a modern day celebrity with his portrait appearing on fans and snuff boxes. Cagliostro was probably born in the 1740s. He was brought up by the head of the Islamic religion at Medina and later lived as a Christian in Europe. He studied in Egypt as a young man. He later was well connected to several royal households. Cagliostro was interested in the Egyptian Rite of Freemasonry, and died in prison as a result of being tried by the Inquisitorial Court for, amongst other things, setting up a Masonic lodge in Rome.

> The real crux of the matter was the Count's attitude towards the traditional institutions of his time. He believed in magic, he claimed and demonstrated supernatural powers. He conjured spirits, predicted future events, and claimed to have medicines, talismanic and

1. *View of Rennes-le-Château from La Pique*

2. *Magdalene Tower, built by Bérenger Saunière with money from the mysterious fortune he acquired*

3. *Bérenger Saunière (1852–1917), parish priest of Rennes-le-Château from 1885 to 1915*

4. *The Shepherds of Arcady by Nicholas Poussin, from the Louvre, Paris*

5. *The last of the clues leading to the Jean Vié tomb; an inscription on the plinth of a wrought iron cross with Virgin and Child outside the door of the church at Rennes-les-Bains. Underneath 'In Hoc Signo Vinces' ('By This Sign Thou Shalt Conquer') are written the words 'Domino Vie Rectore' which Gérard de Sède has translated as: 'To the master who shows the way'*

6. *Jean Vié tomb in the cemetery outside the church at Rennes-les-Bains*

7. *The Apprentice Pillar at Rosslyn Chapel near Edinburgh in Scotland (left);
image of DNA (right)*

8. *Cymatic patterns on the arches of Rosslyn Chapel*

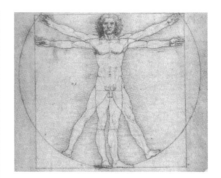

10. 'Vitruvian Man' by Leonardo
da Vinci

9. 'Twelve-year-old Jesus in the Temple'
by Ambrogio Borgognone (1450–1523)

11. 'Our Lady Under-the-
Earth in the crypt at
Chartres Cathedral

12. 'The Last Supper' by Leonardo da Vinci

13. Fern patterns in the fan-vaulting of Exeter Cathedral

14. Fern patterns in frost figures

15. Standing stone on Orkney. The angle of the top is 42°

16. Dr Rudolf Steiner (1861–1925), founder of anthroposophy, or spiritual science

17. 'The Group' wooden sculpture by Rudolf Steiner and Edith Maryon

18. Aurora borealis

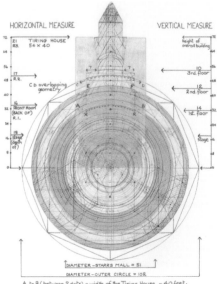

HORIZONTAL MEASURE

VERTICAL MEASURE

19. *The Globe Playhouse (1599). Schematic design*

20. *A very impressive example of the Fibonnacci series leading to fractals within plant growth is reiterated by the florets of broccoli 'Romanesco'. The spirals displayed here lead in alternate opposite directions, having the successive numbers of the Fibonacci series*

alchemical, by which he performed extraordinary cures without remuneration. His free clinics brought upon him the undying enmity of the physicians; his disconcerting remarks irritated the learned; and his dire pronouncements about the future of France disturbed the aristocracy.[11]

Describing the work of Cagliostro in the Lodge at Lyons, Steiner continues by saying:

> The purpose of this lodge was specified by Cagliostro ... Cagliostro was concerned with two things: firstly, with instructions enabling one to produce the so-called Philosopher's Stone; secondly, with creating an understanding of the mystic pentagram. I can only give you a hint of the meaning of these two things. They may be treated with a deal of scorn, but they are not to be taken merely symbolically; they are based on real facts.[12]

Concerning the pentagram and drawing a connection to the Rosicrucians, Steiner says:

> The second lesson was the knowledge of the pentagram. That is the ability to distinguish the five bodies of man one from another ... Only one who knows the pentagram learns to know the five bodies ... Those pupils of Cagliostro who had followed his methods would thereby have achieved what some Rosicrucians achieved who had basically undergone a training with the same orientation. They were in a school of the great European adepts, who taught that the five bodies were realities, and not to remain as mere concepts. That is called 'Knowing the Pentagram' and 'Moral Rebirth.'[13]

Rudolf Steiner's explanation of the nature of the philosopher's stone, Cagliostro's first concern, contains some intriguing information.

> The Philosopher's Stone has a specific purpose, which was stated by Cagliostro; it is meant to prolong human life to a span of 5527 years. To a freethinker that appears laughable. In fact, however, it is possible, by means of special training, to prolong life indefinitely by learning to live outside the physical body ... We are not dealing here with physical death, but with the following. Physical death is

only an apparent occurrence for him who has understood the Philosopher's Stone for himself, and has learned to separate it. For other people it is a real happening, which signifies a great division in their life. For he who understands how to use the Philosopher's Stone in the way that Cagliostro intended his pupils to do, death is only an apparent occurrence. It does not even constitute a decisive turning point in life; it is, in fact, something which is only there for the others who can observe the adept and say that he is dying. He himself, however, does not really die. It is much more the case that the person concerned has learned to live without his physical body, that he has learned during the course of his life to let all those things take place in him gradually that happen suddenly in the physical body at the moment of death. Everything has already taken place in the body of the person concerned, which otherwise takes place at death. Death is then no longer possible, for the said person has long ago learned to live without the physical body. He lays aside the physical body in the same way that one takes off a raincoat, and he puts a new body on just as one puts a new raincoat on.

Now that will give you an inkling. That is one lesson which Cagliostro taught—the Philosopher's Stone—which allows physical death to become a matter of small importance...

I will not say that the pupils of Cagliostro never achieved anything. In general they went as far as comprehending the astral body. Cagliostro was extremely skilful in imparting a view of the astral body. Long before the catastrophe broke over him, he had succeeded in starting a school in Petersburg and a few other places in Europe, in addition to the one in Lyons, out of which later emerged at least a few people who had the basis for some to proceed to the eighteenth, nineteenth and twentieth higher degrees of Freemasonry. Thus Cagliostro at least had an important influence on occult Masonry in Europe before ending his days in the prison in Rome.[14]

These passages highlight two significant references to information that a twentieth or twenty-first century occult group might have been trying to unearth information, on prolonging human life and on the secrets of the pentagram. The pentagram has been prominently featured in some of the major publications in the Rennes saga, particularly and latterly in *The Da Vinci Code*, where the murdered Saunière is found with his arms and legs outstretched in the form of a pentagram. It is interesting to note that in an initiation-cave of the Cathars, situated in the Languedoc, a human-size pentagram was carved into the wall in which the initiate stood, suspended above the ground in the manner of Vitruvian Man.

A critic of the Rennes-le-Château programme of disinformation might argue that all reference to a landscape pentagram discovered there is solely based on these fabrications. However, in Chapter 13 of Puttenham and Wood's book it is conceded that 'Henry Lincoln started to study the geometry of the area around Rennes-le-Château following a suggestion from Professor Christopher Cornford.'[15] This referred to Cornford's analyses of the Poussin painting *The Shepherds of Arcady* to which the parchments refer, and in which Saunière was reported to have taken an interest. Professor Cornford of the Royal College of Art 'had made a particular study of the geometrical structure of paintings and had, indeed, already analysed one of the works of Poussin in this way ... he was surprised to find evidence of the older and long outdated Masonic-geometric system ... What had so startled Cornford was ... [that the] ancient geometric symbol which Poussin had used was the Pentacle.'[16]

Following Cornford's suggestion that 'alignments should be sought in association with the mystery of Rennes-le-Château and, more specifically, those associated with the angles of a pentagon'[17] Henry Lincoln had already established that the horizon depicted in the right-hand corner of the painting very closely resembled four topographical features which could clearly be seen in a modern photograph of the actual landscape, taken from a position where the tomb depicted in the Poussin painting had stood until it was destroyed by explosives a few years ago. He described these four locations as follows: '... the rock of Toustounes. Further to the right is the flank of the mountain of Cardou and then the unmistakable silhouette of the crest of Blanchefort. Most satisfying and exciting of all is to recognize the distant outline of Rennes-le-Château which is visible as an insignificant mound on the far horizon to the right. That mound is exactly placed in the painting.'[18]

When Henry Lincoln had completed his calculations in accordance with Professor Cornford's suggestions he found: 'Three principle mountain features in the immediate locality, each of them relevant to the mystery and on each of which a castle had been built ...'[19] These were the Templar Chateau of Bezu, the Chateau of Blanchefort and the village of Rennes-le-Château. We can thus conclude that at least the landscape pentagram at Rennes really does exist.

★

Information on prolonging human life, as studied in Cagliosto's groups, will be considered in connection with Bérenger Saunière's enigmatic activities and the various specially prepared pieces of information fed to the outside world by the bogus Priory of Sion. As well as parchments, which Saunière was reported to have found in the church at Rennes, were documents which had been planted in the Bibliothèque nationale in Paris. As stated earlier, it had long ago occurred to me that all of these documents upon which the mystery of Rennes has been built might be part of a trawling operation mounted by people who had part, but not all, of a picture which they wished to complete. When I put this possibility to David Wood, author of *Genisis* and *Geneset*, the two books which came after *The Holy Blood and the Holy Grail*, he shook my hand in confirmation and said 'You're there!' In commenting on one of these documents, *The Red Serpent*, in *Genisis*, he stated:

> I have never been totally convinced of the purpose of this pub-
> lication ... it appears to have been the work of someone who had
> far more information than was publicly available and yet could not
> find the complete answer to the riddle. It was certainly composed
> during or after Saunière's time, as it refers to things which did not
> exist prior to his period. In my opinion, the only reason for having
> produced it was to put the 'hounds' on the right scent and then to
> obtain benefits—not necessarily material—from being present at
> the 'kill'.[20]

Robert Richardson's research into the history of French occultism in the eighteenth and nineteenth centuries provides an excellent opportunity for filling in the gap between the time to which Rudolf

Steiner refers at the end of the eighteenth century and that in which Saunière and his group were active at the turn of the twentieth century.

> The French occult revival saw the publication of a vast body of literature in both public and private circulation, which opened up the hidden world of secret societies and hereforeto unknown groups dedicated to the promulgation of guarded knowledge ... The first of these groups appeared in 1838, when Hautpoul family member Jacques Étienne Marconis de Nègre, who was raised at Clat where Bérenger Saunière would later serve as priest before coming to Rennes-le-Château, founded the Rite of Memphis ... During the lifetime of its founder, it claimed structural and philosophical similarities to the Philalethes of Narbonne ... At the turn of the century it was united by the omnipresent Papus with the rite of Misram to form the Rite of Memphis and Misram ... it is also likely that it is the order to which Saunière belonged and which received information about his discoveries ... The order in question is called the Order of the Rose-Croix of the Temple and the Grail ... Its roots appear to begin in Toulouse in 1850, where Charles Eduard de Lapasse founded the Cabalistic Order of the Rose-Croix. Seeking to establish authority for his teachings, Lapasse claimed to have been raised by a prince Balabrin. He alleged the Prince was a disciple of Cagliostro.[21]

It will be remembered that Rudolf Steiner made reference to Cagliostro having been 'successful in Lyons, forming an occult Masonic lodge of Philalethes out of a group of local Masons'. In the above passage a group of the same name is mentioned, while Bérenger Saunière was reported to have made contact with occult groups in Paris and is also described as having possibly stayed in Lyons, lodging in a house in the rue des Macabées a few doors away from the home of one of the Martinist leaders in Lyons; allegedly an underground tunnel connected the two houses. The word 'Macabées' is slang for corpse in French, and there are supposed to be catacombs under the ground there. This may or may not be of use to the investigation as it proceeds. In Picknett and Prince's *Turin Shroud*, Saunière's journeys to Paris are considered:

...whatever went on in that remote Languedoc village must have been impelling, for even today it is a difficult and tedious journey to Paris (we speak from experience). Yet over eighty years ago the cream of Parisian society, including the beautiful and famous opera singer Emma Calvé (who died in 1942), made that journey to see Saunière. Habsburg princes were also among others who visited the tiny hamlet. We do not know why.

What motives would impel such a person to travel that distance: could it be to seek fame, fortune or secret knowledge? It could have been the lure of immortality, the Elixir of Youth or any other chemical by-products claimed for the Great Work. Whatever Saunière had, real or imagined, was obviously worth having. Let us not forget that Sir Isaac Newton was an enthusiastic and unashamed alchemist and he, too, was allegedly Grand Master of the Priory. As were Nicholas Flamel, Robert Boyle, Robert Fludd ... and Leonardo da Vinci? All of these men had the finest minds of their generations, some almost of all time; surely they, of all people, were not duped by a system of hocus pocus?[22]

Earlier in the same chapter Picknett and Prince had referred to Nicholas Flamel of Paris 'who was believed to have lived to at least the age of 400, together with his beloved wife Perenelle. Flamel wrote that he had achieved the Great Work on 17 January 1392.[23] Nicholas Flamel was named as one of the Grand Masters of the Priory of Sion in the *Dossiers Secret*. If we turn to Robert Richardson's research again we find a tenous connection with Emma Calvé, one of Saunière's illustrious associates already mentioned above who, in 1894, 'bought the old Chateau of Cabrières near Millau, where at the end of the 17th century the Cabrières family was alleged to have preserved the book of Abraham the Jew, said to be the prize possession of the alchemist Nicholas Flamel'.[24]

Here it is interesting to remember that Nicholas Flamel figures in *The Philosopher's Stone*, the first of the Harry Potter series. Strange the way that *The Holy Blood and the Holy Grail*, *The Da Vinci Code* and *Harry Potter* books have all risen to be best sellers world-wide! If we continue to read the above passage we learn that Calvé

...restored the Chateau and, like other prominent names in this story, focused her life around the search for esoteric knowledge.

Their relationship with Saunière was that of those who consult with a keeper of secrets, seeking some kind of knowledge from him. The government officials who visited Saunière in the remote village of Rennes-le-Château were high-level Masons, an odd association for a rural priest who railed against the activities of the Masonically influenced Republicans. Unless Saunière and the Masons were philosophical bedfellows through his esoteric interests and discoveries. The reason for the association with these people—who gravitated around the Order of the Rose-Croix of the Temple and the Grail—was because of these overlapping interests. Saunière was thought to be on the trail of information very dear to them—if not the guardian—of long lost, secret knowledge of interest to them all.[25]

What of the other documents, two supposedly ancient parchments which the Priory have also claimed to be part of a practical joke? Gérard de Sède tells us that during February 1964 copies of two of the parchments were given to him, and he subsequently presented their contents to the world in the book which Henry Lincoln bought on his family holiday in France. When Henry Lincoln first met Gérard de Sède he asked him: 'Why didn't you publish the hidden message?' De Sède's answer was: 'Because we thought it might interest someone like you to find it for yourself.'[26]

11.
Saunière's Secret and the Priory of Sion

Part Two: A Kind of Ahrimanic Immortality

It seems that somebody had been waiting for someone like Henry Lincoln to turn up. Having returned home from France with the book he had casually purchased there, he was lying under a tree in his garden on a sunny summer afternoon.

> On my lap the book had fallen open at the page which reproduced one of the curious parchments found by the priest. There was nothing at all exceptional in the text of the document. A few lines from the gospel in Latin: ET FACTUM EST EUM IN SABBATO SECUNDO . . . 'And it came to pass on the second sabbath . . .' My eyes began to close in that comfortable holiday torpor that comes when work, responsibilities, pressures are far away. The Latin text swam meaninglessly before me. Unthinkingly, it seemed randomly, I began to pick letters off the page. A . . . D . . . A . . . G . . . Suddenly I jerked upright. It was as if someone had clashed mighty brazen cymbals two inches from my ear. I was spelling out a message. Not in Latin, but in French! A DAGOBERT II ROI ET A SION EST CET TRESOR ET IL EST LA MORT[1]

Which he eventually translated as: TO DAGOBERT II, KING, AND TO SION BELONGS THIS TREASURE AND HE IS THERE DEAD.[2]

Is it possible that: A DAGOBERT II ROI ET A SION EST CET TRESOR ET IL EST LA MORT could be interpreted as: TO DAGOBERT II, AND TO SION BELONGS THIS TREASURE AND IT IS DEATH? Henry Lincoln certainly considered this initially.

An alternative reading of IL EST LA MORT could be 'It is Death'. Though more dramatic, it is slightly the more questionable of the two renderings. There are no accents in the written text to give firmly 'là' (there) rather than 'la', the definite article for the noun 'la mort' (death). Nevertheless, for a more correct rendering of 'It is death', the French should read: 'C'est la mort'. 'It is death' is certainly more satisfying. It is vague enough to lead nowhere and it avoids the question: who is the 'he' that is there dead? Dagobert's remains are known to be elsewhere.[3]

So, for one reason or other, at that point, Henry Lincoln turned away from pursuing a major piece of bait laid in his path and set out on the route that ultimately led to the bloodline theme, another possible priority on the Priory's agenda.

In the early stages of my research, towards the end of the eighties, a bizarre possibility gradually began to take shape. Long before I read Henry Lincoln's first translation of 'IL EST LA MORT' and several years before finding corroboration in Picknett and Prince's *Turin Shroud*, I began to think that the bloodline was significant—but for a different reason. The painting that Saunière was supposed to have visited in the Louvre on his reported visit to Paris, which was also that from which Professor Cornford found corroboration for the vast pentagram in the landscape around Rennes, *The Shepherds of Arcadia* by Nicholas Poussin, shows a tomb which was later discovered in the landscape there. Shepherds and a shepherdess are grouped around it studying the inscription carved into its side: 'ET IN ARCADIA EGO'. If one looks up this inscription in *Brewer's Dictionary of Phrase and Fable,* one finds the translation from the Latin, 'And I too in Arcadia' along with the information: 'a tomb inscription often depicted in classical paintings. Its author is unknown, and its precise interpretation is disputed. It is possible that in this context "I" is Death.'[4] According to Baigent, Lee and Lincoln:

> In 1656 Poussin, who was living in Rome at the time, had received a visit from the Abbé Louise Fouquet, brother of Nicholas Fouquet, Superintendent of France to Louis XIV of France. From Rome, the abbé dispatched a letter to his brother, describing his meeting with Poussin. Part of this letter is worth quoting. 'He and I described certain things, which I shall with ease be able to explain to you in detail—things which will give you, through Monsieur Poussin, advantages which even kings would have great pains to draw from

him, and which, according to him, it is possible that nobody else will ever rediscover in the centuries to come. And what is more, these are things so difficult to discover that nothing now on this earth can prove of better fortune nor be their equal.[5]

Only in death are all men equal. Knowledge of power over death would be an advantage that even royalty could not confer. However, in this instance, maybe a particular royal bloodline might be supposed to have a slight edge over others. The information in one of the sets of documents lodged in the public library in Paris, *Les Dossiers Secrets*, included genealogical material relating to the ancient Merovingian line of kings. Those who planted them there seemed to know the origin and destination of the bloodline through the ages. What more information could an outsider give? What was important about the presence of the significant local family Hautpoul de Blanchefort in that particular area? (One remembers that it was a member of this family, Jacques Étienne Marconis de Nègre, who was reported by Richardson to have founded the Rite of Memphis in 1838.) To discover the real significance of their bloodline it is necessary to refer back to some of the information we have picked up in the previous chapters.

Over western Europe, before exoteric Christianity had filtered in from the East, there spread the cultures of the early European tribes which included Goths, Visigoths, Lombards, Suevi, Vandals and Franks. 'In this ancient Europe a group of human beings had been preserved who had not been taken away from sharing in the Tree of Life, in whom there lived on, so to speak, the trees of life—ash and elm. In Europe something was left over as it were, like a treasured remnant of the forces of life.'[6] The forces of the Tree of Life to a certain extent still flowed through the blood of these people.

One can here understand how there could be a certain *similarity* between the blood of the Merovingian dynasty in France and the figure of Jesus, the *Luke* Jesus child whose blood was vivified with the full power of the life and chemical ethers, forces of the Tree of Life—an unexpected connection but not a hereditary one. A clue to this may be concealed in a legend that Merovée, after whom the Meriovingian line was named, was born of two fathers. His mother, according to this legend, had been impregnated by both her husband, King Clodio, and by a sea monster. The legend then points out that two bloodstreams flowed in the veins of Merovée, one human, one semi-divine or extraterrestrial. By virtue of his dual blood Merovée was said to have been endowed with an impressive array of superhuman powers. And whatever the historical actuality behind the legend, the Merovingian dynasty continued to be mantled in an aura of magic, sorcery and the supernatural. According to tradition, Merovingian monarchs were occult adepts, initiates in arcane sciences, practitioners of esoteric arts... They were often called 'the sorcerer kings' or 'thaumaturge kings'. By virtue of some miraculous property in the fringes of their robes, they were deemed to possess miraculous curative powers.

The Hautpoul de Blanchefort family had been described as belonging to the Merovingian bloodline. They had lived in the Rennes area for many hundreds of years. According to Robert Richardson 'Blanchefort was the ancestral home of a Cathar noble by that name, not of any Templar Grand Master, few researchers have ever bothered to investigate this ...[7] The four parchments which Saunière was reported to have found in the church at Rennes were supposedly concealed there by Abbé Antoine Bigou, Curé of Rennes-le-Château and chaplain to the Hautpoul de Blanchefort family. Bigou has been said to have composed two of them himself. The content of one was supposed to have been repeated in anagram form on the tombstone that Bigou had drawn up for Marie, Marquise d'Hautpoul de Blanchefort for the churchyard at Rennes in 1783. The official 'Priory story' first related by Gérard de Sède described how, after returning from Paris, Saunière 'spent nights shut up in this cemetery', after which it was discovered that he had 'patiently polished one stone until the inscriptions had been erased'. Again, a little later, he caused the other stone to disappear altogether. Although the story has subsequently been disproved by recent detailed investigation,[8] the fact remains that 17 January was the date of Marie de Hautpoul's death. She shared this death date with other individuals to whom Gérard de Sède draws our attention, describing how several clues lead to a strange tomb, the last of which refers one's direction 'to the Master who shows the way'.[9] On the tombstone may be read (translated):

Here lies
Jean VIE
born in 1808
Appointed Curé in 1840
Died on 1 September 1872
Pray for him.

... What first catches one's eye is the exceedingly unusual format used here to write 1 September, namely, 'le 1er 7bre, which places in prominence the number 17. Can we invoke chance for this? No, because Jean Vié did not die on 1 September (we have taken trouble to verify this in the *State Civil Registers*).

There remains only one solution, that with which someone decidedly wants us to become familiar, namely, that of the rebus and the pun. The writer has skilfully suggested a date, which is the same as that which we have already noticed on the enigmatic tomb of the Marchioness de Blanchefort and which we shall find again though sometimes in different forms.—17 January...[10]

Gérard de Sède describes another tomb to the left of the Jean Vié tomb in which Boudet's mother and sister are buried, then continues:

To the left of the Boudet tomb there is another tomb, that of Paul-Urbain de Fleury, grandson of Françoise and Marie d'Hautpoul de Blanchefort ... It would be a very remarkable occurrence for one to have a double life, but it is a rare one to have a double tomb and still rarer to have a double birth and a double death. Nevertheless if one can believe what is before one's eyes, this is what must have happened to this gentleman. The first stone is engraved as follows:

CI GIT PA	CI GIT PA
UL URBAIN	UL URBAIN
DE FLEURY	DE FLEURY
NE LE 3 MAI	DECIDE LE
1776	7 AOUT
	1836

A little further away to the right, on the other hand, a second stone declares:

IL EST PASSE EN FAISANT LE BIEN
Restes transférés
De Paul-Urbain Compte de FLEURY
Décédé le 7 août 1856
à l'âge de 60 ans

If Paul-Urbain died in 1856 at the age of sixty as the second stone affirms, he cannot have been born in 1776, as the first stone states, but in 1796. If he was born in 1776 as the first stone affirms, he cannot have been sixty years old at his death in accordance with the second stone but eighty.

In reality Paul-Urbain de Fleury was born neither in 1776 nor in 1796 but in 1778.

Double tombstones, double inscriptions on the first stone and double dates.[11]

Here Gérard de Sède is referring to a tombstone which is still clearly to be seen by any passer-by. This strange de Fleury tomb again belongs to a member of the Hautpoul de Blanchefort family.

Both Gérard de Sède and the authors of *The Holy Blood and the Holy Grail* are anxious to emphasize 17 January in relation to Saunière's death which was on 22 January. Descriptions of the cause of his death differ. In *The Holy Blood and the Holy Grail* a stroke is dramatically described by the authors:

On January 17th, 1917, Saunière then in his sixty-fifth year, suffered a sudden stroke. The date of January 17th is perhaps suspicious. The same date appears on the tombstone of the Marquise d'Hautpoul de Blanchefort—the tombstone Saunière had eradicated ... But what makes Saunière's stroke on January 17th most suspicious is the fact that five days before, on January 12th, his parishioners declared that he had seemed to be in enviable health for a man of his age. Yet on January 12th, according to a receipt in our possession, Marie Denarnaud [his housekeeper] had ordered a coffin for her master ... On January 22nd Saunière died unshriven. The following morning his body was placed upright in an armchair on the terrace of the Tour Magdala, clad in an ornate robe adorned with scarlet tassels. One by one certain unidentified mourners filed past, many of them plucking tassels of remembrance from the dead man's garment. There has never been any explanation of this ceremony.[12]

The tassels on the robes of the Merovingian kings have already been described. Thin, red silk cords have been connected with Masonic and Templar ritual in which they symbolize blood. The Red Serpent document mentioned in Chapter 10 described a red snake uncoiling across the centuries. This could be a reference to the Merovingian bloodline holding the transforming power of the four ethers working together with their full original power. Would a ceremony that involved touching these tassels confer these special properties of the Merovingian bloodline to those involved?

The authors of *The Holy Blood and the Holy Grail* say that 'Saunière died unshriven' yet in Gérard de Sède's version: 'It was not until two days after he died that the Curé of Rennes-le-Château received the last sacraments from the hands of Abbé Rivière.'[13] In an article in the April 2005 edition of *Fortean Times*, Paul Smith emphatically states that: 'Saunière *did* receive absolution on his deathbed—and was buried on 24 January 1917 at 10 o'clock in the morning, with a High Mass with deacon and sub-deacon— the story of Saunière's shocking deathbed confessions is another example of modern mythmaking.'[14]

De Sède's version is that on 17 January Saunière was 'struck by an apoplectic fit at the doorway of the Magdala tower'.[15] He describes Saunière's final moments with the priest more accurately but ends on an ominous note:

> What passed between the two priests? We shall never know. But when Rivière left his dying friend he was deathly pale and thrown into confusion.
>
> His emotion was not transitory. He became withdrawn, taciturn and silent. Up to his death, he was not seen to laugh. What terrible secrets had been imparted to him in confidence? What spiritual abyss had he seen gaping before him? Did Bérenger's soul seem to have already changed into one of those stones on which even divine mercy had broken its wings? Did he think that he had abandoned his friend on the very threshold of hell?[16]

What can we find that might throw light on this particular date which has been so energetically highlighted?

There is also an astronomical connection. On January 17, approximately, it may vary slightly from year to year, the sun enters the sidereal constellation (i.e. the actual stars) of Capricorn. In earlier times this constellation was known as the Gate of Death. Capricorn was also associated with an inverted pentagram; note the pentagram stands for the etheric body. Also Eliphas Levi connects the Goat (Capricorn) and the inverted pentagram with Baphomet! Gérard de Sède thinks that Saunière was linked with an occult society of a neo-Rosicrucian type such as one following Levi or Papus. Is it a coincidence that the sun enters *tropical* Capricorn on 23 December (i.e. according to the ordinary zodiac)—the death day of Dagobert II? Could this be connected with what Steiner refers to as 'an ahrimanic transposition of time'?[17] Another such curiosity is Hallowe'en, the ancient Celtic festival of Samhain, festival of the dead. The sun in the ordinary tropical zodiac reaches 7 degrees Scorpio on this date. If we look to see when the sun would reach 7 degrees of Scorpio in the *sidereal* zodiac, now, in the 1990s, the date would be approximately 24 November. However, between 1700 and 1800 the date would have been 22 November![18] And the church of St Sulpice, feast day 17 January, was built in 1746.[19]

We have already mentioned Georges Monti. Monti was secretary to Joséphin Péledan, who founded the Order of the Temple and Rose Cross. A similar order to the Rite of Memphis which Papus united with the Rite of Misram is described as the one through which Monti contacted other orders and learned of the 'discoveries' of Saunière. Monti was reported by de Sède to have kept a surveillance on the anthroposophists in Paris, gaining their confidence by translating Assyrian and Chaldean texts for them.

In connection with all of this it is very interesting to note that Rudolf Steiner, who was giving a course of twelve lectures, *The Karma of Untruthfulness*, between 1 and 30 January 1917, had an interview with a prominent French anthroposophist after a break in the lectures on 15 January and then continued to lecture on 20 January. In the lecture he gave on that date, three days after Saunière's apparent stroke

or apoplectic fit, and two days before Saunière's death, he made the
following statement:

> Those who enter the circle of certain societies practising ceremonial
> magic are securing for themselves a power that reaches beyond
> death, a kind of ahrimanic immortality. For these people this is their
> main concern. For them, the society they enter provides a kind of
> guarantee that certain forces—which should by rights only live in
> them until the moment of death—will continue to live, even
> beyond death. More people than you might think are nowadays
> filled with this idea of guaranteeing for themselves an ahrimanic
> immortality, which consists in exercising influence not only as an
> individual human being, but also through the instrument of a
> society of this kind. Such societies exist in the most varied forms,
> and individuals who have attained certain degrees of advancement
> in these societies know: As a member of this society I shall become
> to some degree immortal because forces which would otherwise
> come to an end at my death will continue to work beyond death.
>
> What these people then experience through this ceremonial
> magic makes them quite oblivious to a thought which would
> concern someone who takes such things truly seriously and in a
> genuinely dignified way. This is that the more the person gains by
> way of materialistic immortality, or rather ahrimanic immortality,
> the more he loses of the consciousness of true, genuine immortality.
> Yet materialism has taken such a hold on many souls today that they
> remain unconcerned about this and are tricked into striving for
> ahrimanic immortality. It could indeed be said that societies exist
> today which, from a spiritual or occult point of view, could be
> called 'insurance companies for ahrimanic immortality'!
>
> It is only a small number of people in each case who understand
> all these things. For as a rule these societies are organized in such a
> way that the ceremonial magic they practise influences only those
> who are unaware of the implications, merely desiring to make
> contact with the spiritual world by means of symbolic ceremonies.
> There are many such people. And those who have this desire are by
> no means necessarily the worst. They are accepted as members of
> the circle of ceremonial magic among whom there are then a few

who simply use the rest of the members as instruments. Therefore one should beware of all secret societies administered by so-called higher grades. These administrative grades usually comprise those who have been initiated to a stage at which they only have a vague idea of what I have just been explaining to you. They comprise those who are to work positively in connection with certain goals and aims which are then realized by the wider group of those who have been merely inveigled into the circle of ceremonial magic. Everything these people do is done in such a way that it leads in the direction required by the higher grades but is strengthened by the forces which come from ceremonial magic.[20]

Was Rudolf Steiner referring to actual events at Rennes-le-Château in this lecture which he gave three days after 17 January 1917, the day when Saunière's stroke or apoplectic fit was reported to have happened and two days before his actual recorded date of death? Was Steiner issuing a warning based on information concerning previously conjectured events, or is this merely a total coincidence, a cosmic joke, issued from beyond a human level to mislead us all yet again?

12.
Opposition to the Grail and its Influence in the Modern World

In *The Holy Blood and the Holy Grail* the authors claim that the Order of the Priory of Sion is a precursor to the Knights Templar. They describe the 'cutting of the elm at Gisors' in 1188 when 'a formal separation supposedly occurred between the two institutions. The Ordre de Sion, which had created the Knights Templar, now washed its hands of its celebrated protégés. The 'parent', in other words, officially disowned the 'child'. This rupture is said to have been commemorated by a ritual or ceremony of some sort.'[1]

Only three years later, 1190, the period of rulership of the archangel Raphael came to an end. It is also the time which Rudolf Steiner has indicated as marking the eventual fading of the esoteric Grail tradition. Steiner has described how each of the archangels rule in turn over a period of 260 years. When the effect of this is studied it can begin to be seen how the particular characteristics of each archangel has influenced the period of its rulership. For example, Gabriel takes Mohammed to the Highest Heaven, dictates the Koran, and also rules over the Victorian era. He is connected with the moon and the preservation of blood ties. The crescent moon is a symbol of Islam, and is also connected with the forces of reproduction and heredity. In Islam and Judaism, both patriarchal religions, the concept of family is strong.

Raphael is the archangel connected with healing. His planet, Mercury, is associated with the elm tree, so that in the 'cutting of the elm' ceremony at Gisors, whatever else the significance of that ceremony might have been, we can see that it marks the end of one epoch and the start of another. The Raphaelic instinct for healing was the birthright of those living during the so-called Dark Ages. The archangel who rules after Raphael is Samael, related to Mars, the planet that energizes the dawning age of increased independence of thought, the age of the consciousness soul.

We have been following the path of the underground stream of exoteric Christianity. As we saw, the Order of Knights Templar was a continuation of this stream. The dawning of the age of Samael, which would span the increasingly materialistic ages to come, would then give birth to the new form of human consciousness which meant that the previous natural access to spiritual realities would gradually fade and there would be very few people in the coming centuries who would be able to keep the ancient wisdom of the mysteries alive in a Christian context. It is therefore understandable that the activities of the Knights Templar are so often misunderstood when seen from the position of twenty-first century consciousness.

It is also possible that the Priory of Sion, which we hear about in current books on the subject, is a modern reconstruction of other groups which formed in the wake of the Templars after their obliteration, rather than having been instrumental in their instigation. These original groups would have used the Grail science, which the inner circle of Templars had intended for the general advancement of evolution, to suit their own purposes. In this way the origins of an 'anti-Grail' stream would have been founded. As the years passed this could have became the secret core of all that stirs under the surface when the various conspiracy theories are investigated today.

The involvement of Bernard of Clairveaux with the founding of the Templars has also been suggested in a scenario put forward by Baigent, Leigh and Lincoln to demonstrate that the aim and purpose of St Bernard in sending out the original nine knights had been for them to rummage about for 'great quantities of bullion, sacred vessels, additional unspecified material and "treasure" of an indeterminate kind . . . twenty-four different hoards buried beneath the Temple itself.'[2] The argument is made to seem plausible when the writers state that, prior to the Templars' expedition to Palestine, the Cistercians were dangerously close to bankruptcy. Under St Bernard's guidance, they underwent a sudden change of fortune. This assumption is not, however, in keeping with the historical facts.

According to James France, a leading expert on the Cistercians and author of *The Cistercians in Scandinavia*, it is not accurate to say that the Cistercians 'were "close to Bankruptcy". It is true that Citeaux was a small and struggling monastery when Bernard joined it with 30 members of his family and friends and that the Cistercians owed a great deal of their subsequent rapid growth to his dynamic personality. The change in their fortunes was to do with recruitment and patronage and nothing whatever to do with the Templars.'[3]

In the time we have just been considering, the time of transition marked by the 'cutting of the elm', the original mystery knowledge was gradually withdrawn, its potency hidden in the Grail legend, which began to be circulated and popularized. Wolfram von Eschenbach's *Parzival* was written sometime between 1195 and 1220. Chrétien de Troyes was writing at almost the same time. Chrétien seems to have been attached, in some indeterminate capacity, to the court of the Count of Champagne, one of the first nine knights of the Order of the Templars. At the Council of Troyes, an exoteric role and Rule for the Templars was instigated. It is fascinating that the Grail Mysteries should have been spun into myth by a member of this same court. One may at this point note that according to James France 'there is no such thing as a Cistercian Rule. The Cistercians followed the Rule of St Benedict, and through the influence of Bernard the Templars adopted this and the degrees and uses of Citeaux.'[4]

Missing from the more orthodox accounts of history has been an account of the Grail family. Walter Johannes Stein, a student of Rudolf Steiner's and a historian, made a deep study of this family line. In his book *The Ninth Century, World History in the Light of the Holy Grail* he relates a plausible link between the Merovingians and the Grail family when referring to Duke Eticho of Alsace, father of St Odilie. He describes how because Odilie was born blind her father sought to kill her, lest the blame for her blindness rest with him. Her mother escaped with the child, who on being baptized regained her sight. Bishop Erhard, who performed the baptism, named her St Odilie, Sol Dei, 'Sun of God. Father and daughter face each other as light and darkness.'[5]

A possibility here is that, as Rudolf Steiner has indicated, the blood of certain early European tribes retained the forces of the Tree of Life, even after the Fall. This force only needed updating to carry legitimate healing power. In other words, Odilie's own hereditary healing forces were permitted to work after she was baptized.

In a letter referred to in *The Ninth Century*, Eliza von Moltke, widow of General von Moltke, commander of the German land-forces during the First World War, quotes from a conversation with Rudolf Steiner:

> The Odilien Cloister on the Odilienberg[6] was originally a seat of pagan Mysteries, later Christianized by the saintly Odilie... More than once she was most wonderfully rescued, thus at one time fleeing before her father's pursuit but under her younger brother's protection, she sought refuge in the hill facing our building at Dornach [the Goetheanum], and was again rescued in a miraculous way on the return journey, and at that time there happened the transformation of the old Mystery Centre into a Christian Cloister. Thence proceeded that Christian stream which Pope Nicholas was concerned to propagate, the stream which was to be in complete opposition to the Byzantine. Later there was a continuous interchange of letters between the Odilienberg and Pope Nicholas. This stream Duke Eticho wished to destroy; he stood in the service of the Merovingians.
>
> This cloister was a source whence the substance of Christianity spread through the West; hence Odilienberg was the centre of so many fights with Alsace.[7]

These passages seem to indicate that the Merovingians were direct opponents of the Grail stream and the true Grail family. This throws further light on the anti-Grail stream that we considered at the beginning of this chapter. Later in Stein's account there is a passage quoted from a biographer of Odilie, Dionysus Albrecht who, writing in 1751, 'shows quite clearly that he was conscious of the mission of the line of Odilie', and describes how, through blood connections, the ducal line of Odilie became widespread. Stein went on to say:

> As a matter of fact most of the ruling families of Europe were of the race of Odilie. And an old tradition emphasizes this. The mission of these family connections was not so much to form a powerful House, i.e. turning a family spirit into a spirit of the times ... its task was to expand what is bound up with the family into what is Cosmopolitan. A Gabriel blood-connection, which, indeed in some of its branches, bore on its coat of arms the Gabriel lily, was to become the vessel of the world-irradiating Sun impulse. Thus was

the Kingdom of God to arise. In the time however during which this should have been accomplished it was neglected . . . those who are connected with the Grail story are . . . linked together in a family relationship . . . One sees, for instance, that Godfrey of Bouillon, whose companions in arms founded the Order of the Knights Templar, stands in a relationship with the family of Odilie . . .[8]

Despite all insistence on the significance of the Merovingian bloodline, we can see how it can no longer have any great significance; all hereditary bloodlines are now merely physical. Supposing that the Merovingian kings were descended from one or other of the alleged Jesus children, their blood would not carry any more significance than that of any other individual. Personal spiritual evolution and self-development are the modern path. Blood ties and the power stemming from them belongs to the regressive anti-Grail stream.

The task of the Grail family was to expand to world-embracing, cosmopolitan dimensions that once lived only in the blood of a particular group of people. The bearers of this bloodline were carefully married into all the royal houses of Europe so that the blood imbued with the power of the Tree of Life, which maintained the sovereignty of individuality, could include all of humanity. It seems that the Grail family created the potential for what the Knights Templar, especially their inner Group, could have stood for. But by their insistence on the continuation of a bloodline perpetrated in the old Gabrielic way, those who clung to their Merovingian origins betrayed the true task and original potential of the Grail family. This may also have been an important factor in the impossibility that the inner group of Knights Templars experienced in maintaining the high ideals for which they strove.

If the central concern of the inner Grail Knights was the universality of Christ's blood, then what route did the other Grail family take? As Walter Johannes Stein mentioned, the line of Clovis, the Merovingian line, had as its emblem the *lily* connected with the archangel Gabriel. Spirituality that arises through heredity has for some time brought decadent supersensible forces into the material world. Odilie's true line would have belonged to esoteric Christianity with the *rose* as its symbol, a genuine brotherhood free of hereditary prerogatives and privileges.

The image of Templar Knights riding together on one horse demonstrates their original ideals of humility.[9] The fact that it has recently been supposed that it was because they indulged in homosexual practices demonstrates how far off course we have wandered.

The archangel Michael became Cosmic Regent during the last third of the nineteenth century. Up to that time human consciousness had passed through the regencies of Samael and Gabriel. Their influences caused the Grail wisdom to become even more obscured as the advance of external science and materialism took an increasing hold on evolution.

As we have seen, the material upon which the authors of *The Holy Blood and the Holy Grail*, and subsequent books, have based their research was concocted by a supposed Priory of Sion. There were documents mentioned in *The Holy Blood and the Holy Grail* that were planted in the Bibliothèque nationale in Paris some time after 1956 and dated 17 January. The most important of these were *Les Dossiers Secrets*, which trace the course of the bloodline later referred to by Beigent, Leigh and Lincoln. In *The Sion Revelation*, Lynn Picknett and Clive Prince concur with the evidence already cited that these documents were put there not for the public at large, but possibly as bait to attract the attention of 'individuals or groups *within French esoteric secret societies*'.[10] Those who penned this document have assumed pseudonyms, the origin of the documents is uncertain and some people connected with them met with mysterious and violent ends.[11] We have already conjectured that one of the reasons a group such as the one going under the assumed name of 'Priory of Sion', whether authentic or not, put out all of these documents was in order to trawl for reactions from the informed who might possess further information stemming from a lost stream of knowledge. This group, whoever they are, also might have a second agenda, for the concealment of which they have obtained further obscurity from recent conclusions which led to claims of their nonexistence. In Picknett and Prince's earlier book, *The Templar Revelation*, the comment is made that:

> ...what better way of attracting attention on the one hand, but filtering out unwanted interlopers or the casually curious on the

other, than to present the public with apparently intriguing but also virtually nonsensical information? It is as if even getting close to what the Priory is about actually constitutes an initiation.[12]

Bill Putnam and John E. Wood reply to the above quote by stating: 'In spite of the false names, the nonexistent addresses, the changes to drawings, the inconsistencies, the invention and the improbabilities to be found in the secret papers, some authors still accept them ... we disagree.'[13] They take the position that there are no grey areas, so that the inconsistencies they have found lead them to discount the possibility that the Priory exists.

There is one author whose research was not initially focused on Rennes-le-Château. She therefore had no agenda connected with the mystery but, in the course of her own investigation, unearthed facts which furnish undeniable proof that some of the claims made by the authors of *The Holy Blood and the Holy Grail* were correct. This is Joy Hancox, author of *The Byrom Collection, The Queen's Chameleon* and *Kingdom for a Stage*. Joy's ongoing research is both meticulous, conscientious and solely based on verifiable facts. Her discovery eventually yielded up corroboration for a section of the list of Grand Masters of the Priory of Sion which were found in the *Dossiers Secrets*.

In unravelling all the complexities of Byrom's story, certain names of people and places recur like themes in music, some more clearly than others... Some of these echoes are coincidental, others are part of a much larger pattern. That pattern extends to events in France which began in 1891 in the tiny French village of Rennes-le-Château.[14]

In the Epilogue to her second book, a biography of John Byrom, *The Queen's Chameleon*, Joy Hancox refers to the alleged discovery of the four parchments by Bérenger Saunière. She then proceeds to identify several of the names connected to the Byrom collection (of drawings) who are also on the list of Grand Masters in the *Dossiers Secrets*.

The relevant people on the list are those whose period of office coincides with the dates of the drawings in *The Byrom Collection*, or whose work is part of its provenance—Robert Fludd, J. Valentin Andrea (also known as Andreae), Robert Boyle, Isaac Newton and

Charles Radclyffe. This section of the pedigree is strikingly apposite.[15]

Of Robert Fludd, who was contemporary with both James I and Charles I, Joy Hancox says he 'was an exponent of the Hermetic tradition. His work owes much to the ideas of Christian Cabalism; Byrom's collection contains drawings directly related to his theories of the universe. One even bears the name of Fludd and his great work *The Microcosm*.'[16]

Joy links Newton and Radclyffe in the following way:

Newton was still president of the Royal Society when Byrom was elected, and spent a considerable amount of time testing the validity of the ideas of the alchemists. Like the Masons, he was fascinated by the dimensions of the Temple of Solomon and its symbolism; Byrom's collection contains a series of drawings which examine the proportions of the Temple. Radclyffe knew Byrom, and, as a senior Freemason in France, would have been conversant with the esoteric ideas which occupied speculative Masonry at the time.[17]

The connection for J. Valentin Andreae came from a letter, forwarded by the publisher, from a reader who owned a copy of Andreae's extremely rare book *Mathematicum Memoriale*. It was published in 1614, and has 110 geometrical drawings. Joy writes: 'I have studied the book and copied drawings from it, and the relationship of Andreae's book to drawings in the Byrom collection is unmistakable.'[18]

Joy has discovered that Robert Boyle was working on a similar set of printed drawings as Byrom, but 30 years earlier. She suggests the link is their mutual interest in the Christian cabbala. One of the prints in Boyle's notebook has, superimposed on the geometrical pattern, a Tree of Life bearing the figure of the crucified Christ.[19] She adds, '...the point is not that the drawings confirm the existence of M. Lobineau's secret society, but that quite independently five of his Grand Masters, one after another, occur in the pedigree of material *known to exist* in one collection and which had for the most part been kept secret to the initiates.'[20]

The connections do not end here as Joy's investigations revealed a more contemporary link: '... in 1955, three Englishmen applied to the

French Consulate in London for an export licence to bring three of Saunière's mysterious genealogies to this country.'[21] One of the men was Hugh Murchison Clowes. In 1953 he had published a history of his family firm of printers in London. This contained a genealogy of the founder members. It shows that the founder's father's great-grandmother was the grandmother of John Byrom as well as Joseph Clowes. Byrom was steward of the Broughton Manor which was part of the Clowes estate in Manchester. The farm Siddal tenanted from 1727 to 1745 was on Clowes's property. Byrom was related to the Clowes family and a close friend of Joseph Clowes. He confided in Joseph and constantly used his chambers when in London. Joseph knew about the Cabala Club, including that part of Byrom's investigation which he thought better to 'suppress'.[22]

The fact that the bogus Priory was privy to information that was valuable to a group in Britain is reinforced by a statement of Robert Richardson's:

Through Father Hoffet,[23] the priory creators had indirect access to the archives at St Sulpice, said to have long been the Catholic Church centre for occult studies in France. And during the war it is likely they also had access to the seized records of Masonic and esoteric organizations. These records, some quite old, were deposited in the occupation controlled Centre d'Action Masonique.[24]

The group in England, as with the bogus Priory in France, may well have been searching for a hidden circle of true Rosicrucians.

From guarded references in these documents and others, they most probably learned of a particular group of people who have attained the status of what is called in occult circles, a Rose-Croix. This term is used to differentiate between a person who has reached a level which foreshadows the next stage in the evolution of humanity and one who is merely a member of a Rosicrucian order or movement. A number of these people are joined together in a group which is very ancient. Its focus is totally spiritual. The members of this group are very rare individuals. Their order is exceptionally discreet and avoids publicity. Its name is little known. It cannot be contacted except in rare cases. The archives of secret societies have documented how the members of this ancient society have acted anonymously behind the scenes of history and through esoteric and exoteric groups, and of the particular sites once associated with them.[25]

Richardson also speculates on the possibility that 'Saunière found a tomb containing the records of an important Rosicrucian group from the 16th century. This would account for his entry into and looting of other tombs and for the interest and support of so many prominent 19th century occultists in the Rennes-le-Château affair.'

A genuine Rosicrucian group of this nature would not be concerned with a hereditary bloodline, only with a connection to the true Grail impulse. So that when in *The Messianic Legacy* Baigent, Leigh and Lincoln again mention the possibility of a bloodline which flows down the generations from the House of David, through Jesus to the present day, they are referring to the 'anti-Grail' impulse. In the Epilogue to that book, they wistfully toy with the concept of royalty as a symbol of meaning in a world which has lost its sense of direction, and then tie up the thread of their argument with the following question:

What, for example, would be the implications for modern Israel, as well as for both Judaism and Christianity, if—on the basis of records or other evidence issuing from the Temple of Jerusalem—Jesus stood revealed as the Messiah? Not the Messiah of late Christian tradition, but the Messiah expected by the people of Palestine two thousand years ago—a man, that is, who was their nation's rightful king, who married, sired children and perhaps did not die on the cross at all... Would it not at a single stroke eradicate the theological differences between Judaism and Christianity and at least some of the antipathy of Islam as well?

In any case and quite apart from the treasury of the Temple, the Prieuré de Sion can promulgate a claim which would enjoy considerable currency even in today's world. On behalf of the families it represents ... [it] can establish ... that the Merovingian Dynasty was of the Davidic line—and was formerly recognized as being so by the Carolingians who supplanted them, by other monarchs and by the Roman Church of the period. Aided by the techniques of modern

public relations, modern advertising and modern political pack-
aging, the Prieuré could thus present to the modern world a figure
who, by the strictest scriptural definition of the term, could claim to
be a biblical Messiah.[26]

The aim of such a *coup d'état* could be to place a modern king
descended from the Merovingian line on the throne in Jerusalem. He
would be acclaimed as a descendent of Jesus, supposedly of the same
hereditary line as the *Matthew* Jesus child.[27] This king would then rule
the world by virtue of the red dynastic blood in his veins. Such a
leader, in solving some of humanity's major problems, would then be
widely hailed and accepted as a world saviour, perhaps even as Christ
himself. The establishment of a European super-state, with an adjusted
astrological chart, would be a massive leap forward towards the
completion of these anti-evolutionary designs. This is even more
clearly hinted at in the following passage from *The Holy Blood and the
Holy Grail* where, according to one of the writers' informants, a M.
Chaumeil, the Secret Society Hieron du Val d'or is described as
planning:

> a theocracy wherein nations would be no more than provinces,
> their leaders but proconsuls in the service of a world occult
> government consisting of an elite. For Europe, this regime of the
> Great King implied a double hegemony of the Papacy and Empire,
> of the Vatican and of the Habsburgs, who would have been the
> Vatican's right arm ... Such a state would have realized the cen-
> turies old dream of a 'heavenly kingdom' on earth, a terrestrial
> replica or mirror-image of the order, harmony and hierarchy of the
> cosmos. It would have actualized the ancient Hermetic promise, 'As
> above, so below'.[28]

13.

Rosslyn Chapel

The Tree of Life and the Holy Grail

It is said that the mortar holding together the stones of Rosslyn Chapel is made from the crushed scallop shells carried there by the many thousands of pilgrims who trod the pilgrim route from Santiago de Compostela over the centuries. The scallop shell is the emblem of St James, brother of Jesus, who together with Mary Magdalene is the leader of esoteric Christianity. The interior of the chapel is crammed with enigmatic carvings relating to secrets of the underground stream of esoteric Christianity. The Tree of Life pillar is the most famous feature of Rosslyn, so in the context of our research it is not surprising that the stonemasons have also created there a plethora of vegetation—nature gone wild in stone, a Green Man's paradise!

The chapel sits on a high rocky position above the River Esk, south-east of Edinburgh in Scotland. The Sinclair family have been connected with this ancient site, sacred to the Saturn Mysteries, since the tenth century. They were originally descended from Rognvald, Earl of More, 'an area on the north-west coast of Norway near the present city of Trondheim'.[1] Their territory stretched over some of the Norwegian coast, the Orkneys and Caithness in Scotland. Rognvald's second son was Hrolf or Rollo, who signed a treaty with King Charles the Simple of France to secure lands in Normandy in 912. The name Sinclair derives from the castle of St Clair-Sur-Epte where the treaty was signed. Saint Clair means *Sanctus Clarus*, Holy Light. Rollo married Gizelle, daughter of the French king, and became the first Duke of Normandy and ancestor of William the Conqueror.

William St Clair arrived in Scotland in 1057 and was eventually given the land at Rosslyn by King Malcolm Canmore of Scotland as a gesture of gratitude for William's success in keeping his borders clear of the English. His son, Henri St Clair, 'accompanied Godfroi de Bouillon to the Holy Land in 1096 and was present at the fall of Jerusalem. He was accompanied by knights from eleven other leading Scottish families. Representatives of all twelve families met regularly at Rosslyn prior to that Crusade and for many centuries afterwards.'[2]

Green Man. Rosslyn Chapel

Hughes de Payne, a founder member of the Knights Templar, was married to Catherine de St Clair of Rosslyn. After their return from Jerusalem some of them travelled to the castle at Rosslyn and were given land at Ballantrodoch in Scotland for their headquarters by the St Clairs.

In *The Holy Blood and the Holy Grail* the Sinclair family are, according to the Priory of Sion documents, reported to be allied to the bloodline. Two of the alleged Grand Masters of the Priory of Sion were St Clairs: Marie de Saint Clair between 1220 and 1266 and Jean de Saint Clair between 1351 and 1366. 'In 1548, the "Prieuré documents" state, Jean des Plantard had married Marie de Saint Clair—thus forging another link between his family and that of the Saint-Clair/Gisors.'[3] Pierre Plantard de Saint-Clair was one of the dominant figures in Baigent, Leigh and Lincoln's research and a supposed current Grand Master of the Priory of Sion when *The Holy Blood and the Holy Grail* was written. Also, according to the statutes the authors obtained from the French Police, Pierre Plantard was listed as Secretary General of the Priory of Sion.

Rosslyn was founded and built as a Collegiate Chapel between 1440 and 1490 by Sir William Sinclair, the third and last Sinclair Earl of Orkney and Royal Chancellor to the Scottish throne. He 'was not only patron of Craftmasonry throughout Scotland but a Grandmaster and an adept of the highest degree'.[4] This was over a hundred years after the fall of the Knights Templar. William St Clair's shield carried an engrailed cross on a background of silver, which indicated that he was a Grail Knight. There was supposedly a hidden Templar initiation chamber underneath Rosslyn.

Rosslyn village was originally built for the stonemasons who were brought from all over Europe to build the chapel. It took a long time to build as Earl William oversaw all the work personally. His son finished the roof but the chapel, which could have been the largest cathedral in Europe, was unfinished. Funds ran out and only the choir was completed, standing on 13 pillars which form an arcade of twelve pointed arches that represent the twelve constellations of the zodiac.

Earl William St Clair, builder of Rosslyn, was appointed Grand Master of the Guild of Craftsmen. 'The Hereditary Grand Mastership of the Masonic guilds remained in the Sinclair family until St Andrew's day 1736 when the then Hereditary Grand Master, yet another Sir William St Clair of Rosslyn, resigned his Hereditary Patronage and Protectorship of the Masonic Craft' to effect the creation of 'the Grand Lodge of Ancient, Free and Accepted Masons of Scotland'.[5] Freemasonry has only been officially in existence since the founding of the Grand Lodge of London in 1717.

Rosslyn Chapel is situated on an ancient and very powerful site. But although the Knights Templar had officially been suppressed for over a hundred years before Rosslyn was founded, there is plenty of evidence in the chapel to indicate a very strong Templar influence there.

The Grail legend concealed information on the path of esoteric Christianity, in order to protect it from the danger of being condemned as heresy by the Church. Rosslyn Chapel was a centre of Gnosticism, of esoteric Christianity. The sometimes enigmatic, intricate carvings and the prospective dimensions of the building provided 'a three-dimensional code which passed on its hidden message in an architectural form of "la langue verte", the green language of initiation'.[6]

Rudolf Steiner, having described the Templars as 'true emissaries of the Holy Grail', also connected them with the Rosicrucian impulse. Manfred Schmidt-Brabant describes how:

> Three hundred years after the founding of the Grail Mysteries, approximately three hundred years after the opening of the Camino [the Compostela pilgrimage], the Crusades began. In 1096, the first wave of Crusades sets out; in 1099, Jerusalem falls. Rudolf Steiner points to the fact that these Crusades actually arose from the heretical movement or, in any case, from movements at the time that were opposed to the official Church of Rome. He describes Godfroy of Bouillon, the leader of the first Crusade, as one who was initiated into the problems that had resulted from Rome's control over Christianity. There was a desire for the famous *Ecclesia non romana,* a non-Roman Church. People wanted to return to Jerusalem in order to found a Christ-centred Church there on the site of the Mystery of Golgotha. Those were the spiritual impulses. Liberation from the infidels was, so to speak, the exoteric aspect.[7]

Rosslyn has been described as a hymn to Templar ideals and as a source of coded teaching for Rosicrucianism and Freemasonry. The chapel was constructed from 1446 onwards. Christian Rosenkreutz[8] went through an initiation in the year 1459 which led to the forming of the Rosicrucian Brotherhood. During this initiation Rosenkreutz received a wound on his forehead. One of the significant carvings at Rosslyn is of an apprentice builder at Rosslyn, who, legend has it, was murdered by the jealous Master Mason on his return from travelling abroad to find inspiration for the crafting of the pillars at Rosslyn. While he was away the apprentice had a dream in which the wonderful design of the Tree of Life pillar was revealed to him, so he created it in stone. On his return the Master Mason was so jealous that he murdered the apprentice by striking him on the right side of his forehead (this could also be seen to signify the suppression of the right-brain, the spiritually creative side of the brain). In the Temple Legend, central to Freemasonry, Hiram, builder of the Temple, is murdered by a similar blow. In that story he is murdered by his apprentices because they want to learn the secret of the Stone-splitting Worm, the Shamir.

Here we see the two mysteries of Rosslyn joined. Nine dragons coil around the base of the Tree of Life pillar there. Dragons are symbols of the powerful energy related to the Tree of Life or Grail-energy. The Tree of Life and the Holy Grail are therefore both present at Rosslyn, which, it is claimed, is a powerful and ancient centre in the etheric earth. The Tree of Life pillar—the apprentice pillar—

> represents the Yggdrasil tree of Norse mythology, the world Ash which binds together Heaven, Earth and Hell... The spiralling branches symbolize the planets and the roots of the trunk dig deeply into the elements of the Earth. At the bottom of the pillar the dragons of Neifelheim can be seen gnawing at the roots of the tree to rob it of its fruitfulness.[9]

This tree seems to illustrate the life ether especially, which at one pole is merged with the Music of the Spheres, while at the other its 'roots dig deeply into the elements of the earth', 'energy-before-matter'. The 'Dragons of Neifelheim' might represent the life ether's 'fallen counterpart', the Third Force, rather than robbing the tree of its fruitfulness. The Stone-splitting Worm could, therefore, be an enigmatic key to building methods used from ancient times, whose secret was guarded by the highest degrees of initiates involved in the construction of many ancient buildings.

The chemical ether manifests in both the Tree of Life and the Holy Grail. How does the chemical ether manifest at Rosslyn? Clues to a connection might be found arising from several directions. The chemical ether works through the fluid medium bringing information into creation. Rosslyn's potency as an ancient sacred site may result from the various springs rising through the carboniferous limestone as they are released from the nearby coal seams. Another clue might be found in the name itself. In *The Sword and the Grail* by Andrew Sinclair, the meaning of the second half of the name *lin* is described as *fall* in the old Scottish language. Therefore *Ros* he translates as *rose* or *rosy*, so the whole name becomes 'Fall of the Rosy blood of Christ'. If we now consider the activity of the chemical ether, which operates together with the life ether as the Tree of Life or Grail-energy, I would venture to suggest 'dewfall' as another possible interpretation of the name of Rosslyn. The word 'dew' is translated as *ros* in Latin, so that Rosslyn or its older name Roslin would give us dew*fall*, with *lin* as the second syllable. Rudolf Steiner explains this in the following words: 'The word dew [German *Tau*] is *ros* in Latin and cross is *crux*. Ros-Crux means at the same time the sign Tau, the cross and the dew on the plants. This is the esoteric meaning of Rose-Cross.'[10]

If we pursue this further we find that the word *Tau* is also the German word for dew. In the next chapter we will investigate the properties of dew further and see how its potency is enhanced where it falls in a location where energies of the Tree of Life, the Grail, predominate in the earth. This is borne out by the ancient name for the site of the Pyramids in Egypt, the Giza plateau, which was Ros-Tau! These connections appear again when we are informed that the pillars at Rosslyn form a perfect *tau*, three interlocking 'T' shapes, and that the entire geometry of the building follows this design in accordance with Masonic ritual.

These multifaceted connections become more than mere coincidence when we begin to look further into the real significance of the Holy Grail at Rosslyn. In the context of our research the abundance of vegetation carved on the walls of Rosslyn Chapel reflects the activity of the Tree of Life or of the Grail which we saw was referred to by Wolfram von Eschenbach as a *cornucopia*. One description of Rosslyn is that the life-forms carved in profusion around the walls by the stonemasons seem more like works of nature than of man, 'something infinitely more than mere art, for something spiritual yet tangible was built into the stone itself'.[11] We here return to an earlier description of the Logos or Cosmic Word, which was referred to in ancient times as the Music of the Spheres. The chemical ether as we have seen is related to the element *water*, and also known as the *sound* or *tone ether*. The Logos, the Cosmic Word, the Christ, sounds through the astral principle, through the chemical ether, bringing *form* to manifestation in matter, causing *differentiation* in the forms of creation. The alchemists and particularly the Rosicrucians understood that *dewfall* at dawn and dusk caused the vegetation to burgeon and proliferate in the spring and early summer. This might have been expected to be especially potent in a sacred location like Rosslyn. To complete this connection, *music, sound* is also featured very prominently at Rosslyn. There are many carvings of musicians with their instruments amongst the vegetation on the walls, while the zodiac arches are decorated with musical notes,[12] indicating that *the Music of the Spheres is sounding at Rosslyn!*

There are more strange parallels to be found at Rosslyn. There is a third connection with an apprentice here. We know that nothing can remain sacred in our present society. Remember the 'Sorcerer's Apprentice' in Walt Disney's *Fantasia*? Micky Mouse thinks he can do the Sorcerer's magic himself. He instructs the buckets and brooms to do the cleaning of the room for him. Chaos ensues as he loses control and is in danger of being swept away in a torrent of water. The Sorcerer returns in time to save the situation. Micky Mouse has also been busy in Rosslyn! Just up the road from Rosslyn, a cloned sheep named Dolly came into existence, amidst much media coverage. We have already come across Rudolf Steiner's warning against the fumblings of mechanistic science in the sphere of life:

> What then is the Holy Grail? For those who understand this legend correctly, it signifies—as can even be proved by literary means—the following. Till now, man has only mastered the inanimate in nature. The transformation of the living forces, the transformation of what sprouts and grows in the plants, and of what manifests itself in animal and human reproduction—that is beyond his power. Man has to leave these mysterious powers of nature untouched. There he cannot encroach. What results from these forces cannot be fully comprehended by him.[13]

Form is normally brought into matter through the Cosmic Word, the Christ, who manifests through the Six Sun Elohim. In nature no two forms are exactly the same. Rudolf Steiner has described how the Elohim work across the threshold from the spiritual world into matter. He also says there are *abnormal Elohim*, disguised as Archai, one rank below the Elohim.

> These beings ... should really according to their essential nature belong to the spaceless. But they enter space, they work in space. And this is characteristic of the ahrimanic—those spiritual beings

who in their true nature are intended to be spaceless have preferred to work in space ... This enables forms to arise in space that do not ray in directly out of the spaceless. Thus the spatial is portrayed in the spatial, so that one spatial form reflects another.[14]

The original Elohim, angelic beings of the Fourth Hierarchy, who combine to manifest the Logos, are responsible for the form principle which is gathered by the Spiritual Sun from all quarters of the sounding heavens. The Elohim then direct this principle across the threshold of the spiritual world into matter. The abnormal Elohim usurp the position usually filled by the Archai, angelic beings one rank below the Elohim. From there they imitate the activity of the true Elohim but can only create into matter from the material side of the threshold. In this way they could be seen to work hand in hand with our blind *exoteric* science which has attempted to plunder the Tree of Life near Rosslyn Chapel, which, however, still conceals the secrets of esoteric science.

When Dolly the Sheep and Rosslyn became news, the *Sunday Times* found a very apt headline:

> 'The Holy Grail of medieval Christian lore meets the
> Holy Grail of science.'

Next to a picture of the 'Apprentice Pillar' was a strikingly similar pillar formed by the DNA spiral. However, when the current research into DNA is investigated with insight gained through knowledge of the Tree of Life, it is found that in his present state of understanding the exoteric scientist behaves in a way strikingly similar to Micky Mouse!

14.
Waters of the Moon

In the last chapter we briefly viewed the function of the chemical ether in bringing the form principle into matter. We also saw that this was effected by the power of the Logos, which passes the many forms of creation into matter from the spiritual world through the medium of sound. Earlier we saw how only as long ago as the seventeenth century the ancient belief in the Music of the Spheres finally died out as a result of the establishment of mechanistic science. As previously mentioned, Shakespeare marked the fading of this knowledge in the *Merchant of Venice*. It is well worth quoting again in the context of this chapter.

> Such harmony is in immortal souls;
> But, whilst this muddy vesture of decay
> Doth grossly close it in, we cannot hear it.[1]

We cannot hear it, but something does hear it. The water systems of our earth! In his brilliant book *Sensitive Chaos*, Theodor Schwenk writes:

> The world of moving water absorbs influences from the con-stellations of the stars in the heavens and passes them on to the earth and its creatures. Cosmic events, the world of water and the living creatures in it form a totality. The latter, as water creatures, simply make visible the cosmic events that live and move in their element. Creatures living on dry land also have a part in these events through the circulation of liquids in them.[2]

He then describes how every stretch of water carries its own char-acteristic vibration, which is close to the vibration of the moon. The closer this is the more easily is the water influenced. The life force, the etheric-force, manifests through this vibration.

> Every water basin, whether ocean, lake or pond, has its own natural period of vibration. This varies according to the shape, size and depth of the basin. The whole morphological character of a lake

finds expression in this natural period of vibration; it is like a 'note' to which the lake is 'tuned'. This 'note' has 'overtones' in its vibration like a flute or the string of a musical instrument. Like these the lake oscillates between the nodes (regions of no disturbance) and the anti-nodes (regions of maximum disturbance) of standing waves ... The natural period of vibration of a stretch of water is in more or less marked resonance with the path of the moon and its tide-producing forces. The resonance is strongest when the natural period of vibration corresponds to the orbital rhythm of the moon ... As the moon passes over different waters of the earth they respond to a greater or lesser degree with their 'note', according to how closely their natural period of vibration is tuned to the rhythm of the moon. All together they are like a great musical instrument spread out over the earth, on which the moon plays an inaudible melody that travels with it round the earth.[3]

The astral is a higher principle that works into the etheric through the *fluid* medium just as the etheric is a higher principle than the physical into which it also enters through the fluid medium. The etheric manifests through a *time* principle, through *rhythms*, while the astral manifests through *pitch*, through the *spaces between things*.

The astral body is the source of our emotions. We express these by the *pitch* of our voice. The *distances between* the notes in our voice exactly indicate the *state of our feelings*. The point through which the astral reaches down into the etheric is where the fluid element is represented. The region of the etheric which receives the higher information from the spiritual cosmos is the chemical, tone or 'number' ether which correlates to the element of water.

The ethers and corresponding elements have gradually come into physical manifestation through four previous incarnations of our earth. The activity of the chemical ether originated with the Ancient Moon evolution. Ancient Moon evolution also marks the stage in creation when the astral body appeared for the first time. So there is a special connection between the astral body, the chemical ether and the moon. The astral principle, which is connected to the moon, 'receives' the information and passes it through the etheric down to the physical. The astral principle can only be found in the human and animal

kingdoms. It takes its name from the region from which this qualitative information comes—the turning, sounding heavens—and passes
through to the fluid systems of the human and animal kingdoms. The
astral as the seat of our feeling life gives rise to tears of joy and grief,
demonstrating the close connection with the fluid element.

Steiner gives us a description of the time after the Fall when only
earth and moon were left together, when the forces of the chemical
ether worked powerfully through the earth, which at that time had
only condensed as far as the watery state. At the beginning of our
present Earth evolution the entire planetary system was contained
within the earth in a repetition of the earliest times in its three previous
incarnations. This was the time referred to in the Bible as paradise. At
the Fall, six Elohim, beings of the Fourth Hierarchy, removed the sun-
forces, the life ether, from the earth to form a new sun sphere in the
cosmos.

> ...and the tone had remained in the earth. So when the light
> departed the water became dark but also drenched with tone. It was
> tone that gave form to the water ... We see that tone is something
> formative, a shaping force, since through tone the parts are arranged
> in order. Tone is a shaping power, and it is this that formed the body
> out of the water. This was the force of tone which had remained in
> the earth. It was tone, it was sound that rang through the earth, out
> of which the human form (manifesting the whole of creation)
> shaped itself.[4]

Some time after the Seventh Elohim, Yahweh, removed these forces
of tone from the earth to form a new moon sphere; these were the
forces of the chemical ether.

Over ten years ago a course was given in England by Austria's top
authority on humus research, Professor Gernot Gräfer, with his colleague Maria Felsenreich. Their discoveries concerning the role of
water on earth ran almost parallel with Steiner's statements on the Fall.
They stated that:

> ...in its natural healthy state water can be dowsed for nine clearly
> identified resonance formations. The transformation of these reso-
> nance formations leads to the build-up of corresponding infor-

mation fields, which stand in relation to specific chemical elements, vital functions and magnetic patterns.[5]

This would seem to be saying that healthy water contains all necessary information for life, an echo of the paradise state at the beginning of our present Earth evolution when all the influences of the heavenly bodies were sounding from within the earth. During the course, Gernot and Maria often used the same expression, referring to the fact that healthy water belonged to the 'paradise state'—but this statement was solely based on their own observations. They also stated:

> Energy transfer has to be understood as the basis for life on earth. Our planet was shaped by the evolution of water which was, is and will be the media for the transport of vibrational energy . . . the earth body's most characteristic feature is its resounding quality which differs . . . from region to region and from one level of evolution to another. We may call this resounding quality of the earth body Music.[6]

Compare this with Steiner's previously quoted descriptions of the beginning of our present Earth evolution when he speaks of how the earth was 'drenched with tone', how 'tone, sound, rang through the earth creating the life forms'.

Gernot and Maria used a basalt pendulum to detect up to nine mysterious resonance patterns which could be dowsed in the purest water to be found on earth. After the course was over, Alan Hall of the Live Water Trust in Gloucestershire made a resumé of their work in a lecture where he considered that these nine patterns might be 'hieroglyphs' for the notes of the musical scale. Here we have the possibility of direct experience with the Music of the Spheres in visible form.

In his book *The Music of the Spheres*, Jamie James points out that:

> The elder Pliny . . . tells us in detail exactly how Pythagoras conceived of the music of the spheres. Counting outward from the earth to the outermost sphere of the fixed stars, Pythagoras fixed the musical intervals as follows: from the earth to the moon was a whole step; from the moon to Mercury, a half step; Mercury to Venus, another half step; from Venus to the sun was a minor third; which is

equal to three half steps; the sun to Mars, a whole step; Mars to Jupiter, a half step; Jupiter to Saturn a half step; and from Saturn to the sphere of the fixed stars another minor third. Thus the musical scale to which Aristotle referred, the so-called Pythagorean Scale, runs: C, D, E♭, E, G, A, B♭, B, D.[7]

Jamie James quotes Plato's description of these forces:

These intricate traceries in the sky are, no doubt, the loveliest and most perfect of material things, but still part of the visible world, and therefore they fall far short of the true realities—the real relative velocities, in the world of pure number and all perfect geometrical figures, of the movements which carry round the bodies involved in them. These, you will agree, can be conceived by reason and thought, not seen by the eye.[8]

At the Fall the pure tones were thrust out of the earth, to ray inwards from the periphery where the solid planets are formed as physical markers for each border between tone and tone. When dowsed this scale produces all nine resonance patterns in order.

A few years after the course this possibility was put to the test during the eclipse of the sun in the summer of 1999. By this time it had been established that if one watered a plant of a particular species and then tested it for resonance patterns with the pendulum a set sequence of patterns was received. A small basil plant was watered and tested for patterns before the eclipse began. The patterns took on the sequence pertaining to that particular plant. As the eclipse progressed the pendulum's movements reduced until it was perfectly still at total eclipse. As the sun was uncovered the pendulum gradually began to move again until the original sequence continued. From this it was possible to assume that as the sun's effect was lessened cosmic information gradually ceased to be transferred to the organic systems of the earth.

It was especially after the event at Chernobyl, in 1986, that Gernot Gräfer and his colleague Maria Felsenreich discovered that the resonance patterns, which they had monitored in healthy water in previous years, were almost non-existent. They were driving down an autobahn and spied a little church in the distance; they somehow felt compelled to leave their route and visit it. The church was dedicated to the Virgin Mary. Underneath was a running spring. When they dowsed over its water they found it had not been affected by Chernobyl. Concerning the nine clearly identified resonance formations found in water in its natural healthy state, they say: 'The transformation of these resonance formations leads to the build-up of corresponding information fields, which stand in relation to specific chemical elements, vital functions and magnetic patterns.'[9]

The 'paradise' situation had been preserved in the spring under the church! What might be the reason for this? We have also seen that, in scientific terms, these places have been recognized as centres of magnetic and electromagnetc energy. In terms of the etheric world these are centres of potentially powerful subtle energy. They have also come to be connected with or dedicated to the Goddess, and she, both in her ancient and Christian form, is a representation of the etheric world. Having once learned the resonance patterns personally it has been fascinating to find that water in locations sacred to the Goddess registers all nine patterns when investigated. One of the most exciting experiments was carried out on two separate trips to Ephesus in Turkey. From ancient times Ephesus had been sacred to the Goddess. There was a shrine of Isis there and the Temple of Artemis at Ephesus was one of the Seven Wonders of the Ancient World. The Virgin Mary spent the last years of her life in Ephesus. In the nineteenth century a German nun, while dying, had a vision of the Virgin Mary. In the vision she was told the exact location of the Virgin Mary's house in Ephesus and, although she had never travelled out of Germany, she was able to give such a precise description that the house was eventually found. The foundations were buried below ground level on a high spot above the ancient ruins of Ephesus. Running under the house is a spring which had been sacred since pagan times. On two separate visits it has been possible to dowse all nine patterns in the water there.

★

The name Roslin, or Rosslyn has been interpreted as meaning dewfall. Dew is a very potent manifestation of the chemical ether which was recognized by the alchemists. Form originates at the periphery of the cosmos, where it is held in the circle of the zodiac and brought into matter through the Music of the Spheres. The sun then gathers these forces from the periphery. The sun's light is reflected by the moon, which we now see is particularly connected with the activity of the chemical ether and the fluid element. A further possibility is that this formative information package is next picked up and held by the ionosphere. If we venture outside at dawn or at dusk we are all familiar with the increased moisture that hangs in the air at that time, namely, the dew, which was so revered by the alchemists. At dawn it is caused by the belt of chemical ether rising up from within the physical earth, which by midday reaches the upper reaches of the atmosphere. It then returns on its downward path, reaching the surface of the earth by evening. Gardeners in the past knew that the best time to tend their plants was at dawn or dusk. They mistrusted midday for the care of their gardens, calling it 'the time of the Noontide Witch'. They knew that the up-building formative forces present in the moisture which were leaving the surface of the earth at dawn were no longer around to sustain the living vegetation which was left to its own devices at midday.

In spring and summer, when the vegetation is enlivening all around us, we are particularly aware of the birdsong rising in the morning and returning at evening. In this music of the birdsong could we be hearing part of the secret of the process whereby sound carries the formative forces needed for the qualitative differentiation of life—the shapes, scents, tastes, colours and healing qualities—from the cosmic periphery? The formative information is collected by the chemical ether, rising together with the dawn chorus of the birds, and returned at evening to bathe the vegetation with music-permeated dew.

When one considers the quality of the British countryside in spring and early summer, especially at the time around dawn and dusk, it becomes understandable that so much of the Grail legend originated in these islands. Although the progress of the chemical ether at morning and evening takes place to a greater or lesser extent all over the globe, one may observe that there is a special quality, a greenish-blueness in the air and around all the vegetation, that is characteristic of dawn and dusk in Britain. The ancient parish church nestling in depths of lush young vegetation takes on the ambience of a Grail chapel on the edge of some enchanted forest. The glen below Rosslyn Chapel has been described as a magical place—surely this is where its hidden Grail lies.

Here science and legend meet. It will be remembered that the interpretation of the Grail that we are pursuing sees the two ethers represented by the Tree of Life as living symbols of the Grail. The daily bathing of vegetation by the chemical ether and the silent activity of the Music of the Spheres brought earthwards in the morning and evening chorus of the birds bear witness to the blending of fact and legend that belong to the 'science of the Grail'.

At this point it is possible to bring knowledge of the significance of dew into connection with *The Da Vinci Code* pentagram, the Golden Section and the Fibonacci series. The form of the pentagram runs as a connecting theme through all of the processes connected with the descent of cosmic information into matter. The path of Venus in relation to the sun—the great pentagram in the heavens—appears to be central to the process, while the skeletal structure of the human etheric body is also pentagonal. The seedheads of certain flowers also mirror this form. The Golden Section holds pentagonal dimensions and is also related to the Fibonacci series. In the Golden Section we find that in an asymmetrical division the smaller part shows the same proportional relationship to the greater part as the latter does to the whole, undivided segment. The same relationship may be seen in areas and in angles. Human proportions and features, works of art and architecture created in these proportions always look harmonious and well balanced. The entire human body follows Golden Section dimensions when it is divided at the navel. The knee divides the whole leg, eyebrows divide the head, the elbow divides the arm. Leonardo's Vitruvian Man demonstrates these proportions.

> The laws of the Golden Section can be found in nature in the arrangement of the leaves on the stems of many plants. In the time of Goethe, botanists noted that the spiral sequence of leaves moving up the stem and their rhythm involves specific angles that are always greater than 90°. At the Sorbonne in Paris, the Bravais brothers measured the angles of divergence in hundreds of plants and found the average to be 137°30′48″. At the time this seemed to be a random result, requiring no further discussion.[10]

In a paper which appeared in an anthroposophical medical journal, Walter Bühler describes how the earth is divided into zones of light, dark, sunrise and sunset in Golden Section proportions. The Golden Section is related to pentagonal geometry and therefore also to the path of Venus, which describes a perfect pentagram into the zodiac in relation to the sun during a period of eight years:

> Calculations show that the ratio of the potentially sunlit surface and the actual area of starry night is that of major to minor, i.e., the divine ratio. This is due to the additional area covered by the dawn and dusk belt. The generative zone belonging to the rainbow sphere shows Golden Section principles everywhere, as will be shown briefly below. In this zone the sun is always at an angle of less than 42° ... The myriads of dewdrops arising from the green plant world sparkle in all the colours of the spectrum, especially in the mornings. Every sun-glowing dewdrop therefore holds the laws of the Golden

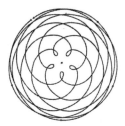

The curving course of an orbit of Venus over an 8-year period. The earth is shown at the centre, drawn to scale

The pattern of a silver thistle-blossom

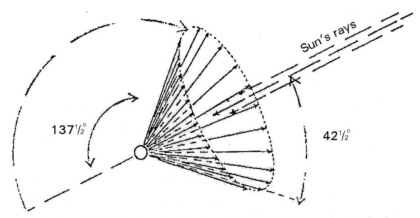

Refraction and reflection in a droplet of water. Fanlike colour cone seen in dewdrops and raindrops

Section within it... Every drop is an image of the macrocosmic world around it and of its spherical bodies. In terms of physics, it reflects the light which passes through it because of diffraction and reflection, producing a circular colour cone. The delicate 'flower of light' holds all the colours of the spectrum. Deviation from the central sun ray is always approximately 42°. We have to have the sun at our backs and look at the drop from this angle if our pupils are to capture the play of colours ... The observer has to find exactly the right position relative to the incoming ray of the morning sun if its light is to change into all the colours of the rainbow![11]

This has been interpreted in relation to pentagonal geometry:

At a first glance there is a rigorous mathematical and geometric correspondence between the pentagon, 137° and the 42° referred to. What is so remarkable is that this reflects a unification between, on the one hand, the geometry of the pentagon (the root of 5 + 1) and, on the other, the electromagnetic waveforms emanating from the sun; these are 'sine' and 'cosine' waves.[12]

On a trip to Orkney in 2004, I was intrigued to see that some of the standing stones in the Ring of Brodgar, rather than being straight at the top, were cut off at an angle. I measured the angle and found it to be approximately 42 degrees. Is this merely a strange coincidence?

These divine ratio proportions also hold good for the beneficial 'morning' and 'evening forces' which are favoured for the timing of important planting and gathering in biodynamic gardening and farming. The 'morning' and 'evening' of the year—April and May, September and October—relate to growing and dying back respectively.

Tau is the German word for dew. This interesting connection between the ancient, mysterious knowledge of the *Tau* and 'dew' is brilliantly illustrated in *Clairvoyance and Consciousness* by the Swiss anthroposophist T.H. Meyer. His description of the *Tau* echoes the passage from Steiner that was quoted earlier, and together with it fits perfectly with the reference to 'the earth body's resounding quality' made by Gernot and Maria in reference to the earliest stages of the earth:

Filled with the sound of the Tau—this was the experience in Atlantis throughout millennia ... 'Tau', this was what sounded for thousands of years and the bodily form of man was built up in response. To the man of ancient Atlantis the Tau once sounded forth from all things, then in the post-Atlantean time it seemed to die away into silence, and yet in times to come it will be heard again in a new way; it will resound within man himself.[13]

In the branching arches of the Gothic cathedrals, built according to knowledge held by the Templars, we find forms which remind one of the fern patterns seen in frost formations. Frost forms when the moisture in the atmosphere, caused by the chemical ether at morning, freezes and leaves the 'formative patterns' it is carrying on the surfaces of windows or, as in the case of Plate 14, on the roofs of cars. David Elkington, in his book *In the Name of the Gods*, asks concerning the organic, fernlike forms found in churches and cathedrals: 'What do they really represent?'

The original experiment was performed by Father Andrew Glazewski, a Polish physicist based in Britain. Father Glazewski was also a Jesuit priest whose main interest was crystallography and plant growth and their relationship to sound. All organic matter is made up of crystals and compounds; what Glazewski set out to demonstrate was that plants composed of specific crystals followed the same harmonics as the crystals themselves, extending off-shoots from their stems proportionate to the same musical phrases and tonalities. His experiments showed that the flutings on the columns of the Gothic cathedrals also followed the same harmonics ... There is strong evidence that they reflect the same ratio in the swelling and narrowing of growing plant stems, as well as the flutings on the columns of Gothic cathedrals.[14]

These forms make their appearance again in *Rhythmic Formative Forces of Music*, published by Borderland Sciences Research Foundation. In it Michael Theroux illustrates the work of Margaret Watts Hughes, who at the end of the nineteenth century perfectly illustrated the special activity of the chemical ether in relation to the fluid element:

In 1885, a woman by the name of Margaret Watts Hughes developed an instrument which, in combination with the human voice, was able to create the branching figures of flowers, ferns, trees and other organic forms into physical manifestation. She called this invention the *Eidophone*. The Eidophone was constructed of a hollow tube which opened into a large, bell-like chamber. The top of the bell chamber was covered with a thin membrane of india-rubber. Singing into the tube produced a variety of tone signatures on the surface of the membrane. In her earlier experiments, Watts Hughes used differing qualities of *Lycopodium* powder to sprinkle on the surface of the membrane which, when sung into, produced simple vibrational geometric patterns. She noted that it was not only the pitch and magnitude, but the *tonal quality* of the voice which induced varying characteristics in the shape of the figures. Not long after her initial experiments, she began using liquid substances to coat the membrane, and to her astonishment, the organic forms started to appear. These forms were not composed out of simple variation in vibrational structure, but were characteristic themselves ... Her experiments justify the claims that information of this

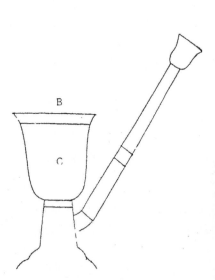

Margaret Watts Hughes's design for the Eidaphone

The 'Hugh-Lloyd Fern Variety' of voice figures

compositional nature is transmitted in eido-dendritic (branching, tree-like) form ... The medium of transmission (as in the Eidaphone's liquid forms) must naturally be dendrite-receptive in order for the correct formation to arrange itself. Thus, from the philosophical viewpoint of Rudolf Steiner's four ethers, these eido-dendritic forms find their natural habitat in the chemical or tone ether. The four ethers—Warmth, Light, Chemical and Life—are endowed with formative processes, and the chemical/tone ether possesses the requisite living, liquid substance of which all vocal and musical composition finds its medium. This chemical/tone ether is the living, breathing substance of the earth itself.[15]

In a simple but extremely effective way the fern and treelike patterns formed on the drum of the Eidophone and the shapes made by frozen dew on such modern surfaces as the car roof in the illustration are contemporary manifestations of the esoteric knowledge that found expression with the Templars and the Rosicrucians. They are manifestations of the science of the Grail.

15.
The Chalice and the Blade

The Aurora and the Blossom of the Divine Chalice

'If you want to find the Holy Grail, you might look into the depths of a Norwegian fjord!' Years ago these words were spoken to me at a time when they bore no particular significance. What lies buried in the northern fjords and lakes on winter nights? The reflected radiance of the aurora borealis! How does this relate to our understanding of the Holy Grail as a manifestation of the two higher ethers?

Harald Falck-Ytter, in his beautiful book *Aurora*, describes how the aurora is a phenomenon that takes place whenever the high-speed plasma of the solar wind interacts with the electromagnetic field of the earth.

> It is justifiable within the meaning of present-day science to look for the aurora's origin in the neighbouring regions of the earth. In this case the decisive question arises as to whether the solar wind's outgoing effect is not so much the cause of the aurora as rather the occasion for an as yet unknown, sun-related structure within the terrestrial organism, including its surrounding spheres, that gives rise to the aurora's mysterious revelation.[1]

Falck-Ytter's book very skilfully moves between a detailed scientific explanation of the aurora and a demonstration of it as a manifestation of the etheric realm. In his investigation it becomes possible to see how the mysteries that were hidden in the Grail legend are corroborated by science when seen from the point of view of spiritual science.

He describes how the solar wind and the solar plasma originate within the corona of the sun. As we know, the Tree of Life was removed to the interior of the sun at the Fall. The solar wind is further described as streaming through and filling the entire planetary system; it does not create light there for plasma is dark and 'not even, like the corona, light related'.[2] This 'stream of ions and protons is related to matter'.[3] As we further read that it 'carries ionized particles, such as hydrogen and helium, along with it'[4] we can turn to Gunther Wachsmuth's account of the activity of the life ether, the Tree of Life, in the creation of ozone.

1) Experimental research establishes the fact that the substance which makes its appearance in the *vanishing* of matter, in its spontaneous radioactive decay, is the same as that which we discover at the boundaries of our earth organism, in the *coming into existence* of matter; that is, helium (He).

2) When the forces radiating inward into the earth organism penetrate more deeply into the material world, the sun force then forms ozone, the threefold oxygen.[5]

Here the sun force can be seen to be one and the same as the sun-related structure described by Falck-Ytter, both descriptions being of the activity of the life ether—the Tree of Life removed from the earth to form a new sun sphere at the Fall. Falck-Ytter further describes how the solar wind's 'relationship to all material substance is demonstrated in its being bound to magnetic forces ... As plasma in the earth's magnetosphere, it produces light and colour in the terrestrial darkness in the form of the aurora, by colliding with highly refined terrestrial matter.'[6]

The aurora is created when the sun forces come into contact with the earth's magnetism, which we can also understand to be the concentrated realm of the fallen life ether at the poles. As Wachsmuth points out: 'There must be points within the earth's organism where the constant concentration of life ether and its unmodified action reach their maximum. Such points, then, of the heightened activity of the life ether are the magnetic poles.'[7]

We could describe the aurora as a manifestation of the sun-related forces of the life ether dipping down into its earthbound, fallen counterpart in the same way that the etherized blood of Christ is caught in the Grail. This cup is formed by the electrical and magnetic forces above the earth's surface which also belong to the fallen, earthly counterparts of the etheric forces.

This picture of the aurora as the Grail is increasingly corroborated by Falck-Ytter as we follow his descriptions of the aurora's formation: 'Shining auroral ovals take form as light and coloured blossoms above the earth's polar regions. Into the centre of these blossom structures, pale red plasma flows from the high realms of the sun. It fills the chalice structure, invisible to the naked eye, with solar processes which pass out of the heights into the depths.'[8]

Falck-Ytter then describes how 'the stream of solar particles now penetrate into the regions of the open lines of magnetic force above the geomagnetic pole directly into the terrestrial environment; in doing so it fuses with the funnel-shaped converging lines of force which act as a powerful brake on it. This gives rise to the barely perceptible, high aurora which fits into the vault of heaven, like a delicate pink cupola, even during the polar "day" in winter.'[9]

Both the chalice and the plasma which fills it arise through interaction between the sun and earth forces. At this point we can maybe link this picture of the aurora borealis as a manifestation of the Holy Grail with a mystery centre, north of today's Russia, with which the historical Parzival was connected and where sacred Grail knowledge was related to the 'power which brings new plant life into being in the spring, a power which is innocent in the plant kingdom but entangled with passion and desire in the animal and human kingdoms'.

Here Rudolf Steiner is once more referring to the Holy Grail as the two higher ethers or the Tree of Life. He further tells us:

> ... in certain post-Atlantean mysteries the initiates looked forward to a distant time when animal nature bound by the Fall would be transformed to a state where, as the ray from the sun goes right down into the plant, so will man's now purified power unite itself with this divine chalice which will manifest like a blossom hanging down from the sky—a reversal of the chalice of the earthly plant: man's transformed nature rising from the earth like the sun's ray.[10]

Very little is known of this centre. If it was north of Russia, it would be situated near or within the Arctic Circle, north of latitude 60°, where at the time of the historical Parzival, in the ninth century, the aurora borealis was most visible.

'The centre of the northern lights shifts slowly in relation to the North Pole. It is assumed today that in about 700 BC this centre lay somewhat north of Spitsbergen and in about AD 1200 lay near the New Siberian Island [*Novosibirskie Ostrova*].'[11] During the ninth century the mystery centre on the shores of the White Sea would have been situated between these two points in an area corresponding to northern Russia. This would mean that the aurora was a frequent *outer* phenomenon in that location at that time. However, it is valuable to consider that, as one goes back in time, the *outer* phenomenon in nature could also appear as *inner* experience. In his book *Aurora*, Falck-Ytter describes how Plutarch gave the first and exact description of the northern lights, which appeared in the West in 467 BC, and then also mentions:

> Many earlier accounts include descriptions that could refer to the aurora borealis. For instance, biblical passages have been quoted. However, in such cases, the nature of human consciousness which in earlier millennia was pictorial and mythical, has, for the most part, not been reckoned with. Psychic and spiritual facts were described. In these circumstances, outer perceptions such as the northern lights could have been stimulating or rousing, but they would be imaginatively experienced.[12]

In the case of Rudolf Steiner's description of the *inner pictures* perceived in the mystery centre on the shores of the White Sea, it could be possible that the results of initiation produced an *inner picture* that corresponded to the *outer* phenomenon of nature manifesting in that area at that time in history.

Here we can possibly make a connection between the above-mentioned mystery centre and the aurora. In his book Falck-Ytter relates lightning, the rainbow and the aurora to God the Father, God the Son and to the Holy Spirit respectively.

> Like the aurora, the spirit has always been hidden and unknown in the historical periods of human evolution. Before the Christian era the Spirit could be found only in the secrecy of the world beyond. And since that time it is only slowly penetrating the sphere of human experience. In the same way the aurora shows itself to human beings; it was only in the twentieth century, when humanity became a comprehensive and interrelated society, that the being of the aurora came fully into appearance ... The aurora's nature is—like the yet unveiled spirit—of the future.[13]

In the Grail legend the dove of the Spirit hovers over the Grail chalice. The pre-Christian initiates waited in secret dark caves to perceive the spiritual sun shining at the midnight hour on the deepest night in winter. This was not a physical manifestation of the sun's light but its spiritual counterpart, which to be seen requires an inner effort of human activity.

The poles are the least inhabited areas on the earth's surface; therefore the phenomenon of the aurora has rarely been observed until comparatively recently, when the spiritual mysteries are secret no longer. As a result of the progress of modern science, travel to the remote corners of the earth is now a possibility for anyone. In the dark sky above the polar regions the inverted chalice is openly displayed over sparsely inhabited territory. The aurora can be seen and reported by any human being who journeys near there. Could the aurora be an outward manifestation of the inverted blossom, the Grail, seen by the very few ninth-century initiates inhabiting the terrain north of latitude 60°?

The Holy Grail is a symbol for the reproductive forces in nature. Since the beginnings of evolution power over these forces of life was given to mankind as a gift over which there was no conscious control. The first human beings were of one gender, *more female than male*. When the Fall occurred and the human race was divided between male and female these unconscious forces of reproduction were entrusted to the female. Rudolf Steiner has described how this unconscious gift, the Holy Grail, has been symbolized by the Grail initiates since early times in the form of an inverted triangle.

This symbol might also represent the form of a dove, or the Holy Spirit. In the Grail legend, the Holy Spirit hovers over the Chalice and could be seen as the same inverted triangle.

Steiner has also spoken of the 'Lost Word', hidden knowledge, which pointed to a future time when mankind would be permitted to have *conscious control* over the living forces once more, control over the Tree of Life—the chemical and life ethers. In this future time when humanity has reversed the effects of the Fall, the living forces—the Grail—will create new life-forms through human speech, by the 'Word'. This will take place through the male larynx, for in that future time the perfected human being will once more be of one gender which will be *more male than female*. In a beautiful television programme in the late 1960s the embryologist Thomas Weiss demonstrated with accurate medical drawings that this same triangular form that we see in the form of the inverted dove, the Holy Spirit hovering over the Grail, can be perceived in

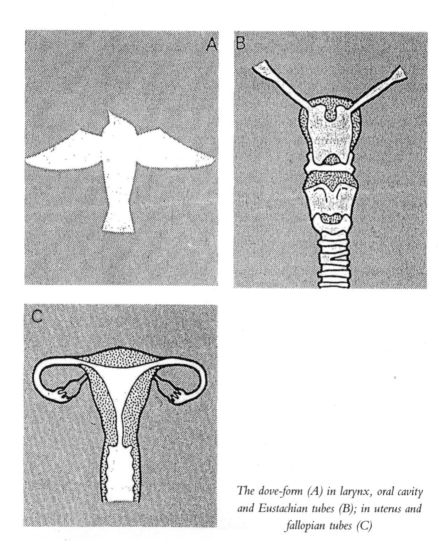

The dove-form (A) in larynx, oral cavity and Eustachian tubes (B); in uterus and fallopian tubes (C)

the triangular form of the womb and the male vocal organs. There is no rejection of the Goddess here. In Chapter 4 we saw how in the future the triple Goddess will be transformed to the Divine Sophia, a manifestation of the Holy Spirit.

We begin to understand the significance of the Chalice and the Blade, referred to in *The Da Vinci Code*, when we realize that the forces thrust down into the earth and man's lower nature—the Holy Lance—which reach redemption in the future are symbolized by another triangle with its point facing upwards.

These two triangles are described at the end of *The Da Vinci Code* when the hero, Langdon, discovers the 'inverted pyramid' at the Louvre, described as 'a breathtaking V-shaped contour of glass . . . The Chalice'! At its tip he sees the tiny structure of a miniature pyramid, only three feet tall. He notes that the two pyramids point at one another, perfectly aligned, with their tips almost touching. 'The Chalice above. The Blade below.'[14]

We have just seen that Steiner likened the divine Chalice to a blossom hanging down from the sky, symbolized as the triangle below.

The Templars and the Rosicrucians worked to keep alive the knowledge that every individual can eventually attain to the Christ energy within and, by actively engaging in the process of manifesting the Christ, can eventually control that divine power. We have just quoted Steiner's description of this future possibility, 'man's transformed nature rising from the earth like the sun's ray', which can be symbolized as the triangle below.

By transforming the reproductive forces we re-attain our position as spiritual beings with an immortal soul, and in that re-attainment we conquer death.

As we have seen, this then is the work of the Bridal Chamber, the Great Work, the quest for the Grail and the final goal of the alchemists—the achievement of conscious immortality, which we saw illustrated in the final plate of the Codex Rosae Crucis in Chapter 8. The left side of the plate represented the divine nature and the right side the earthly nature. These opposites were combined in a circle entitled 'By This Sign Thou Shalt Conquer'. Within this quartered circle were the symbols of the elements, the colours and the numbers that pointed towards the completion and the consummation of all things. The divine and earthly nature reconciled and equilibrated 'on the scales of R. C.' resulted in the perfected adept, a son of light, an embodiment of the Christos. The perfected man revealed the purpose of the Great Work: the achievement of conscious immortality. We remember that the inscription 'By this sign thou shalt conquer' appeared twice amongst the Rennes clues, but in the church at Rennes-le-Château an extra word had been added: 'By this sign ye shall conquer him',[15] meaning 'death'.

The word plasma is used in the scientific description of the aurora phenomenon and also for the fluid constituent of blood. A further possible reference to this invisible solar plasma can be found in Rudolf Steiner's lecture cycle *Christ and the Spiritual World and the Search for the Holy Grail*:

> In the gold gleaming sickle of the moon—as any close observer can see—the dark part of the moon emerges and is as though marked off by the bright sickle ... The gold gleaming sickle becomes apparent because the physical rays of the sun fall on the moon. The illuminated part of the moon shines out as the gold gleaming vessel. Within it rests the dark Host: physically, this is the dark part not reached by the sun's rays; spiritually there is something else. When the rays of the sun fall on part of the moon and are reflected in gold gleaming light, something else does nevertheless pass through the physical matter. This something is the spiritual element that lives in the sun's rays. The spiritual power of the sun is not held back and

reflected as the sun's physical power is; it goes through and, because it is resisted by the power of the moon, what we see at rest in the golden vessel is actually the spiritual power of the sun.[16]

Could a connection be made here with the solar plasma as it is scientifically described in *Aurora* and 'the spiritual power of the sun' described above? If so, one might see in the Grail chalice itself a symbol for the forces of life and chemical ethers retained in the earth after the Fall, together with the chemical ether which still proceeds from the moon.

In connection with the magnetic earthly forces of the aurora phenomenon, one could imagine the chalice as a symbol for the forces of the life and chemical ethers retained in the earth after the Fall. Here again there is a connection with the Mothers, the triple Goddess. In this connection might be found a tenuous link with the claims of these recent books that refer to Mary Magdalene's womb as the Holy Grail.

The awesome undercurrent of low notes in the Grail theme from Richard Wagner's *Parsifal* hints at the depths in which these forces lie, both in the centre of the earth and within human nature as well. On his way to the Grail castle the innocent Parzival is put through many temptations by the beautiful flower maidens who, together with Kundry, were held in thrall by the evil Klingsor whose aim was to lure the Grail Knights from their high goal of purity. By themselves they are the innocent vessels of energy which would only become threatening if the one aspiring to the Grail were to fall prey to the frailty of his lower nature. This lower nature can be recognized as a residue of the moon influences left behind at the Fall, both in the human being and within the earth. These moon forces belong to the previous Moon evolution of the earth. Rudolf Steiner elaborates on this in the course of lectures quoted above:

> In the moon festivals of the Jews it was made clear that the Lord of the Earth shines down symbolically in his reflection from the moon ... When all that has come over into Earth evolution from the Saturn, Sun and Moon periods is grasped in its natural aspect, then we find it symbolized in the old Hebrew tradition through Eve. Eve—the vowels are never clearly pronounced—Eve! Add to it the sign for the divine being of Hebrew antiquity who is the

Ruler of Earth-history, and we have a form which is quite as valid as any other—Jehve-Jahve, the ruler of the earth who has his symbol in the moon. If we bring this into conjunction with what has come over from the Moon period and with its outcome for Earth evolution, we have the ruler of the earth united with the Earth Mother, whose powers are a result of the Moon period—Jahve! Hence out of Hebrew antiquity there emerges this mysterious connection with the moon forces which have left their remains in the moon known to astronomy and their human form in the female element in human life. The connection of the Ruler of the Earth with the Moon Mother is given us in the name Jahve.[17]

The moon forces described as the human forces in the female element are explained further in a lecture given at Dornach, 27 January 1923:

What the Moon is able to reflect from the whole universe forms the sum-total of the forces which sustain the animal world of the Earth, especially the forces that are connected with the sexual nature of animals; these forces also sustain the animal element in man and are connected with his sexual nature in its physical aspect. So the lower nature of man is a product of what radiates from the moon, while the highest wisdom once possessed by the earth lies concealed within the moon fortress.[18]

In his Grail lectures Rudolf Steiner gives us a picture of the forces of sun and moon united once more '... the gold-gleaming sickle of the moon, as it appeared in the heavens, with the dark moon like a great disc dimly visible within it ...'[19] where 'in truth the Spirit of the sun rests in the vessel of the moon'.[20] Earlier in the lecture Steiner describes this in such a way that we can see the chalice of the Grail— the 'moon' nature of the earth personified by the 'Earth Mother'. Here he describes an experience he had after visiting the Sistine Chapel:

... I was coming out of St Peter's in Rome under the strong impression made on me by Michelangelo's work that you find on the right-hand side as you enter—the Mother with Jesus, the Mother who looks so young, with Jesus dead already on her knees.

And under the after-effect of looking at this work of art ... there came to me, not as a vision but as a true Imagination from the spiritual world a picture ... showing how Parzival, after he has gone away for the first time from the Castle of the Grail, where he had failed to ask about the mysteries which prevail there, meets in the forest a young woman who is holding her bridegroom in her lap and weeping over him. But I knew that, whether it is the mother or the bride whose bridegroom is dead (Christ is often called the Bridegroom), the picture had a meaning, and that the connection thus established ... had a meaning also.[21]

The way forward to the Grail castle, the high goal of the Templars, is found through the re-establishing of sun and moon together, through the moon forces of the lower nature which are transformed to hold the Host. These are the deepest forces both within the earth and within the human nature which needs to undergo such catharsis that the depths into which Earth evolution has descended becomes the Grail through which the transforming power of Christ can shine.

At the poles the still unredeemed earthly forces rise up to meet the pure life ether as it streams down from the sun. The force that rises up from the earth and from our lower nature must in both cases be transformed by human effort. It was the highest ideal of the Rosicrucians that the deepest, darkest regions both of ourselves and the earth would one day become a light that would shine out into the cosmos from the earth whose depths have once more become a sun.

16.
Healing the Grail King

Working with the Christ Energy in the
Twenty-first Century

One of the central concerns of anthroposophy is to awaken humanity to the reality of Christ's presence in our midst; to indicate how a conscious entry to the etheric world is now possible for the first time since the closing of Paradise after the Fall of Man. Rudolf Steiner outlined the manner in which this would happen on many occasions:

> ...let us now picture the vision of Christ as it will appear to the first forerunners during the next 2500 years and as it appeared to Paul on the way to Damascus. Men will ascend to knowledge of the spiritual world permeated by a *new country, a new realm*. Man will enter an etheric region which is here now, but which he must first learn to perceive. This etheric region is even now spread out before the eyes of those who have carried out their esoteric training as far as 'illumination'.
>
> It is visible for the initiate up to its lofty heights, and he draws thence at certain intervals the forces that he requires. Thus, when he has to carry out some special work, he draws forces from this realm within the earth's circuit—*which is here*, but only for the human beings who can see into it. A part of that land will be spread before a great portion of humanity during the next 2500 years. Formerly, in the days of a primeval clairvoyance, man could see into the spiritual world, so that he has already been able to see what he will now see again, but with his new self-consciousness.[1]

The experience of crossing the threshold is not an easy one. Rudolf Steiner predicted that many people would be caused great distress towards the end of the twentieth century because they would not possess the necessary spiritual faculties to understand what they were experiencing. The opposing powers have anticipated this event with great cunning, so psychedelic drugs made their appearance just at a time when the possibility of attaining this new dimension was beginning to be experienced naturally. Crossing the borders of the spiritual world is rather like being cast out into the ocean in a boat without oars or a compass. To know where one is and to be able to stay on course makes great demands on that part of our being still in its infancy—the ego, our eternal spiritual core, which only came into existence during the present Earth evolution.

Rudolf Steiner constantly spoke of the urgency for each human being to begin to strengthen these forces of the ego so that humanity would be able to cross this frontier without losing itself. All individuals will experience this whether or not they are prepared. Therefore it is a matter of the greatest urgency that they are ready to face it in clear consciousness and with the strength to fulfil their destinies. Christ is the medium through which we find our own total individual humanity, our own unique being. The more we find that, the less we need to focus on Christ. We become focused in our own centre. Christ is an activity; he is the becoming of the highest in oneself. Recognition of Christ is therefore a personal experience which cannot be forced on humanity; we must all find Christ in our own time. To say 'I am a Christian' is merely paying lip service if the recognition of Christ is not a *personal* experience. Turning the message of Christ into 'fire insurance' and frightening people into accepting Christianity is a direct example of how the opposing powers operate.

After death, regions of the spiritual world are reached where a certain aspect of Christ can be perceived, but those individuals who on earth have as yet had no inner experience of Christ cannot see him there. When they move into the spiritual region of the sun after death, for them the 'throne of the sun' is empty. They then lose consciousness and enter a cosmic sleep which lasts until they return to earth in their next incarnation. From this it can be understood why there is as yet so little understanding of Christ prevalent in the world.

From the middle of the twentieth century onwards it became possible for more and more human beings to begin experiencing the effects of conscious participation in the activity of the two higher ethers, the Tree of Life. This can be illustrated in connection with a direct experience of the Music of the Spheres by a pupil of Steiner's, Ehrenfried Pfeiffer, when he was a boy.

Around age nine and again at twelve Ehrenfried (Pfeiffer) consciously experienced the music of the spheres. As he was looking at the starry sky it suddenly withdrew from sight—in its place the essence of the heavens appeared and he heard a wonderful music which took a hold of his entire being and connected it with the harmony of the spheres.[2]

Ehrenfried Pfeiffer later found his way to Rudolf Steiner and, through following Steiner's indications, turned his descriptions of the new knowledge of the sphere of life into concrete facts in the application of biodynamic gardening, farming and also in medicine.

In 1938/39 Pfeiffer accepted an invitation from the Medical College of Philadelphia to establish a crystallization lab there for evaluating the blood crystallizations of cancer patients using scientific criteria. Subsequently he was given an honorary degree in medicine from Philadelphia University. His work has, to a certain extent, recently been taken up again by individual researchers.

The range of practical activities founded by Rudolf Steiner provide a demonstration of the possibilities that come into being as the return of the Tree of Life, the science of the Grail, begins to take effect— anthroposophical medicine, biodynamic agriculture, the movement for a Threefold Commonwealth, the Camphill movement, Waldorf schools, and curative eurythmy, to name just a few. In some cases, Steiner indicated possibilities which were subsequently taken up by his pupils, as with Ehrenfried Pfeiffer mentioned above. There is also the case of Hans Jenny, who opened up research into the field of Cymatics, which has attracted much interest as it developed in various ways by people outside the anthroposophical movement. A detailed description of some of these other applications of the Grail science can be found in Appendix 4.

The new Tree of Life faculties will be centred in an organ which is especially adapted for perceiving the activity of the etheric world, one that is linked to the sun: the human heart.

In *The Heart Lectures*, Ehrenfried Pfeiffer outlines this development:

In our time there are certain changes taking place in the heart, by which a fifth chamber will develop. In this fifth chamber man will have a new organ which will allow him to control life forces in a different way than is possible at the moment ... the heart is not a pressure pump, but an organ in which etheric space is created so that the blood is sucked to the heart rather than pumped ... With every pulse of the heart a certain amount of substance is absorbed, is taken away as physical pressure and added to the etheric substance. This then begins to radiate outward ... The radiation from this etheric organ of the heart is actually developing into a spiritual sense organ.[3]

A time is developing when enormous qualitative changes are taking place between the physical and the etheric world. These changes will gather momentum as individual human beings work on themselves and gradually step into a hitherto hidden dimension, the Grail castle, as a result of their individual resonance with and response to the Grail quest.

In Chapter 8 there is a description by Maria Schindler of how it takes about twelve hundred years for the pentagon formed by the conjunctions of the earth and Venus to perform one complete rotation through the zodiac. (The *pentagram* is formed by the inferior and superior conjunctions of Venus with the *sun*.) Her book was written towards the end of 1975 when, in a later chapter, she continued this description:

> As at the end of a solar year of 365 days the sun shines forth from the same group of stars as twelve months earlier, so meetings of Earth and Venus, having passed round almost the entire Zodiac since the ninth century, are now approaching the places they had during Parzival's life. The star rhythms are expressions of divine thoughts. The Venus rhythm indicates that the end of a cycle is near and that seeds sown in that earlier time can now put forth their shoots.[4]

'Brother, what ails thee?' This was the question that was needed to heal the Grail King.

When we, as human beings, begin to realize that the suffering of Creation has been caused by ourselves, then responsibility for the healing process can be entrusted to us and the secrets of the Tree of Life handed back for the first time since the Fall. However, this time still lies in the far distant future. The greater the possibility for light the darker are the shadows it throws. This might explain why, just when many new encounters with the etheric world are increasingly experienced, terrible events are reported on a daily basis and we are forced into a compulsory attitude of fear, distrust and scepticism.[5]

What lies ahead? The undercurrents of history are never simple; as a result, problems which arise in evolution often have very different sources to the ones that at first appear obvious. We have been introduced to Ahriman, god of darkness, the Zoroastrian opponent of the *true Sun Being*, Ahura Mazda, who is also *Christ*. Ahriman has been described by Steiner as the lord of materialism. Another, more powerful being has also been described, Sorat, the Sun Demon. Sorat's main intention is to oppose the effect of Christ in human evolution and to prevent humanity from the possibility of returning to the paradise state.

One of the special characteristics of an ahrimanic being is that it causes impulses that belong to a later time to unfold prematurely. At Ghondi Shapur knowledge, for which human consciousness was not yet ready, would have been given to mankind out of step with the healthy course of evolution.

We have seen how, at the academy of Ghondi Shapur, knowledge of nature and of the spirit, which would later be attained as a personal discovery, began to be instilled prematurely into the students' still immature understanding. For the last 500 years we have been meant to acquire science and wisdom through our own efforts in strict natural-scientific research before discovering the spiritual background to nature. During this time the Rosicrucians fostered the true knowledge of nature, while encouraging the human being to eventually find his way through to a new-found individual realization of these hidden laws. The first attack of Sorat the Sun Demon was intended to give knowledge of the subtle workings of nature into our undeveloped concepts 2000 years too soon and in a harmful way. It was Sorat's plan to cut off humanity from the spirit. As we have seen, the moment for its accomplishment was to be about AD 666.

Amazing inventions had been planned there which would have made the need for machines or experiments unnecessary. The year 666 was to have brought in a culture for which humanity would only be prepared during the third millennium. This danger was deflected by intervention from the spiritual world.

In comparison with the plainly feeble Christianity of the seventh century as against the powerful impulse of 666, what the spiritual world set going through the visionary Mohammed represented an extraordinary strong movement.[6]

Islam rescued mankind from the fate which would have been brought about by the impulse of Ghondi Shapur. In the year 666, the peoples of western Europe who were later to develop ideal conditions of consciousness for the development of the Grail impulse were still unsophisticated. Semitic peoples had become more civilized in comparison. At a time when human beings were too immature to find equilibrium from within as individuals, one extreme pole had to balance the other extreme pole in order to redress this imbalance.

Ahriman and Lucifer represent these two poles. Ahriman rushes us too quickly into the future whereas Lucifer holds events back beyond their natural duration. In this way a luciferic impulse was used by the spiritual world in 666 as a counterbalance to the attack of Sorat which has an ahrimanic dynamic.

In the Goetheanum in Switzerland, the centre of anthroposophy, Rudolf Steiner's wood carving 'The Representative of Man' has this central figure holding the balance between the two others, Lucifer and Ahriman in polarity. After Christ's intervention in evolution mankind had the possibility of gradually achieving the maintenance of that balance for himself. Through the influence of the third attack of Sorat, in 2001, the Templars' goal has again been temporarily delayed, making it extremely difficult for each of us not to succumb to all of the many prejudices that are forced on us daily by the shadows lurking behind Government and the media.

The old Grail King is suffering from an affliction caused by his immersion in matter. Parzival will become the new Grail King if he fathoms the problem of the old King's affliction. When we begin to see through the veil cast over fallen nature by Ahriman the spiritual origins of creation will again be revealed and the healing process can begin.

The Parzival legend culminates with his second arrival at the Grail castle, where he heals the wounded Amfortas and replaces him as the Guardian of the Grail. Amfortas has been mortally wounded, but is kept alive by the power of the Grail. He wishes for death, but it never comes. This is the present condition of many modern people who believe that death will bring the solution to all their problems by bringing an end to their existence. Unaware that they are immortal souls, they do not know that there is no end, that the spiritual world is ever renewed and never at rest. Like Parzival every person must put right the wrongs they have done and complete the task that destiny has laid upon them down to the smallest detail.

In Christ, humanity becomes one race. Once the Grail is returned to the earth 'the healing of the nations' can take place. The Knights Templar as guardians of the Grail also have the mission to bridge the gulf that separates races and religions.

Before Parzival can enter the Grail castle for the second time, he meets a strange Black and White Knight. They fight before they realize that they are half-brothers. Feirefis is Parzival's older brother, born to his father Ghamuret and his first wife, a Moslem princess. After she died Ghamuret married Parzival's mother, the Christian Herzeloid,

> And then they recognized one another, although they were born of different mothers. And however different in the different peoples of the earth the earthly mother may be they are nevertheless child of one spirit. How could men fail gradually to recognize each other in their true heritage? Then it dawns on Parzival that this is his brother.[7]

It has been described that our Black and White Brother represents the entire human race, who may not be left behind at the point where any one of us begins to cross the threshold into the Grail castle. Parzival is only allowed to enter when he approaches it in Feirefis's company. There is still much to be done. Since the last attack of Sorat, which was 1998, precisely three years from 11 September 2001 (9/11), the polarity between Islam and Christianity has become unbearable. Materialism and scepticism seem to be stronger than ever before. Is anyone confident that the gates of the Grail castle will open if they arrive on the threshold alone?

When Parzival becomes the Grail King, Feirefis marries the Grail Maiden. The first child of this marriage is Prester John, an enigmatic figure who lives somewhere in the East and who in some legends is mentioned as the founder of the Templars. At a time when the Church had become visibly corrupt, the legend of Prester John abounded. He was a wise king in whose kingdom there was neither injustice nor poverty.

One can see in this figure a prophetic dream of the time when religious intolerance has ended through a synthesis of all that is noble in all the great religions. The Templars worked towards this goal, forging a union between the religion of the sun—Christianity—and religions of the moon—Islam and Judaism—reminding us that on one level the Grail motif shows the fully realized interpenetration of sun and moon.

The forces that remained in the earth after the moon's departure began to cause matter to crystallize and harden. This is the definition-forming activity of the chemical ether which calcifies matter when the vivifying activity of the life ether is absent. On the other hand the life ether cannot function effectively without the chemical ether to add definition and form to the profusion of emerging life. The two activities are mutually inter-creative, but destructive if isolated.

At the beginning of Earth evolution, when all that had been achieved during the previous evolutionary stages was recapitulated, the creation of the new earth was brought about by the *Father*, the principle which represents creation as it comes into being from the spiritual world. The symbol of this initial creation, as it manifested in the 'paradise' stage of evolution, originates from the form of a six-pointed-star, which may be explained as follows. In outlining a six-pointed-star one travels around the periphery; the centre remains unsullied like untrodden snow. A six-pointed-star is recreated in the petals of Gabriel's flower, the *lily*, which is also sometimes associated with the Virgin Mary, representative of the lost innocence of creation.

The six-pointed Star of David is a symbol of Judaism, the patriarchal religion which had the task of linking its followers to the Godhead, to the *Father* principle, when as a result of the Fall the blood of generations became the only link with the spiritual world. Heredity and blood ties were the last fading connection that mankind had with the creative principle of the *Father*. As this connection diminished mankind was faced with severance from the spiritual world unless the effect of the Fall could be reversed. There was then no possibility of regaining the lost innocence of Paradise, of returning up the old road that led from the Creation, from the *Father*. A new impulse had to begin, that of the *Son*, which would enable humanity to return once more to the *Father* but this time, as a result of the Fall, in freedom and with the faculty of independent thought. This new impulse was fostered by esoteric Christianity, whose symbol is the *rose*.

The Templars knew that a time would come when the forces of the *lily* and *rose*, and of the moon and the sun, would join. But as they and the Cathars faced torture and the fire, they had to be content that this possibility must be reserved for a later date. The promise of this transformation was preserved through the centuries in the symbolism and cryptic writings of the Rosicrucians.

The cover of the Foxcroft edition of *The Chymical Wedding* shows Dürer's *The Virgin on the Crescent*.[8] The Virgin stands on the crescent moon holding the child in her arms; both figures radiate the light of the sun. The prophecy of 'Day Four' of *The Chymical Wedding* pronounces: 'The light of the Moon shall be as the light of the Sun and the light of the Sun shall be seven times lighter.'[9]

The earth and mankind will one day be changed so that the transformed moon forces will shine out into the cosmos as the Grail, which holds the Host, the spiritual light of Christ, the one-time light of the sun now shining with a still greater brightness from the earth.

But the Grail must first be won, then Feirefis can wed the Grail Maiden. The moon impulse permeating Islam was instrumental in bringing materialism and scientific thinking into evolution—just as the moon forces bring crystallization and definition to matter. The chemical ether adds differentiation to emerging life by drawing in the formative influences of the planets and the zodiac. It can be argued that Islamic culture has brought evolution to a necessary deeper involvement in matter than would have been the case had esoteric Christianity prevailed in the early centuries.

The Temple in Jerusalem was a prefiguring of the New Jerusalem. The dimensions of Solomon's Temple represented the future physical body of humanity in the next epoch. This next epoch is in fact the beginning of the gradual transformation of the earth towards a new paradise state, where we find the Tree of Life once again. This is the New Jerusalem of the Book of Revelation.

> In the midst of the street of it, and on either side of the river, *was there* the Tree of Life, which bare twelve *manner of* fruits, *and* yielded her fruit every month: and the leaves *were* for the healing of the nations.[10]

It is therefore important to reflect that St John, the writer of the Book of Revelation, experienced a vision of this future state of the earth when the effects of the Fall would be reversed. Before the Fall the sexes were undivided. As the Tree of Life forces gradually begin to permeate evolution, not only will mankind re-attain the paradise state in a new individual consciousness, but the division between the sexes will also be ended. Therefore we can consider that the John figure is portrayed by Leonardo da Vinci in *The Last Supper* not as a woman, but as the future human being.

Earlier, on p. 170, it was mentioned that before the Fall humanity was not divided into male and female—there was only a gender that was predominantly female. Following the Fall, the female womb retained the unconscious forces of procreation. When mankind overcomes the forces of the Fall, transforming the lower nature, humanity will once more be of one gender, but this time predominantly male, creating new life through the conscious activity of the organs of speech. This is the secret of the 'Lost Word'. Having realized this we can also understand how the disciple who tells us of the future state of the earth—the New Jerusalem—also speaks of the Creative Word at the beginning of his Gospel.

The ideal human being is represented in Leonardo's Vitruvian Figure. This could also be understood as the harmonious balance of both sexes—which might be corroborated by our spiritual-scientific knowledge of the role of the ethers at the Fall. If we study the symbols of the ethers we find the circle, denoting the warmth ether, and the square, denoting the life ether, drawn together squaring the circle with the human form extended to form a pentagram within them. These two symbols of the warmth and life ethers each represent one of the poles of the ethers, which were divided at the Fall. We might see their representation in Leonardo's Vitruvian Figure as a clue to the eventual harmonious reintegration of the two sexes.[11] The figure of the man is standing in the shape of a pentagram. Rudolf Steiner described the pentagram as the form of the skeletal structure of the etheric body.[12]

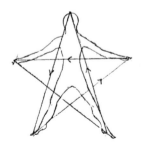

...the substances of the physical body group themselves in the manner natural to them, and the body becomes a corpse and falls to pieces. The etheric body, therefore, continually combats the destruction of the physical body. Each organ of the physical body has behind it this etheric body. Man has an etheric heart, an etheric brain, etc., which holds together the corresponding physical organ. One is naturally tempted to picture the etheric body in a material way, somewhat like a thin cloud, but in reality the etheric body consists of a number of currents of force. The clairvoyant sees in the etheric body of man certain currents that are exceedingly important. Thus, for example, there is a stream which rises from the left foot to the forehead [see diagram], to a point which lies between the eyes, about half an inch down within the brain; it then returns to the other foot; from there it passes to the hand on the opposite side; from thence through the heart into the other hand, and from there back to its starting point. In this way it forms a pentagram of currents of force.[13]

This was understood by Hiram when he built the Temple in Jerusalem, where the pentagon was represented as a realistic representation of the future body of humankind. In his lecture cycle *The Temple Legend*, Steiner says:

Mankind has now progressed from the stage of fourfoldness to that of fivefoldness, as five-membered man, who has become conscious of his own higher self. The inner divine Temple is so formed as to enclose the fivefold human being. The square is holy. The door, the roof and the side pillars together form a pentagon.[14]

In the following lecture Steiner takes the description further by saying:

The human etheric body will provide the basis, at a higher stage, for the immortal man, who will no longer be subject to death. The etheric body at present still dissolves with the death of the human being. But the more man perfects and purifies himself from within, the nearer will he get to permanence, the less will he perish. Every labour undertaken for the etheric body contributes towards man's immortality. In this sense it is true that man will gain more mastery, the more evolution takes place naturally, the more it is directed towards the forces of life.[15]

The Knights Templar worked towards this high ideal. As we have already understood, the Temple in Jerusalem was a prototype for the transformation which each human being has to achieve individually and, in so doing, eventually create the New Jerusalem—the earth returned to the paradise state in a new form. This is the true Grail quest and the ultimate goal of the order of the Knights Templar. In the past they were as yet only able to *guard* the Grail. No one knew whether it could be won or not.[16]

The mystery of Rennes-le-Château, which was discovered for English-speaking people by Henry Lincoln four decades ago, started an impulse which sent great numbers of people on a new Grail quest. Was the whole thing a huge practical joke, or was it spun as a modern myth by people who needed missing information to complete their understanding of subjects which could offer them great benefit? Whatever the ultimate answer, it has certainly sent thousands of people on a journey which began in a quiet and ancient village nestling in the foothills of the Pyrenees and grew to focus the attention of the masses on the enigmatic roots of Christianity.

There *is* no easy answer; it depends on whether one can accept that there were once secret teachings which could not be given to the public at large but which individuals in today's society may now be ready to investigate for themselves. It depends on *every human being's personal relationship* to the events of two thousand years ago.

By the time the Mystery of Golgotha took place, spiritual impulses had long ago ceased to be carried through hereditary bloodlines. Christ, incarnate in the Luke Jesus body, brought to mankind a renewed blood, revitalized with the original potential due to us in Paradise. Because of the Fall we had lost our connection with Paradise, but gained the possibility to be free individual human beings. The renewed blood which we can now incorporate through relating to Christ is resonant with the spiritual force from which we have been estranged for so long. As a result we can now re-attain our lost position in the spiritual world. Rudolf Steiner has described the nature of hereditary blood in the present time:

> Blood sets human beings at variance with one another. Blood fetters to the earthly and material that element in man which descends from heavenly heights. In our century, especially, people have gravely sinned against the essence of Christianity, inasmuch as they have turned again to the principle of blood.[17]

Rudolf Steiner indicated the present and future role of blood in evolution. He spoke of a new type of spiritual being that has been active among human beings since about the fourth and fifth centuries AD. He said that these beings 'will one day be the greatest helpers of the individual human being' and that 'they will help him to build a new earth planet out of his moral impulses'. He named them 'earth spirits':

> ... the particular tendency of these beings is to help man to become very individual, so as to shape the whole organism of a man who has within him a strong moral idea that this moral idea can become part of his very temperament, character and blood, that the moral ideas and individual morality can be derived from the blood itself. [These beings] can render significant help to men who are acquiring individual freedom in ever greater measure. [However they] feel especially deflected from their aim by the factor of human heredity. When the superstition of heredity is very potent this runs counter to all [their] inner inclinations and propensities.[18]

We need no bloodline, no United Europe, or united anything else that has been imposed externally. For although we have been isolated from the spiritual world since the Fall we can now find our way back as individual human beings, by resonating to the Christ event of two thousand years ago as a personal inner experience. In this way we form a different 'community' built according to the impulses of individuals interacting through common humanity. We can then begin to create foundations for the New Heaven and Earth which will be the next incarnation of this earth planet—the New Jerusalem.

Appendix 1

Mani's Teachings

The following is a free rendering by Walter Johannes Stein of a description of Mani's teachings in a book by Konrad Kessler,[1] together with indications Rudolf Steiner made on the subject, in *The Ninth Century and the Holy Grail*.[2]

Evil has not existed as evil from the beginning but only in its elements. For what is good and right is different for different times. Thus, what at first worked for good because it belonged to the time later works injuriously. Taken merely in its elements evil is of the same origin as good, and it too therefore is without end. As evil it does end. But it determines its own end, being placed in a position to do so by the sacrificial act of the good which freely mingled with it. In order that good shall be able to redeem evil, it develops to the extent that, while separated from it, it has the power, through partly uniting with evil, to place it in the position of becoming good also, out of free will stimulated by the radiant light of the good. Now because evil has five members while good has seven, the good only remains by itself at the beginning and end. But during the middle period of its evolution it dips down into the five and redeems the harmony of the twelve-foldness. [Here reference is made to the seven light and the five dark constellations in the sun's course.] Therefore the Godhead, King of the Paradise of Light, adopts five members. His members are: Gentleness, Knowledge, Understanding, Silence and Penetration. Five other members are, however, concerned with the heart [*das Gemüt*]: Love, Faith, Fidelity, Bravery, Wisdom. As the evolution of the world brought about the severance of the world of the Light, of the heights, from the dark flood of the depths, there arose Satan from the depths. He was not himself without beginning but was nevertheless without beginning in his parts and elements; thus it was these parts which came together out of the elements and formed themselves into Satan. His head was that of a lion, his trunk that of a dragon, his wings were like those of a great bird, his tail was that of a water animal, his four feet however resembled those of a land animal. As this being had formed itself out of the darkness it was called the Dragon, the Old Serpent. Then he began to destroy, to swallow and to injure other beings, stalking hither and thither to right and left and penetrating down below into the depths where he continually brought injury and destruction to all who sought to overpower him. Thereafter he darted upwards into the heights and catching sight of the radiance of the light felt a repugnance towards it. When he further saw that this radiance was only strengthened by coming into contact with its opposite, he was alarmed, crumpled up together limb by limb and withdrew into his basic elements.

But now once again he darted up into the heights, and now the Light-Earth observed the activity of Satan and his intention to attack and destroy. And as the Earth observed this, behold the world of Insight, the world of Knowledge, then the world of Silence, then the world of Understanding, then the world of Gentleness also observed it. Thereupon the King of the Paradise of Light observed it and considered by what means Satan might be met.

His hosts truly were powerful enough, but in the realm of light there was only good. Therefore He with His righteous Spirit, with His five worlds and with His twelve elements, created a race—the original race of men. This race he sent below that it might mix itself with darkness. And this race was to fight the Dragon.

Then primeval man armed himself with his five supporters, the five Gods—with the lightly fluttering breath, with the wind, with the light, with the water and with the fire. The first thing with which he clothed himself was the breath. Over the fluttering breath he wrapped the mantle of light that undulated downwards, and over the light he drew the veil of welling water and protected himself with the blowing wind. Then he took the fire as a shield and lance in his hand and hastened to descend from Paradise.

Then the Dragon armed himself with his five supporters—with the smoke, the flame, the darkness, the scorching wind, the suffocating fumes—he armed himself with them, took them for his shield and went forth against primeval man. They fought for a long time and the Dragon won the victory over man, devoured some of his light and surrounded him with his supporters and his Elements. Then arose the storm, the whirling dance and death, and hell consumed itself. Thus arose the human race. Man however recognized the Friend of Light, the King of the Paradise of Light and this radiance filled him with delight. For the light of primal man that the Dragon had swallowed caused the Dragon to feel pleasure in light. 'May light be kindled by light' rejoiced man, and the abyss rose even higher and higher, radiating, sparkling, shining and emitting light like a sun. Thus were the Spirits of darkness, together with all their dependents and their substances redeemed, uplifted, illumined and warmed, so that gentleness proved stronger than hatred. In man gentleness redeemed the Dragon from hell.

Appendix 2

The Arabianizing of Aristotelianism

In the legend of Flore and Blanscheflur, a young knight goes to an Arabian court to rescue the maiden betrothed to him who has been sent to work in this court as a slave. The pure love of Flore and Blanscheflur eventually melts the hardened heart of the Caliph who has imprisoned the young girl, so that they are allowed to return together to the west. According to Walter Johannes Stein, Flore symbolically represents Charibert of Laon, grandfather of Charlemagne, who inspired his daughter Bertha and King Pippin her husband to send ambassadors to the court of Mansur in Baghdad. This embassy departed from the land of the Franks during Christmas 765 and returned in 768. What they brought back from the court of al-Mansur was symbolized by Blanscheflur: the true soul of Europe, the teachings of Aristotle.

Tragedy befell the Zoroastrian impulse after this embassy left for Europe. The wisdom that had been preserved by the Persian Barmacides was lost when al-Mansur was succeeded as Caliph by Harun-al-Rashid who was painfully aware of the importance of the Persian element and of the power of the Barmacides. Harun-al-Rashid gave orders for the Persian prime minister to be seized from his home and beheaded. Stein relates how:

> They tore him violently from his seat and dragged him outside. When half an hour later the Christian physician Gabriel ... came before the Caliph, he observed that the severed head of the Barmacide lay on a dish before the chief of the believers. This was the sign for the downfall of the family. All who belonged to it were taken captive that evening and thrown into prison. Messengers were sent in haste and by order to overthrow their authority in the provinces and all their possessions were taken from them ... Through the beheading of the Persian Minister, through the extermination of the family of the Barmacides, a stream of culture

was destroyed. It is the stream of the continued influence of the Zarathustra element which Manichaeism wished to renew, to Christianize, and which in its union with the Greek wisdom would have brought about a synthesis between Christianity and the ancient Mystery wisdom.[1]

A spirit-denying materialism had been injected into the Arabic intellectual world many centuries before this event. It was the Anti-Grail stream that continually sought to eliminate the Persian impulse with its deep teachings concerning the spiritualization of matter. According to Rudolf Steiner, it was this Arabic impulse which became the basis of modern materialistic science.

Appendix 3

The Spiritual Hierarchies Described by Rudolf Steiner
From a Commentary by Ernst Lehrs in *Man or Matter*[1]

Rudolf Steiner first published information concerning the nature and activity of the Hierarchies in 1909 in his book *Occult Science— an Outline*.[2] This work is mainly devoted to describing the evolution of the earth as part of the planetary system, and with it that of man, from their creation up to the present, along with a survey of the coming stages of this evolution. Detailed information is given concerning the four great cosmic periods, designated as 'Old Saturn', 'Old Sun', 'Old Moon' and 'Earth'. Each of these periods, in sequence, served, as far as man is concerned, for the creation and initial development of his physical body, his etheric body, his astral body, and the implanting of the germ of his Ego. At the beginning of each period, a specific Hierarchy is active in the emanation of the substance in question, while other Hierarchies approach in order to organize and shape the vehicles we wear today as the various bodily organizations. In describing these activities, Rudolf Steiner calls the Hierarchies by definite names formulated by himself, but he always also joins to these the names which have been customary in 'esoteric Christology'. The latter are the names which Dionysius, going partly back to older nomenclatures, had given them. As the following synopsis shows, the nine Hierarchies form three groups, generally designated in spiritual science as the First, Second, and Third Hierarchy. On a certain occasion Rudolf Steiner gave expression, through particular names, to the common characteristics shared by each of the three groups. These are shown in the first column. The synopsis also shows, alongside the spiritual-scientific and esoteric Christian names for the various ranks, the customary translations of the names into present-day language. Finally it shows the creative contributions made by the Hierarchies, out of their own substance, to the building up of the world and of the human being.

I. Hierarchy

Spirits of	Spirits of Love	Seraphim	Seraphim	
Strength	Spirits of Harmony	Cherubim	Cherubim	
	Spirits of Will	Thrones	Thrones	Donors of the Physical[3]

II. Hierarchy

Spirits of	Spirits of Wisdom	Kyriotetes	Dominions	Donors of the Etheric
Light	Spirits of Motion	Dynamis	Powers	Donors of the Astral
	Spirits of Form	Exusiai	Mights[4]	Donors of the Ego

III. Hierarchy

Spirits of	Spirits of Personality	Archai	Principalities
Soul	Spirits of Fire	Archangeloi	Archangels
	Sons of Life	Angeloi	Angels

. . . [The] beings of the two lowest ranks of the Third Hierarchy—the Spirits of Fire and the Sons of Life—had not yet, during the first great period of evolution, Old Saturn, taken part in the common work of creation. This was because they had not yet attained, in their own evolution, to the stage necessary for such activity. They were still objects of the creative activity of Higher Beings—the Seraphim and Cherubim. All of this is set forth in detail in *Occult Science* and in other works by Rudolf Steiner.

Appendix 4

The Science of the Grail—Some Modern Practitioners

This is a brief summary of some modern pioneering work that has been encountered during the research for this book. The individuals listed below have rediscovered the Tree of Life energies. Many of them were making their discoveries, as far as one knows, outside the influence of Rudolf Steiner's spiritual science, yet their findings fully corroborate all that Steiner predicted for the turn of the twentieth and twenty-first centuries. Their work is independent of any spiritual or scientific orthodoxy.

The Music of the Spheres and Healing

By implementing the Tree of Life energy we are once again entering the domain from which all healing proceeds. Negative space is that dimension which opens up when the borders of physical existence are crossed. Negative space forces bring the forms, scents and colours into matter via the astral and etheric bodies. When this process is interrupted illness occurs. The aim of all true healing and therapy is to restore the full effect of these forces. For example, the aromatherapist is working backwards by applying a scented oil directly to the physical body, enabling its effects to reach the cosmic source of its origin, either from the sphere of a particular planet or from the influence of a specific position in the zodiac. A direct contact is then established between the physical body and the specific area in the spiritual cosmos from which healing is required for the particular problem.

Gernot Gräfer and Maria Felsenreich—Nine resonance patterns in water

There is an intimate relationship between water and the etheric negative space forces. In the work of Gernot Gräfer and Maria Felsenreich water, in its natural healthy state, was shown to be capable of nine clearly identified and dowsable resonance formations. The transformation of these resonance formations leads to the build-up of corresponding information fields, which stand in relation to specific chemical elements, vital functions and magnetic patterns. These fields are required by living bodies in the process of building their tissues. The whole of life on earth together with water, which is its chief constituent and carrying element, is a transformation matrix for the energy radiations originating from the cosmos and the earth itself.

Gernot and Maria's resonances were identified first of all through dowsing. Steiner spoke against dowsing as a method of questioning, which works below the threshold of consciousness. Steiner at all times warned against all but fully 'conscious' methods of obtaining knowledge for contemporary mankind. However, it would be out of character with Rudolf Steiner's intentions for serious students of anthroposophy not to consider these new findings, provided that they do so with a clear knowledge of the influences with which they are dealing, whether they investigate below the surface of consciousness with dowsing or enter the realm of Ahriman when dealing with phenomena obtained through electricity.

Sharry Edwards—Signature Sounds

It has been thought possible that the resonances could be a manifestation of the Music of the Spheres. A consistent body of practical, therapeutic and scientific evidence for this position was found in the work of Sharry Edwards. Sharry, a housewife from Ohio, USA and a former university instructor in the field of parapsychology, had unusual hearing abilities. She first became aware of her unique hearing when reading about tinnitus, a disease involving ringing in the ears. Tests revealed that she had extremely acute hearing—well beyond the normal human range of 20 to 20,000 cycles per second. When asked to demonstrate what she was hearing, it was discovered that she could produce pure tones (sine waves) with her voice. She was told that this was impossible for a human voice, and agreed to do a research study that would substantiate what she was hearing.

The results of the study concluded that she not only could produce pure tones but also duplicate them within her vocal range with exact precision. It was then discovered that these tones were able to affect blood pressure. The questions left unanswered by that first project prompted Edwards to probe further.

Two decades of investigation have led to some startling conclusions. In 1982 Edwards discovered that the sounds she was hearing and duplicating could be related to musical notes missing from a person's speaking voice. Working with an emphysaema patient in a critical condition, Edwards discovered that, much like vitamin therapy, essential sounds could be replaced with astounding results. Preliminary studies completed by Edwards show that when a person's missing sounds are returned the body begins to rebuild itself—even from previously incurable diseases.

Very early on, Edwards saw that her work could provide a necessary paradigm for a unifying field theory of subtle energy medicine. According to Edwards each individual has what she has defined as a *signature sound* that is distinctive. A signature sound is a specific individual frequency or series of frequencies thought to emanate from living systems which may indicate physical, spiritual and emotional status. These individualized frequencies are apparently created from a combination of genetic coding, geographic locale, brain and neural functions, biochemistry, emotions, physical structure and environment. Signature sounds correspond to physiological and psychological status. Vocally missing tones also correspond to physiological and psychological status.

Signature sounds and vocally missing tones have been found to correspond to notes traditionally assigned to individual astrological signs. Forty per cent of the time a person's sound has been found to correspond to the musical note assigned to that person's sign by traditional astrology. Forty per cent of the time the sound matches the musical note assigned to the sign six signs away. Twenty per cent of the time there is no correspondence. The diatonic musical scale was designed using the ratios of the planets at their farthest distance from the sun. The harmonics of the diatonic tempered musical scale, in frequencies below normal hearing range, correspond to brain wave cluster patterns.

Brain dominance plays an important part in determining what tone formulation to use in support of signature sound techniques. Indicators of physical distress and emotional states can be categorized according to missing vocal notes and octaves. A *musical scale designed from the atomic weights of elements found in the human body closely correlates to the already established diatonic scale designed by Kepler.* A musical scale using the atomic weights of elements as a foundation emulates brain wave clusters at lower octaves. To date, *frequency formulas* based on signature sounds have been able to assist in such conditions as emphysaema, high blood pressure, epilepsy, multiple sclerosis, traumatic pain, eye disorders, depression, drug dependency and biochemical disorders.

Man-made electricity and electromagnetic energies seem to be the most influential factors in causing a signature sound to change its originating boundaries. Polluted food and water, negative emotions and environments, all have about equal effect, depending on the body's vulnerable characteristics. Geographic incompatibility, partner unsuitability and unhealthy habits, such as drugs and alcohol, are also affecting factors.

Edwards stated that she did not know all of the implications of her work, nor did she understand the complexity of the techniques involved. 'I'm not a medical practitioner, a physicist, a musician, nor an engineer. What I do is "backwards science". Normally you construct a theory and attempt to prove its merit. In my case, I have an auditory and vocal talent that seems to affect people psychologically and physiologically. My work is an attempt to create an avenue for others to duplicate, by mechanical means, what I first began to do vocally.' (Quoted from publicity literature.)

A.A Tomatis

Dr Alfred Tomatis was an ear, nose and throat surgeon, a pioneer in understanding the neuro-physiology of the human listening process. He discovered the 'Tomatis Effect', which operates in such a way that we can produce vocally the frequencies we are able to hear. He has invented the 'Electronic Ear', a device which gradually filters out the lower frequencies from the music of Mozart and Gregorian Chant, leaving a balanced sequence of high frequencies which exercise the tiny muscles of the inner ear, thus bringing about a re-education of the listening capacity and returning to us the frequencies we have shut out from our hearing through life's trauma. This 'Tomatis Method' has been successfully used to help singers and actors who have lost or damaged their voices. The neurological connection of the inner ear with the brain and the entire nervous system means that this method can be used to help a wide variety of ear related disorders ranging from deafness, tinnitus, Menière's vertigo and stuttering to depression, learning difficulties and brain damage. It can also be used to re-energize the whole system.

The Grail Energy and Cancer

Iscador

Iscador is a preparation derived from mistletoe specifically for the treatment of cancer. It was developed by anthroposophical medical practitioners following the indications of Rudolf Steiner. The mistletoe is gathered at midsummer and midwinter and then spun out of earth's gravity in a centrifuge. Iscador is usually given to the patient as an injection; it brings vitality and support to the immune system.

Mistletoe also relates to the research carried out in this book, as it is often to be found growing on points of intensified etheric/earth-energy. If you're on the trail of a Templar site, look up at the trees where you will most likely see clumps of mistletoe.

Wilhelm Reich (1897–1957), Orgone and the etheric

The researches of Wilhelm Reich were carried out independently from those of Steiner and Wachsmuth. However, the fact that there is a connection between their respective findings is confirmed by a passage from a biography of Reich, *The Man Who Dreamed of Tomorrow*, by W. Edward Mann and Edward Hoffman:

> Although Reich apparently had no knowledge of Steiner, his latter-day excursions into religion and science ... suggest that he was moving inexorably towards a similar philosophical standpoint ... It may be that the Orgone corresponds to one of [the] four 'etheric' forces, although at this stage of our understanding it is difficult to say precisely which one. However, Trevor James Constable, a prominent student of Reich and a leading practitioner of Reichian cloud busting, feels that the Orgone is equivalent to the chemical ether. On the other hand, there also seem to be suggestions that

Orgone is akin to the life etheric forces [the life ether] since this force comes from the sun, as Reich once posited Orgone does, and is responsible for the rhythms of day and night and of the seasons, variations that Reich also ascribed to the Orgone energy envelope (the atmospheric Orgone ring surrounding the planet).[1]

Perhaps the Orgone is best seen as the working in tandem of *both* the Tree of Life energies.

Royal Raymond Rife (1888–1971), the Rife microscope and cure for cancer

Having studied at John Hopkins and Heidelberg Universities, Rife worked with the Leitz and Zeiss optical companies as well as undertaking missions for the US Government in Germany during the First World War. He returned to the USA and took up his search for the bacteria that were causing the dread diseases of the time. By the late 1920s, dissatisfied with the limited performance of the best available research microscopes, he had designed and built several of his own. These far exceeded the optical resolution of earlier microscopes, and enabled him to identify and grow cultures of the bacteria responsible for all of these diseases except cancer.

During this time he discovered that different types of bacteria each have one or more very precise resonant frequencies. He invented his frequency instrument, an electronic machine which could be set to radiate that particular resonant frequency; it would selectively destroy the bacteria causing the disease without harming the patient. Typhoid, polio, diphtheria, tuberculosis and syphilis were just a few of the diseases he cured. Finally in 1932 he discovered the filterable micro-organisms which caused cancer, the smallest he had seen. The rats he inoculated with these micro-organisms rapidly developed tumours, and he cured them using the frequency instrument.

In 1934 a clinical trial was organized under the auspices of the University of Southern California, supervised by a committee of America's top doctors including the president of the American Society of Pathologists. Of the 16 terminally ill cancer patients (who were so ill they had to be brought by ambulance), 14 were pronounced clinically cured within the ten-week trial, and the remaining two were treated and cured over the following weeks by a local doctor who had bought the Rife machine.

Rife blocked the attempts of the president of the AMA to obtain the rights of the frequency instrument, which was by then being bought and successfully used by a growing number of doctors. He regarded the AMA as a corrupt organization under the control of a powerful and equally corrupt drug industry. In 1939 Rife's company, Beam Ray, won a prolonged legal case allegedly instigated by the AMA, but was bankrupted and destroyed in the process. Due to the stress of the trial Rife had become an alcoholic and he died a pauper in 1971.

Water

Viktor Schauberger (1885–1958), the nature of water and many discoveries which ran parallel with Rudolf Steiner's scientific indications

Schauberger was an ardent and gifted naturalist who was employed in about 1918 by Prince Adolf Schaumberg-Lippe to look after 21,000 hectares of almost untouched forest land in Bernerau, Steyerling. In this environment, where human intervention had not begun to destroy the natural patterns and activities of the forest, Schauberger was able to observe a wide variety of natural phenomena that had been unobserved by the scientists and naturalists of his day. Water was Schauberger's passion and his close, daily study of the rich phenomena of nature alerted him to natural laws that had slipped past the attention of others.[2] Often these observations contradicted the supposed laws discovered by modern science. Schauberger derived workable and superior technology from the conclusions he reached through his observations, and this earned him the hatred of many in the scientific community. Schauberger discovered that cool water carries loads better than warm water, that even the smallest change in temperature would dramatically affect the log-carrying capacity of a river. Schauberger applied this insight to the building of logging flumes, much to the contempt and derision of the local experts. The flumes Schauberger designed also followed the course of rivers and imitated their meandering flow. Special mixing stations replaced warm with cool water. Schauberger first proposed this design as part of a competition. His idea was instantly rejected as moronic and out of step with the development of modern knowledge. Schauberger's ability to solve insoluble problems with his self-gained and 'forbidden' knowledge was demonstrated for the first time when the flume was built, becoming the first of many.

Brown's Gas

Yull Brown, an Australian citizen, was born in Bulgaria on the stroke of midnight on Easter Eve. Brown discovered how water can be 'cracked back into its two fundamental components, returned once again to a gaseous state'—its 'constituent gases' hydrogen and oxygen—and how to ignite and burn them safely without risk of explosion (a result widely if not almost universally held to be impossible). Properly mixed in stochiometric proportion, the gases were non-explosive and therefore as safe as any conventional fuel in current use. The word stochiometric—impossible to find in most dictionaries—means that Brown's Gas, as it is now familiarly called, is stable because the ratio between the hydrogen and oxygen is very nearly the same 2:1 as in the fluid, chemically represented as H_2O, from which it is derived.

None among the many novel uses for Brown's discoveries is more remarkable than the one which can harness the 'free' power of atmospheric pressure. This, in turn, is directly related to the *implosive* nature of Brown's Gas. 'In a length of pipe 18.60 inches long filled with gas, and sealed and sparked as described, the imploded gas would leave behind only enough water to fill a tenth of an inch in the pipe the remaining volume of which, taking up 18.59 inches of its length, would be filled with a vacuum . . .' With the instant creation of a high vacuum, as so easily affected by simply igniting Brown's Gas, the door is opened to 'triggering atmospheric pressure as a source of energy'.

The implications of this take us out of the realms of the formerly accepted laws of physics. One of Brown's inventions was a flame which alters its temperature depending upon the material with which it comes into contact. 'The most unusual property of this flame is that it is not formed as a set of explosions, as are ordinary flames, but as a set of implosions. Consequently, all classical theory about combustion products, highest temperature regions, and other specifics are up for revision.'

It is interesting to read the comments of two Japanese scientists— one a professor of physics, the other a professor of chemistry—who enthusiastically wrote to Brown in 1986 from the International Christian University, Mitaka, Tokyo: 'We suspect that you may have found some way to keep the originally formed hydrogen atoms and the oxygen atoms at their atomic state (H and O) so that the energy loss in the molecular formation (H_2 and O_2) could be avoided and, at the same time, you have solved the problem of storing a large amount of highly explosive gas in a molecular form. Are we right?'

In this present Earth evolution, at the 'atomic state', before the atoms have combined to form the molecules of gases, the life ether predominates, which is why the Tree of Life energy rushes into the tube when the two gases, hydrogen and oxygen, are separated. This is also why the flame they produce when ignited has properties so different from the usual Tree of Knowledge form of energy.

BioCeramica

Nearly three thousand years ago Japanese villagers used to keep drinking water in vases made from a very special clay. No one knew why, but the water in these vases stayed fresh much longer than water kept in vases made of ordinary clay. Sometime in the late twentieth century two Japanese businessmen, looking for some way to use their wealth and expertise for the benefit of all humanity, discovered segments of this seemingly miraculous ceramic in the Japanese Natural History Museum. The ceramic was known to Japanese archaeologists as *Jyomoun-Doki*, and the two businessmen, Mr Fukazawa and Mr Mori, decided to see if they could reproduce it. The ceramic is made from a clay which is found near Niigata Mid-West on the Japanese mainland, and it took them 20 years to perfect the firing process. They gave the end result a simple but elegant name—BioCeramica.

The Ministry of Agriculture and Fisheries in Japan carried out intensive experiments that showed that fields of rice irrigated with BioCeramica will grow stronger plants that are more resistant to disease and damage. It was also shown that fish bred and reared in water treated with BioCeramica grow larger and are exceptionally healthy. Elsewhere it was discovered that when introduced into cooking oils BioCeramica causes the cooking oil to remain fresher longer, and food to be cooked more thoroughly.

One of the most exciting discoveries occurred when Bio-Ceramica was introduced into a public swimming bath in Japan. Observers noticed that strange vortices were appearing in the water. Film was taken, which, when studied, revealed what has been called the 'embryo of water'. The vortices of 'empty space' appeared to be the process of 'matter in creation' made visible—the activity of the etheric as 'negative existence' working creatively into the manifest world.

Experimentation and research have shown that the effects of Bio-Ceramica are not related to atomic radiation and are impossible to evaluate within the context of materialistic science.

Concluding Note

It is important to say that the author is very aware there have probably been many more candidates for this Appendix since the first edition of this book came out. Time does not allow for further research in this area. But there are two comments that need to be made in retrospect. It has been reported that Rudolf Steiner once indicated that the four ethers work together in full strength and perfect harmony in the location of Vienna in Austria. The whirling and turning of the Viennese Waltz follow the dynamic of a vortex. It is interesting to note that Gernot Gräfer and Maria Felsenreich were working in Vienna and both Wilhelm Reich and Victor Schauberger also originated from that region. I believe there may be others.

It is also sad to note that the Opposition to the Grail has worked very effectively in ending the lives of many of the people who have begun to research the Tree of Life energy. Wilhelm Reich was found dead in his prison cell on 3 November 1957, having had his books burned and his laboratory partly destroyed by the United States Government in 1956 before being taken into custody. Victor

Schauberger died of a broken heart on returning to Austria after relinquishing the patents of his life-work to a large American oil company. There is a continuing list of similar happenings involving others working in the same field.

Notes

Chapter 1 (pages 4–10)

1. *Le Trésor Maudit*, by Gérard de Sède, first appeared under the title *L'Or de Rennes ou la vie insolite de Bérenger Saunière, Curé de Rennes-le-Château*, Editions Juillard, Paris 1967, and Le Cercle du Nouvelle Lire d'Histoire, Tallendier 1968. It later appeared in English as *The Accursed Treasure of Rennes-le-Château*, translated by Bill Kersey.
2. Welburn, A., *The Beginnings of Christianity*, p. 21.
3. Pagels, E., *The Gnostic Gospels*, p. 101.
4. Steiner, R., 'Christmas at a Time of Grievous Destiny', lecture, Basle, 21 December 1915, in *The Festivals and Their Meaning*, p. 56.
5. Ibid.
6. Ibid. pp. 56–7.

Chapter 2 (pages 11–25)

1. Steiner, R., *Building Stones for an Understanding of the Mystery of Golgotha*, pp. 23–4.
2. Ibid, p. 30. Also the courts and administration were in the hands of the Sadducees.
3. Steiner, R., *The Temple Legend*, Lecture 6, p. 61.
4. See Appendix 1.
5. Stein, W.J., *The Ninth Century. World History in the Light of the Holy Grail*, p. 84.
6. Manfred Seyfert-Landgraf, 'Islam and the Development of Modern Consciousness', *New View*, Autumn 2006, p. 28.
7. 'The Impulse of Jundi Sabur', three articles by Sigismund von Gleich published in *Blätter für Anthroposophie*, 1963, translated by Mabel Cotterell, typescript, Rudolf Steiner House Library, London, Chapter 1, p. 9.
8. See Appendix 2.
9. Stein, W.J., *The Ninth Century*, p. 277.
10. Steiner has also given other interpretations of this number in connection with Sorat.
11. Steiner, R., *The Book of Revelation and the Work of the Priest*, lecture of 12 September 1924, Dornach, pp. 113–14.
12. Steiner, R., *Theosophy*, p. 83.
13. Ibid. pp. 57–8. The entire human being is subdivided into the following members:

A. material, physical body
B. etheric body (life body)
C. soul body (astral body)
D. sentient soul
E. mind (intellectual soul)
F. consciousness soul
G. Spirit Self
H. Life Spirit
I. Spirit Man

The astral body (C) and sentient soul (D) are a unity in earthly human beings, as are the consciousness soul (F) and the Spirit Self (G). This yields seven components of the earthly human being:

(i)   material, physical body
(ii)   etheric or life body
(iii) sentient soul body
(iv)   mind (or intellectual) soul
(v)   the spirit-filled consciousness soul
(vi)   Life Spirit
(vii) Spirit Self

If we look at the mind soul and the consciousness soul as the two garments of the 'I' that belong together with the 'I' as their central core, then the human being can be differentiated into physical body, life body, astral body and 'I', with the term 'astral body' designating the union of the soul body and the sentient soul.

14. Steiner, R., *Karmic Relationships*, Vol II, lecture of 12 April 1924.
15. Wertheim Aymès, C.A., *The Pictorial Language of Hieronymus Bosch*, New Knowledge Books. 1975, pp. 12–13.
16. Ibid. p. 12.
17. Ibid.
18. Ibid.
19. Ibid. p. 11.
20. Zeylmans van Emmichoven, F.W., *The Foundation Stone*, p. 36.
21. Bailey, E., *Daily Telegraph*, colour supplement, August 1990.
22. Ibid.
23. Ibid.
24. Steiner, R., *The Temple Legend*, p. 167.
25. Steiner, R., *The Festivals and their Meaning*, lecture 'The Michael Impulse and the Mystery of Golgotha', pp. 373–4.
26. Goethe, W. von, *The Metamorphosis of Plants*.
27. Steiner, R., *The Philosophy of Freedom*, p. 32.

Chapter 3 (pages 26–43)

1. Rudolf Steiner often refers to the etheric body as a 'time' organism. It also has to do with the preservation of memory. In reports of near-death experiences a common comment is on the experience of the individual's life laid out before them in the form of a tableau, embracing past, present and future. This is an experience that takes place within the etheric realm, into which we pass immediately after death. See Ritchie, G., *Return from Tomorrow* for a classic example of this.

2. Steiner, R., *The Temple Legend*, p. 167.

3. Steiner, R., *The Festivals and their Meaning*, lecture 'The Michael Impulse and the Mystery of Golgotha', pp. 373–4.

4. Steiner, R., *The Temple Legend*, p. 301.

5. Steiner, R., *Wonders of the World*, lecture of 20 August 1911, Munich, p. 58.

6. Ibid. p. 59.

7. See Appendix 3.

8. Steiner, R., *Occult Science—An Outline*, p. 121.

9. Steiner, R., *Man as Symphony of the Creative Word*, p. 59.

10. Steiner, R., *Occult Signs and Symbols*, p. 28. It will also be remembered that the bee is a symbol connected to the Rennes mystery.

11. Steiner, R., *Genesis*, lecture of 21 August 1910, Munich, pp. 65–6.

12. Steiner, R., *The Gospel of St John in Relation to the Other Gospels*, pp. 38–9.

13. Steiner, R., *Genesis*, Munich, 21 August 1910, p. 64.

14. This period in Earth evolution is referred to as the Hyperborean period.

15. Steiner, R., *Egyptian Myths and Mysteries*, Lecture 5, pp. 71–3.

16. Ravenscroft, T., *The Cup of Destiny*, p. 91.

17. Eschenbach, W. von, *Parzival*, pp. 126–7.

18. Steiner, R., *Egyptian Myths And Mysteries*, Lecture 5, p. 73.

19. John 1:1.

20. Lehrs, E., *Man or Matter*, p. 473.

21. Steiner, R., *The Spiritual Beings in the Heavenly Bodies and in the Kingdoms of Nature*, p. 92.

22. Wachsmuth, G., 'The Etheric World in Science, Art and Religion' (unpublished translation), Chapter 7.

23. Ibid. Chapter 12.

24. Ibid.

25. Ibid.

26. Steiner, R., *Genesis*, lecture of 24 August 1910, Munich, pp. 118–19.

27. Steiner, R., *Occult Science—an Outline*, p. 166.

28. Steiner, R., *Gospel of St John*, p. 52 (1969 edition).

29. Genesis 3:24.
30. Blattmann, G., *The Sun*, p. 71.
31. Stein, W.J., *The Ninth Century in the Light of the Holy Grail*, pp. 78–9.

Chapter 4 (pages 44–48)
 1. Shakespeare, W., *The Merchant of Venice*, Act V, Scene 1.
 2. Steiner, R., *The Etherization of the Blood*, lecture, Basle, 1 October 1911.
 3. Cotterel, M., 'The Undiscovered Third Force', *Anthroposophical Quarterly*, Autumn 1961.
 4. Steiner, R., 'The Problem of Faust', lecture, Dornach, 2 November 1915, typescript R.55, pp. 5–6, 10, Rudolf Steiner House Library, London.
 5. The heroine of *The Da Vinci Code* is aptly named Sophie.
 6. Steiner, R., Basel, lecture of 20 November 1907, *Isis Mary Sophia. Her Mission and Ours*, edited and introduced by Christopher Bamford, SteinerBooks, 2003, p. 59.

Chapter 5 (pages 49–62)
 1. Bock, E., *The Childhood and Youth of Jesus*.
 2. Steiner, R., GA 94, lecture of 28 October 1906, 'Art as a Spiritual Activity', quoted by S.O. Prokofieff in *The Spiritual Origins of Eastern Europe and the Future Mysteries of the Holy Grail*, p. 24.
 3. Prokofieff, S.O., *The Spiritual Origins of Eastern Europe and the Future Mysteries of the Holy Grail*, p. 25.
 4. Translated from the Avesta by Hermann Bekh.
 5. Wachsmuth, G., 'Etheric Formative Forces in Cosmos, Earth and Man', Book 2, Chapter 12, typescript, Rudolf Steiner House Library, London.
 6. Baigent, M., Lee, R., Lincoln, H., *The Holy Blood and the Holy Grail*, Corgi paperback edition, p. 332.
 7. From *Testament of Simeon* 7:2–3. A translation of the *Testaments* is to be found in J.H. Charlesworth (ed.), *The Old Testament Pseudepigrapha*, I, London 1983, pp. 77 ff.
 8. Welburn, A., *The Beginnings of Christianity*, pp. 128–9.
 9. Steiner, R., *The Gospel of St Luke*, pp. 87–8.
10. Gospel of St Luke, 1:78–9 (New International Version).
11. It is interesting to note here that the Greek word for ratio is *logos*, which also means thought, word. One of the activities of the chemical or sound ether is connected to comparative ratios as creation proceeds into matter through sound—the Music of the Spheres. Clement of Alexandria and the other early Church Fathers who wrote on music could argue that Pythagorean identification of ratios, or logos, with the divine principle of

universal order harmonized with the Gospel's identification of Logos with God, of which Christ was the manifestation.

12. Steiner, R., *From Jesus to Christ*, p. 57.

13. Steiner, R., 'The Death of a God and its Fruits in Humanity', Easter lecture, Dusseldorf, 5 May 1912, in *The Festivals and Their Meaning*, p. 164.

14. Ibid. p. 160.

15. Steiner, R., *The Gospel of St John in its Relation to the Other Three Gospels, Particularly to the Gospel of St Luke*, 14 lectures, Kassel, 24 June–7 July 1909, Lecture 13, p. 207.

16. Matthew 17:2 (New International Version).

17. Heidenreich, A., *The Etheric Christ and the Risen Christ*, p. 21.

18. Steiner, R., *The Temple Legend*, p. 26.

19. Steiner, R., *The Fifth Gospel*, p. 33.

20. Transcript of unpublished lecture given by Rudolf Steiner at Munich, October 1911, Rudolf Steiner House Library, London.

21. Corinthians 13:4–12. Many of Paul's texts seem to have suffered from additions made by a later editor. Also, as Emil Bock demonstrates in his book *Saint Paul*, Luther's translation of Paul's writings often *reverses* the meaning of the original text. The current view of Paul as a paranoid schizophrenic with manic tendencies hardly fits in with the emphasis in Paul's writings on love as the authentic dimension of inner moral freedom.

22. Blattman, Georg, *Radiant Matter, Decay and Consecration*, pp. 33–4.

Chapter 6 (pages 63–74)

1. Wyatt, I., 'The Black Virgin of Chartres', *Anthroposophical Quarterly*, Vol. 17, No. 4, Winter 1972.

2. My personal notes from a RILKO lecture by C. Dudley, 'The Sacred Geometry of Canterbury Cathedral.

3. Sease, V., and Schmidt-Brabant, M., *Paths of the Christian Mysteries*, p. 140.

4. Ravenscroft, T., *The Cup of Destiny*, p. 91.

5. Steiner, R., *The Temple Legend*, p. 150.

6. Lievegoed, B.C.J., *Mystery Streams in Europe and the New Mysteries*, p. 58.

7. Ibid. p. 57.

8. Charpentier, L., *The Mysteries of Chartres Cathedral*, p. 57.

9. Ibid. pp. 57–8.

10. Steiner, R., *The Gospel of St Matthew*, Lecture 3, p. 56.

11. Ibid. p. 58.

12. Sease, V., and Schmidt-Brabant, M., *Paths of the Christian Mysteries*, p. 138.

13. Steiner, R., *The Gospel of St Matthew*, Lecture 3, pp. 61–2.
14. Morizot, P., *The School at Chartres*, pp. 5–6.
15. See note 1.
16. Anderson, W., and Hicks, C., *The Green Man*, p. 68.
17. Steiner, R., *The Knights Templar*, lecture, Dornach, 2 October 1916.
18. Steiner, R., *An Occult Physiology*, Lecture 2, pp. 42–4.
19. Steiner, R., *The Knights Templar*.
20. Wachsmuth, G., 'The Face of the Earth and the Destiny of Mankind', a lecture given at Dornach on 27 December 1923. This was later published in *Gaia-Sophia*, the first yearbook issued by the Section for Natural Science at the Goetheanum.
21. Steiner, R., *The Temple Legend*, p. 26.
22. John 14:12.
23. Morizot, *The Templars*, pp. 22–3.
24. Ibid.
25. Steiner, R., *The Book of Revelation and the Work of the Priest*, pp. 1–14.

Chapter 7 (pages 75–88)

1. Welburn, A., *The Beginnings of Christianity*, p. 19.
2. The former leading Council member of the General Anthroposophical Society, Manfred Schmidt-Brabant, offered some intriguing suggestions in a lecture given on 29 July 2000, which was subsequently printed for members in *What is Happening in the Anthroposophical Society*, Vol. 23, 1/2002. Whether from his own research or from unpublished archive material it is not known, but he suggests that a former incarnation of Mary was the Queen of Sheba. In the *Temple Legend* we learn how Solomon called upon Hiram Abiff to build his great temple. The Queen of Sheba—formerly called Balchis—came to visit and fell in love with Hiram instead, breaking off her engagement with Solomon. We find from Steiner's spiritual research that Hiram was a former incarnation of St John and we can thus see that the close karmic bond that existed between Hiram and the Queen would have had some kind of fulfilment during the next incarnation of St John. (From an article 'Who was Mary Magdalene?' by Margaret Jonas in *New View*, Summer 2003.)
3. Lievegoed, B.C.J., *The Battle for the Soul*.
4. Steiner, R., *Mystery Knowledge and Mystery Centres*, Lecture 9, pp. 158–9.
5. Steiner, R., *The Mission of the Folk Souls*.
6. Steiner, R., *Karmic Relationships*, Vol. 2, Lecture 2, pp. 28–9.
7. There have been several verbal reports of this, including a possible one from Walter Johannes Stein.
8. René Querido, personal transcript of a lecture given at the St John's

Community, East Hoathly, Sussex. It has been suggested that 'M' might represent 'Mundi'.

9. Yates, F., *The Rosicrucian Enlightenment*, pp. 1–2.
10. Ibid. p. 27.
11. Ibid.
12. Ibid. p. 29.
13. Ibid.
14. Hancox, J., *The Byrom Collection*, dust jacket, 1992 edition.
15. Hancox, J., *Kingdom for a Stage*, p. 36.
16. Ibid. p. 115.
17. Ibid. p. 87.
18. Theroux, M., *Rhythmic Formative Forces of Music*, The Borderland Research Foundation.
19. Brown, D., *The Da Vinci Code*, Chapter 72, p. 403 (paperback edition).
20. Hancox, J., *Kingdom for a Stage*, pp. 89–90.
21. Adams, G., and Whicher, O., *The Plant Between Sun and Earth*, p. 35.
22. Ibid.
23. Schwenk, T., *The Basis for Potentization Research*, p. 6.
24. Ibid. p. 6.
25. Ibid. p. 7.
26. Steiner, R., and Wegman, I., *Fundamentals of Therapy, An Extension of the Art of Healing through Spiritual Knowledge*, p. 17.

Chapter 8 (pages 89–103)

1. The Fibonacci sequence of numbers goes 1, 1, 2, 3, 5, 8, 13, 21 . . . Each number is the sum of the two before it. The Fibonacci series is often exhibited in the forms of nature, e.g. the spiral growth of fir cones and leaves on trees.
2. Sease, V., and Schmidt-Brabant, M., *Paths of the Christian Mysteries*, p. 84.
3. Wallace-Murphy, T., and Hopkins, M., *Rosslyn, Guardian of the Secrets of the Holy Grail*, p. 132.
4. Sease, V., and Schmidt-Brabant, M., *Paths of the Christian Mysteries*, pp. 88–9.
5. Schindler, M., *Europe—A Cosmic Picture*, p. 39.
6. Ibid.
7. Andreae, J.V., *The Chymical Wedding*, Minerva Books, p. 84.
8. Ibid.
9. Steiner, R., Lecture 4, Munich, 21 August 1911, in *Wonders of the World, Ordeals of the Soul, Revelations of the Spirit*, p. 77.
10. Mann, E., *Sacred Architecture*, p. 22.
11. Sease, V., and Schmidt-Brabant, M., *Paths of the Christian Mysteries*, p. 88.

12. Pagels, E., *The Gnostic Gospels*, p. 66.
13. The Gnostic Gospel of Philip, from *The Other Bible*, Harper and Row, San Francisco.
14. Steiner, R., Christmas lecture, Basle, 21 December 1916, 'Christmas at a Time of Grievous Destiny', in *The Festivals and their Meaning*.
15. Steiner, R., from *Inhaltender Esoterischen Stunden*, vol. 1, November 1906.
16. Welburn, A., *Gnosis, the Mysteries and Christian Writings*, p. 286.
17. The Gospel of Philip.
18. Hall, M., *Codex Rosae Crucis*, Plate 27.
19. Ibid.
20. Ibid.
21. Henry Lincoln's interpretation of the extra word 'him' is the obvious one; it refers to the representation of 'earth' in the alchemical group, the demon Asmodeus. See *The Holy Place*, p. 35.
22. Wachsmuth, G., *The Formative Forces in Cosmos, Earth and Man*, Chapter 8.
23. Hall, M., *Codex Rosae Crucis*, from Plate 27.
24. Steiner, R., lecture, 20 November 1907, in *Isis Mary Sophia, Her Mission and Ours*, pp. 58–9.

Chapter 9 (pages 104–111)
1. Simonze, W.C., *Doppelgänger des Menschen* (the *Doppelgänger* in Man), private translation by Dorothea Pratley.
2. Ibid.
3. Hauschka, R., *The Nature of Substance*, p. 106.
4. Ibid, pp. 106–7.
5. Ibid. p. 109.
6. See Steiner, R., *The Etherization of the Blood*.
7. Simonze, W.C., see note 1.
8. Steiner, R., *An Esoteric Cosmology*, p. 114.
9. Steiner, R., *Mysteries of the East and of Christianity*, p. 66.
10. Ibid. p. 66.
11. Trevor, M., *Newman—The Pillar of the Cloud*, pp. 120–1. 'Bugs, bandits, foreign food, foreign talk, loneliness, nothing put him off... One of his secret reasons for going was to see what it was like "to be solitary and a wanderer". He *wanted* [author's italics] to rough it alone. *At least part of him wanted it* [my italics]; at moments he dreaded it... What was more, it was to be no easy tourist's visit. He would take a servant and mules and his own provisions and walk and ride round the island, visiting all the most famous ancient sites. This was really an extraordinary plan for an Oxford don who had never been out of England before, and was worthy

of the toughest professional travellers of the time. Newman knew this was a strange episode in his life from start to finish, but this aspect never seems to have struck him. Either he took his own courage for granted, or it did not occur to him that he needed courage to undertake an expedition so unlike anything he was accustomed to do. But he knew that Sicily was a wild place and that people quite frequently got murdered there. Yet the only thing that worried him before going seems to have been the inevitable discomforts.

'Much stranger was the complete break with the whole habit of his mind. For years all his acts had been ruled by duty and determined by circumstance, which he had accepted as God's will. But no duty called him to Sicily. Circumstances rather suggested a return with the Froudes to the duties at home. It was perhaps the only time in his life he acted upon an urgent wish of his own, and yet he hardly knew himself why he was so determined on it. In the event the whole adventure perfectly realized in action the psychological and spiritual crisis within, resolved the uncertainties and renewed the life in him, so he went back to England charged with a new power. Perhaps that obscure intuition of his drove him back to the beautiful island he called "man's tomb".'

12. Ibid. p. 121.
13. Ibid. p. 123.
14. Ibid. p. 139.
15. Welburn, A., *Gnosis, the Mysteries and Christian Writings*, p. 275.

Chapter 10 (pages 112–123)
1. De Séde, Gèrard, *Le Trésor Maudit de Rennes-le-Château*. See Chapter 1, note 1.
2. Baigent, M., Leigh, R., and Lincoln, H., *The Holy Blood and the Holy Grail*, pp. 35–6.
3. Putnam, B., and Wood, J.E., *The Treasure of Rennes-le-Château. A Mystery Solved*, Preface, p. xi.
4. Richardson, Robert, *The Unknown Treasure: The Priory of Sion Fraud and the Spiritual Treasure of Rennes-le-Château*, p. 1.
5. Ibid, p. 12.
6. Picknett, L., and Prince, C., *The Sion Revelation*, p. 192.
7. Richardson, Robert, *The Unknown Treasure: The Priory of Sion Fraud and the Spiritual Treasure of Rennes-le-Château*, p. 13.
8. Ibid.
9. Steiner, R., *The Temple Legend*, Lecture 9, p. 101.
10. Ibid. p. 102.
11. Hall, M.P., 'Cagliostro and the Rite of Egyptian Freemasonry', *The*

Phoenix Illustrated Review of Occultism and Philosophy, 1960, p. 154, Philosophical Research Society, Los Angeles.

12. Steiner, R., *The Temple Legend*, Lecture 9, pp. 102–3.
13. Ibid. pp. 104–5.
14. Ibid. pp. 103–6.
15. Putnam, B., and Wood, J.E., *The Treasure of Rennes-le-Château, a Mystery Solved*, Chapter 13, p. 133.
16. Lincoln, H., *The Holy Place*, pp. 62 and 63.
17. Ibid. p. 66.
18. Ibid. p. 56.
19. Ibid. p. 66.
20. Wood, D., *Genisis, The First Book of Revelation*, Baton Press, Tunbridge Wells, 1985, p. 42.
21. Richardson, R., *The Unknown Treasure: The Priory of Sion Fraud and the Spiritual Treasure of Rennes-le-Château*, pp. 14–15.
22. Picknett, L., and Prince, C., *The Turin Shroud. In Whose Image?* p. 97.
23. Ibid. p. 100.
24. Richardson, R., *The Unknown Treasure: The Priory of Sion Fraud and the Spiritual Treasure of Rennes-le-Château*, p. 24.
25. Ibid.
26. Lincoln, Henry, *The Holy Place*, p. 13.

Chapter 11 (pages 124–133)
1. Lincoln, H., *The Holy Place*, p. 11.
2. Baigent, M., Leigh, R., and Lincoln, H., *The Holy Blood and the Holy Grail*, p. 26.
3. Lincoln, H., *The Holy Place*, p. 24.
4. *Brewer's Dictionary of Phrase and Fable*, Millennium Edition.
5. Baigent, M., Leigh, R., and Lincoln, H., *The Holy Blood and the Holy Grail*, p. 38.
6. Steiner, R., 'The Tree of Knowledge and the Tree of Life', a lecture given at Dornach, 24 July 1915, in *The Golden Blade*, 1965.
7. Richardson, R., *The Unknown Treasure: The Priory of Sion Fraud and the Spiritual Treasure of Rennes-le-Château*, p. 14.
8. De Sède, G., *The Accursed Treasure of Rennes-le-Château*, p. 20.
9. Ibid. p. 114.
10. Ibid. pp. 115–16.
11. Ibid. pp. 118–19.
12. Baigent, M., Leigh, R., and Lincoln, H., *The Holy Blood and the Holy Grail*, p. 30.
13. De Sède, G., *The Accursed Treasure of Rennes-le-Château*, p. 41.

14. *Fortean Times*, April 2006.
15. De Sède, G., *The Accursed Treasure of Rennes-le-Château*, p. 40.
16. Ibid. p. 41.
17. 'Ahrimanic transposition of time'—bringing events forward in time out of their natural position.
18. 22 November, Ophiucus, the thirteenth sign of the zodiac, mentioned in *Le Serpent Rouge*.
19. Margaret Jonas, unpublished writing.
20. Steiner, R., *The Karma of Untruthfulness*, Lecture 21, 20 January 1917, Dornach, pp. 147–8.

Chapter 12 (pages 134–144)

1. Baigent, M., Leigh, R., and Lincoln, H., *The Holy Blood and the Holy Grail*, pp. 120–1.
2. Ibid. p. 87.
3. Personal correspondence from James France.
4. Ibid.
5. Stein, W.J., *The Ninth Century. World History in the Light of the Holy Grail*, p. 287.
6. Lynn Picknett and Clive Prince made the following connection between the Odilienberg and a supposed Grand Master of the Priory of Sion, Iolande de Bar, in turn a daughter of Grand Master René d'Anjou. Iolande 'married one of René's knights, Ferri, the lord of an important pilgrimage centre of Sion-Vaudémont in Lorraine, where she spent most of the rest of her life. The mountain of the tellingly named Sion-Vaudémont has been deemed sacred since pre-Christian times, originally in honour of the goddess Rosemerta but by Iolande de Bar's day it was dedicated to Our Lady of Sion. There was also the Abbey of Notre-Dame de Sion, to which was attached the chivalric order called the Knights or Brotherhood of Sion, founded by Ferri's grandfather in 1396 ... Sion-Vaudémont's status as a pilgrimage centre suffered as a result of the French Revolution, but in the 1830s three brothers—all Catholic priests, Léopold, François and Quirin Baillard—made it their life's work to restore it as a sacred centre along with its "twin", Mont Sainte-Odile in Alsace, about 60 miles (100 km) away.' *The Sion Revelation*, pp. 21–2.
7. Stein, W.J., *The Ninth Century. World History in the Light of the Holy Grail*, p. 290.
8. Ibid. p. 292.
9. Rudolf Steiner has stated that the image of two Templars riding together on one horse indicates that one is a 'Grail Knight', an excarnate Templar working across the 'threshold' of death with a living Knight. The Grail

Knight has also been described by Steiner as a 'Swan Knight', see *The Mystery of the Trinity and the Mission of the Spirit*, Lecture 1, Dornach, 23 July 1922.

10. Picknett, L., and Prince, C., *The Sion Revelation*, p. 192.

11. 'Whatever their point, the authors of *Le Serpent Rouge*—or, rather, the alleged authors—met with a fate as gruesome as that of Fakhar ul Islam. On March 6th, 1967, Louis Saint-Maxent and Gaston de Koker were found hanged. And on the following day, March 7th, Pierre Feugère was found hanged as well. (Baigent, Leigh and Lincoln, *The Holy Blood and the Holy Grail*, p. 102.) Fakhar ul Islam's decapitated body 'was found on the railway tracks at Melun, having been hurled from the Paris–Geneva express', on 20 February 1967. (*Holy Blood*, p. 99.)

12. *The Templar Revelation*, pp. 46–7.

13. Putnam, B., and Wood, J.E., *The Treasure of Rennes-le-Château*, p. 112.

14. Hancox, J., *The Queen's Chameleon*, p. 232.

15. Ibid. p. 234.

16. Ibid.

17. Ibid.

18. Ibid. p. 235.

19. Paraphrase from *Joy Hancox, The Byrom Collection*, p. 232 (1992 edition).

20. Hancox, J., *The Queen's Chameleon*, p. 235.

21. Ibid.

22. Paraphrase of facts taken from pp. 230 and 232 of *The Queen's Chameleon* by Joy Hancox.

23. Father Hoffet, connected to the church of St Sulpice in Paris. In the original story of Rennes-le-Château he was described as a Paris contact of Saunière's. This has subsequently been contested on the grounds that Hoffet would have been too young to have met Saunière when he visited Paris.

24. Richardson, R., *The Unknown Treasure*, pp. 23–4.

25. Ibid. p. 24.

26. Baigent, M., Leigh, R., and Lincoln, H., *The Messianic Legacy*, p. 322.

27. If we turn back to Chapter 5 we find that the Jesus child of the kingly line, mentioned in Matthew's Gospel, sacrificed his individuality to the child of the priestly line, of Luke's Gospel, and then died.

28. Baigent, M., Leigh, R., and Lincoln, H., *The Holy Blood and the Holy Grail*, p. 207.

Chapter 13 (pages 145–152)

1. Wallace-Murphy, T., and Hopkins, M., *Rosslyn, Guardian of the Secrets of the Holy Grail*, pp. 198–9.

2. Ibid. p. 200.

3. Baigent, M., Leigh, R., and Lincoln, H., *The Holy Blood and the Holy Grail*, p. 184. The Priory documents supposedly state that both the Plantard family and the St Clairs belonged to the bloodline.

4. Wallace-Murphy, T., *The Templar Legacy and the Masonic Inheritance within Rosslyn Chapel*, p. 30.

5. Ibid. pp. 22–3.

6. Wallace-Murphy, T., and Hopkins, M., *Rosslyn, Guardian of the Secret of the Holy Grail*, p. 113.

7. Sease, V., and Schmidt-Brabant, M., 'The World Mission of the Templars as Emissaries of the Holy Grail', in *Paths of the Christian Mysteries*, p. 134.

8. This was during the second incarnation of Rosenkreutz.

9. Wallace-Murphy, T., and Hopkins, M., *The Templar Legacy and the Masonic Inheritance within Rosslyn Chapel*, p. 34.

10. Steiner, R., in *Concerning the History and Content of the Higher Degrees of the Esoteric School. 1904–1914*, Etheric Dimensions Press, 2005, p. 370 (CH 1669, Les Sciernes-d'Albreuve, Switzerland, and Hu's Gate, Tobermory, Isle of Mull, PA75 6NR).

11. Wallace-Murphy, T., *Rosslyn, Guardian of the Secret of the Holy Grail*, p. 10.

12. On the underside of some of these notes one can see the Chladni sound patterns.

13. Steiner, R., *The Temple Legend*, p. 301.

14. Steiner, R., *Three Streams in the Evolution of Mankind*, Lecture 1, p. 22.

Chapter 14 (pages 153–165)

1. Shakespeare, W., *The Merchant of Venice*, Act V, Scene 1.

2. Schwenk, T., *Sensitive Chaos*, p. 70.

3. Ibid. p. 30.

4. Steiner, R., *Egyptian Myths and Mysteries*, p. 73–4.

5. Gräfer, G., and Felsenreich, M., information from *Forstellung für Bioenergie*, Austria.

6. Ibid.

7. James, J., *The Music of the Spheres*, p. 40.

8. Ibid. p. 52.

9. Gräfer, G., and Felsenreich, M., information from *Forstellung für Bioenergie*, Austria.

10. Bühler, W., 'The Sparkling Droplet', *Journal of Anthroposophical Medicine*, Vol. 13, No. 2, 1996. (Original title 'Der funkelride Tropfen', *Merkurstabe*, special suppl., translated by A.R. Meuss.)

11. Bühler, W., 'The Powers of Morning and Evening. Cosmologic

Aspects', *Journal of Anthroposophical Medicine*, Vol. 3, 1994, extracted from *Das Pentegramm und der Goldene Schnitt als Schoepfungsprinzip*, by Walter Bühler, Freies Geistesleben, Stuttgart 1994, reprinted in the journal with the author's permission. (Original title 'Zum Problem der Morgen-und-Abend Kraefte—Kosmologiste Aspekte', from *Merkurstab* 1993; 46:606–611, translated by Anna Meuss.)

12. Correspondence from Peter Welsford, FCA, researcher and writer on Hidden Harmonics, the HH Factor and the DNA Genome. Email: pawelsford@hotmail.com

13. Meyer, T.H., *Clairvoyance and Consciousness*, p. 17.

14. Elkington, D., *In the Name of the Gods*, p. 195.

15. Theroux, M., 'Dendrites—The Structural Archetype of Communication. The Eido-Dendritic Experience of Composition', in *Rhythmic Formative Forces of Music*, Borderland Sciences Research Foundation, pp. 48–9.

Chapter 15 (pages 166–176)

1. Falck-Ytter, H., *Aurora*, p. 82.

2. Ibid. p. 99.

3. Ibid.

4. Ibid.

5. Wachsmuth, G., *Etheric Formative Forces in Cosmos, Earth and Man*, Book 1, Chapter 4, p. 109.

6. Falck-Ytter, H., *Aurora*, p. 99.

7. Wachsmuth, G., *Etheric Formative Forces*, p. 81.

8. Falck-Ytter, H., *Aurora*, p. 112.

9. Ibid. p. 79.

10. Steiner, R., 'Parzival', typescript of a lecture given in London on 29 July 1906, Rudolf Steiner House Library, London.

11. Falck-Ytter, H., *Aurora*, p. 50.

12. Ibid. p. 44.

13. Ibid. pp. 134–5.

14. Brown, D., *The Da Vinci Code*, pp. 591–2.

15. See Chapter 8, note 21.

16. Steiner, R., *Christ and the Spiritual World and the Search for the Holy Grail*, pp. 114–15.

17. Ibid. p. 118.

18. Steiner, R., 'The Spiritual Individualities of the Planets', lecture, 27 July 1923, Dornach, published in *The Golden Blade*, 1966, p. 22.

19. Steiner, R., *Christ and the Spiritual World and the Search for the Holy Grail*, p. 111.

20. Ibid. p. 115.
21. Ibid. pp. 99–100.

Chapter 16 (pages 177–190)

1. Steiner, R., *The Christ Impulse and the Development of Ego Consciousness*, AP, 1976.
2. Selawry, A., *Ehrenfried Pfeiffer, Pioneer of Spiritual Research and Practice*, p. 4.
3. Pfeiffer, E., *The Heart Lectures*, Lecture 1, pp. 2 and 10.
4. Schindler, M., *Europe—A Cosmic Picture*, p. 220.
5. An example of this new insight into the etheric world is reported in an article by Dorian Schmidt in the Winter 2005 edition of the Biodynamic Agriculture Association's journal *Star and Furrow*. Dorian's workshop, which took place at the Hatch Camphill Community in Thornbury, July 2005, was reported in the Summer issue 2005. His first article and subsequent ones were also published in the Research Into Lost Knowledge Journals, Nos. 67, 68 and 69. As far as terror and distrust are concerned, the author feels that none of her readers need any more information on these subjects!
6. Von Gleich, S., *The Academy of Ghondi Shapur*, typescript from Rudolf Steiner House Library, London.
7. Stein, W.J., *The Ninth Century in the Light of the Holy Grail*, p. 259.
8. Andreae, J.V., *The Chymical Wedding of Christian Rosenkreutz* (Johann Foxcroft translation, 1690).
9. Ibid. 'Day Four', p. 43.
10. Revelation 22:2.
11. This comparison is made solely from the author's point of view, being fully aware that the Vitruvian Figure was drawn by Leonardo da Vinci to illustrate 'one of the earliest written documents dealing with human proportions' by Marcus Vitruvius Pollio, 'the first-century Roman architect and writer. He begins his *Ten Books on Architecture* with the recommendation that temples, in order to be magnificent, should be constructed on the analogy of the well-shaped human body, in which he says, there is a perfect harmony between all the parts.'

    In this context '. . . the relatedness of the human body to the circle and the square rests upon the archetypal idea of "squaring the circle", which fascinated the ancients, because these shapes were considered perfect and even sacred, the circle having been looked upon as a symbol of the heavenly orbits, the square as a representation of the "foursquare" firmness of the earth. The two combined in the human body suggests in the language of symbolic patterns that we unite within ourselves the diversities of heaven and earth, an idea shared by many mythologies and religions.' (Doczi, György, *The Power of Limits. Proportional Harmonies in Nature, Art and Architecture*, Shambhala, Boston and London 1994, p. 93.)

12. Steiner, R., *Occult Signs and Symbols*, lecture, Stuttgart, 13 September 1907.

13. Steiner, R., *Gospel of St John*, lecture, Basel, 17 November 1907, type-script ENSO, Rudolf Steiner House, London.

14. Steiner, R., *The Temple Legend*, Lecture 12, 'The Lost Temple and its Restoration', pp. 150–1.

15. Ibid. p. 174.

16. When Trevrizant first counselled Parzival no one had yet been able to follow Christ to where the deepest powers lie, guarded by the backward beings of Ancient Saturn. Because of this Trevrizant later admits that before Parzival set out for the Grail castle he had lied to him about the fallen angels being redeemable. 'Whoever desires to have reward from God must be in feud with those angels. For they are eternally damned and chose their own perdition.' (*Parzival*, Penguin Classics, Chapter 16, p. 396.) It was then, and still is, unknown whether humanity will be capable of overcoming the deepest fallen forces. However, in the context of this book the author's personal aspiration is that, in the Manichaean sense, even these darkest powers are ultimately redeemable!

17. Steiner, R., lecture, Basle, 26 December 1921, in *Festivals and their Meaning*, p. 106.

18. Steiner, R., lecture, 23 September 1922, Dornach, in *Supersensible Influences in the History of Mankind*.

Appendix 1

1. Kessler, K., *Mani, Forschungen über die manichäische Religion*, Vol. I, p. 306, Berlin 1889.

2. *The Ninth Century, World History in the Light of the Holy Grail*, by Walter Johannes Stein, Temple Lodge Press, London 1988, Chapter 4, pp. 81–3.

Appendix 2

1. Stein, W.J., *The Ninth Century, World History in the Light of the Holy Grail*, pp. 86–7.

Appendix 3

1. Lehrs, E., *Man or Matter*, Faber & Faber, 1958, pp. 426–7; RSP, 1985, pp. 466–7.

2. Also published as *An Outline of Esoteric Science*.

3. Physical matter had previously been described as cosmic will that has become old.

4. In the Old Testament they bear the name of Elohim. One of them, called Yahweh in the Bible, undertook the leadership of the Hebrew people as a Divinity working at the same time in nature and in human history.

Appendix 4

1. Mann, W.E., and Hoffman, E., *The Man Who Dreamed of Tomorrow*, pp. 168–9.

2. These phenomena are now lost forever due to the spread of industrial cities and the wholesale destruction of the natural landscape. One of the reasons for the success of materialistic theories has been the eradication of those areas in which the etheric forces worked with the greatest vitality.

Bibliography

Abbreviations:

AP   = Anthroposophic Press (New York)
MER = Mercury Press (Spring Valley, New York)
RSP = Rudolf Steiner Press (London/Forest Row, Sussex)
SBC = Steiner Book Centre (Canada)
SGP = St George Publications (Spring Valley, New York)

Rudolf Steiner

The Book of Revelation and the Work of the Priest, RSP, 1998
Building Stones for an Understanding of the Mystery of Golgotha, RSP, 1972
Christ and the Spiritual World and the Search for the Holy Grail, RSP, 1963
The Christ Impulse and the Development of Ego Consciousness, AP, 1976
Christianity as Mystical Fact, AP, 1997
Concerning the History and Content of the Higher Degrees of the Esoteric School, 1904–1914, Etheric Dimensions Press, 2005 (CH 1669, Les Sciernes-d'Albreuve, Switzerland, and Hu's Gate, Tobermory, Isle of Mull, PA75 6NR)
Cosmic Christianity and the Impulse of Michael, RSP, 1953
Egyptian Myths and Mysteries, AP, 1971
Esoteric Christianity and the Mission of Christian Rosenkreutz, RSP, 1984
An Esoteric Cosmology, SGP, 1978
Esoteric Development, AP, 1982
The Etherization of the Blood, Lecture, Basle, 1 October, 1911, RSP, 1971
The Fall of the Spirits of Darkness, RSP, 1993
The Festivals and their Meaning, RSP, 1981
The Fifth Gospel, RSP, 1968
From Jesus to Christ, RSP, 1973
From Symptom to Reality in Modern History, RSP, 1976
Fundamentals of Therapy (with Ita Wegman), RSP, 1983
Genesis, Secrets of Creation, RSP, 2002 ·
Goethean Science, MER, 1988
Gospel of St Luke, RSP, 1988
Gospel of St John, AP, 1948
Gospel of St John in Relation to the Other Gospels, AP 1948

Gospel of St Mark, AP, 1986

Gospel of St Matthew, RSP, 1965 (reprinted 1985)

Harmony of the Creative Word, RSP, 2001

How to Know Higher Worlds, AP, 1994

Inner Impulses of Evolution—The Mexican Mysteries, The Knights Templar, AP, 1984

The Karma of Untruthfulness, Vol. 2, RSP, 1992

Karmic Relationships, Vol. 11, RSP, 1997

The Knights Templar, the Mystery of the Warrior Monks, RSP, 2007

Isis Mary Sophia. Her Mission and Ours, SBC, 2003

Man as Symphony of the Creative Word, RSP, 1970.

Manifestations of Karma, RSP, 1969.

The Mission of the Archangel Michael, AP, 1961

The Mission of the Folk Souls, RSP, 2005

The Mysteries of the East and of Christianity, RSP, 1989

Mystery Knowledge and Mystery Centres, RSP, 1997

The Mystery of the Trinity and the Mission of the Spirit, AP, 1991

An Occult Physiology, RSP, 1983

Occult Science, RSP, 1969

Occult Signs and Symbols, AP, 1980

An Outline of Esoteric Science, AP, 1997

The Philosophy of Freedom, RSP, 1979

The Reappearance of Christ in the Etheric, AP, 1983

The Riddle of Man, MER, 1990

Rosicrucian Esotericism, AP, 1978

Rosicrucianism and Modern Initiation, RSP, 1982

The Spiritual Beings in the Heavenly Bodies and in the Kingdoms of Nature, AP, 1992

Supersensible Influences in the History of Mankind, Rudolf Steiner Publishing Co., 1956

The Temple Legend, RSP, 1985

Theosophy, AP, 1994

Three Streams in the Evolution of Mankind, RSP, 1985

Wonders of the World, Ordeals of the Soul, Revelations of the Spirit, RSP, 1963

World Ether—Elemental Beings—Kingdoms of Nature (text from Rudolf Steiner compiled and with commentary by Ernst Hageman), MER, 1993

General Bibliography

Adams, George, *Physical and Etheric Spaces*, RSP, 1978

Adams, George, and Whicher, Olive, *The Plant Between Sun and Earth*, RSP, 1980

Alexandersson, Olof, *Living Water—Victor Schauberger and the Secrets of Natural Energy*, Gateway Books, Bath 1990

Anderson, William, and Hicks, Clive, *The Green Man—The Archetype of Oneness with the Earth*, HarperCollins, London 1990

Andreae, Joseph Valentin, *The Chymical Wedding of Christian Rosenkreutz* (trans. Foxcroft, E., 1690), Minerva Books, London

Ashe, Geoffrey, *Mythology of the British Isles*, Guild Publishing, London 1990

Baigent, Michael, and Leigh, Richard, *The Messianic Legacy*, Jonathan Cape, London 1986

Baigent, Michael, and Leigh, Richard, *The Temple and the Lodge*, Jonathan Cape, London 1989

Baigent, Michael, Leigh, Richard, and Lincoln, Henry, *The Holy Blood and the Holy Grail*, Corgi, 1983

Baring, Anne, and Cashford, Jules, *The Myth of the Goddess*, BCA, London 1991

Barnstone, Willis (ed.), *The Other Bible*, Harper & Rowe, New York 1984

Begg, Ian, and Begg, Duke, *In Search of the Holy Grail and the Precious Blood*, HarperCollins, London 1995

Bittleston, Adam, *Our Spiritual Companions*, Floris Books, Edinburgh 1980

Blattmann, Georg, *Radiant Matter, Decay and Consecration*, Floris Books, Edinburgh 1983

Blattman, Georg, *The Sun—The Ancient Mysteries and a New Physics*, Floris Books, Edinburgh 1985

Bock, Emil, *The Childhood and Youth of Jesus*, Floris Books, Edinburgh 1997

Bock, Emil, *St Paul: Life, Epistles and Teachings*, Floris Books, Edinburgh 1993

Boehme, Jacob, *The Signature of All Things*, James Clarke & Co. Ltd., Cambridge 1981

Brewer's Dictionary of Phrase and Fable (Millennium Edition), London 1999

Brown, Dan, *The Da Vinci Code*, Corgi, 2004

Charlesworth, James H. (ed.), *The Old Testament Pseudepigrapha*, Vol. 1, Doubleday, London 1983

Charpentier, Louis, *The Mysteries of Chartres Cathedral*, RILKO Books, 1972

Churton, Tobias, *The Gnostics*, Wiedenfield and Nicholson in association with Channel Four Television Company and Border Television plc, London

Collins, Andrew, *The Seventh Sword*, Century, London 1991

Corbu, Claire, and Captier, Antoine, *L'Heritage de l'Abbé Saunière*, Belisane, Nice 1985

Coveny, Peter, and Highfield, Roger, *The Arrow of Time*, W.H. Allen, London 1991

Dawkins, Peter, *Zoence, the Science of Life, Discovering the Sacred Spaces of Your Life*, Samuel Weiser, New York 1999

De Sède, Gérard, *The Accursed Treasure of Rennes-le-Château* (translated by Bill Kersey from the French edition, *Le Trésor Maudit de Rennes-le-Château*), DEK Publishing, Worcester Park, Surrey 2001

De Sède, Gérard, *Rennes-le-Château, les Dossieres, les Impostures, les Phantasomes et les Hypothèses*, Editions Péladon Robert Laffont, Paris 1988

Eastern, Stewart, *Rudolf Steiner—Herald of a New Epoch*, AP, 1980

Emmichoven, F.W. Zeylemans van, *The Foundation Stone*, RSP, London 1983

Eisenman, R., and Wise, M., *The Dead Sea Scrolls Uncovered*, Element, Dorset 1992

Elkington, D., *In the Name of the Gods*, Green Man Press, 2001

Eschenbach, Wolfram von, *Parzival*, Penguin Books, 1980

Falck-Ytter, Harald, *Aurora—The Northern Lights in Mythology, History and Science*, Floris Books, Edinburgh 1985

Foster, Richard, *Patterns of Thought*, Jonathan Cape, London 1991

France, James, *The Cistercians in Scandinavia*, Cistercian Publications, Michigan

Godwin, Joscelyn, *Arktos—The Polar Myth*, Thames and Hudson, London 1993

Godwin, Malcolm, *The Holy Grail—Its Origins, Secrets, and Meaning Revealed*, BCA, London 1994

Goethe, J.W. von, *The Metamorphosis of Plants*, Biodynamic Farming and Gardening Association, 1974

Gräfer, G., and Felsenreich, M., from *Forstellung für Bioenergie*, Austria

Hall, Manly, *Codex Rosae Crucis*, Philosophical Research Society, Inc. 1974

Hancox, Joy, *The Byrom Collection*, Jonathan Cape, London 1992; paperback edition with new Preface, Jonathan Cape, 1997

Hancox, Joy, *Kingdom for a Stage*, Sutton Publishing Ltd, Thrupp, Stroud, Gloucestershire 2001

Hancox, Joy, *The Queen's Chameleon*, Random House, 1994

Hauschka, Rudolf, *The Nature of Substance*, Stuart and Watkins, London 1967

Hauschka, Rudolf, *Nutrition*, Stuart and Watkins, London 1967

Heidenreich, Alfred, *The Etheric Christ and the Risen Christ*, RSP, 1969

Heyer, Karl, *The Middle Ages*, Steiner Schools Fellowship, 1994

Hutton, Ronald, *The Pagan Religions of the Ancient British Isles*, Blackwell, London 1991

James, Jamie, *The Music of the Spheres*, Little Brown, London 1994

Lehrs, Ernst, *Man or Matter*, Faber & Faber, 1958, RSP, 1985

Lievegoed, Bernard, C.J., *The Battle for the Soul*, Hawthorn Press, Stroud 1994

Lievegoed, Bernard, C.J., *Man on the Threshold*, Hawthorn Press, Stroud 1985

Lievegoed, Bernard, C.J., *Mystery Streams in Europe and the New Mysteries*, AP, New York 1982

Lincoln, Henry, *The Holy Place*, Jonathan Cape, 1991, Corgi, 1992

Loomis, Roger Sherman, *The Grail—From Celtic Myth to Christian Symbol*, Constable and Constable, Suffolk 1992

MacCulloch, J.A., *The Religion of the Ancient Celts*, Constable and Constable, London 1991

Mann, A.T., *Sacred Architecture*, Element Books, Dorset 1993

Mann, Edward, and Hoffman, Edward, *The Man who Dreamed of Tomorrow*, J.P. Tarcher, Los Angeles 1980

Matthews, Caitlin, *Sophia—Goddess of Wisdom*, Aquarian Press, Harper Collins, London 1992

Meyer, T.H., *The Bodhisattva Question*, Temple Lodge, London 1993

Meyer, T.H., *Clairvoyance and Consciousness*, Temple Lodge, London 1991

Morizot, P., *The School at Chartres*, SGP, 1987

Morizot, P., *The Templars*, AP, 1960

Oakley, I.C., *Masonry and Medieval Mysticism*, Theosophical Publishing House, London 1900

Pagels, Elaine, *The Gnostic Gospels*, Weidenfeld and Nicolson, London 1980

Pfeiffer, Ehrenfried, *The Heart Lectures*, MER, 1989

Picknett, Lynn, and Prince, Clive, *The Sion Revelation. Inside the Shadowy World of Europe's Secret Masters*, Time Warner Books, London 2006

Picknett, Lynn, and Prince, Clive, *The Turin Shroud. In Whose Image?* BCA by arrangement with Bloomsbury Publishing Ltd., 1994

Prokofieff, Sergei O., *The Cycle of the Year as a Path of Initiation*, Temple Lodge Publishing, London 1991

Prokofieff, Sergei O., *The Spiritual Origins of Eastern Europe and the Future Mysteries of the Holy Grail*, Temple Lodge Publishing, London 1994

Putnam, Bill, and Wood, John Edwin, *The Treasure of Rennes-le-Château. A Mystery Solved*, Sutton Publishing, Gloucestershire 2003

Querido, René, *The Golden Age of Chartres*, Floris Books, Edinburgh 1987

Ravenscroft, Trevor, *The Cup of Destiny*, Rider and Co., London 1981

Ravenscroft, Trevor, *The Spear of Destiny*, Neville Spearman, London 1972

Richardson, Robert, *The Unknown Treasure: The Priory of Sion Fraud and the*

Spiritual Treasure of Rennes-le-Château, North Star Publishing Company (PO Box 940562, Houston Texas, 77094-7562), 1998

Ritchie, George G., with Elizabeth Sherrill, Fleming H. Ravel, *Return from Tomorrow*, Grand Rapids, Michigan, 1983, 1994

Robinson, John J., *Born in Blood—The Lost Secrets of Freemasonry*, Guild Publishing, London 1989

Schindler, Maria, *Europe—A Cosmic Picture*, New Knowledge Books, Sussex 1975

Schwenk, Theodor, *The Basis of Potentization Research*, MP, 1988

Schwenk, Theodor, *Sensitive Chaos, The Creation of Flowing Forms in Water and Air*, RSP, 1996

Sease, Virginia, and Schmidt-Brabant, Manfred, *Paths of the Christian Mysteries*, Temple Lodge Publishing, 2003

Seddon, Richard, *The Mystery of Arthur at Tintagel*, RSP, 1990

Selawry, Alla, *Ehrenfried Pfeiffer, Pioneer of Spiritual Research and Practice*, MP, 1992

Shepherd, A.P., *Rudolf Steiner—Scientist of the Invisible*, Floris Books, Edinburgh 1983

Simonis, Werner Christian, *Doppelgänger des Menschen* (The *Döppelganger* in Man), Verlag die Kommenden GmbH, Frieberg 1973. Private translation by Dorothea Pratley

Sinclair, Andrew, *The Sword and the Grail*, Century, London 1993

Stein, Walter, J., *The Death of Merlin*, Floris Books, Edinburgh 1989

Stein, Walter, J., *The Ninth Century. World History in the Light of the Holy Grail*, Temple Lodge Publishing, 1991

Strachan, Gordon, *Christ and the Cosmos*, Labarum Publications, Scotland 1985

Theroux, M., *Rhythmic Formative Forces of Music*, Borderland Sciences Research Foundation, California 1995

Trevor, Meriol, *Newman, The Pillar and the Cloud*, Macmillan, London 1962

Wachsmuth, G., *Etheric Formative Forces in Cosmos, Earth and Man*. Book 1, Anthroposophical Publishing Co., 1932

Wachsmuth, G., *The Etheric World in Art, Science and Religion*, Book 2, unpublished translation typescript, Rudolf Steiner House Library, London

Waite, Arthur Edward, *The Real History of the Rosicrucians*, London 1887

Wallace-Murphy, Tim, *The Templar Legacy and the Masonic Inheritance within Rosslyn Chapel*, published by 'The Friends of Rosslyn', Rosslyn Chapel, Roslin, Midlothian EH25 9PU

Wallace-Murphy, Tim, and Hopkins, Marilyn, *Rosslyn, Guardian of the Secret of the Holy Grail*

Weinberg, Steven, *Dreams of a Final Theory*, Random House, London 1993

Wertheim Aymès, C.A., *The Pictorial Language of Hieronymus Bosch*, New Knowledge Books, 1975

Welburn, Andrew, *The Beginnings of Christianity*, Floris Books, Edinburgh 1991

Welburn, Andrew, *Gnosis, the Mysteries and Christian Writings*, Floris Books, Edinburgh 1994

Wood, David, *Genisis—The First Book of Revelation*, Baton Press, Kent 1985

Wood, David, and Campbell, Ian, *Geneset—Target Earth*, Belleview Books, Middlesex 1994

Wyatt, Isabel, *From Round Table to Grail Castle*, Lanthorn Press, Sussex 1979

Yates, Frances A., *The Rosicrucian Enlightenment*, Routledge, London 1999

Picture Credits

Thanks are due to the following for photographs and illustrations:

Mercury Press, Spring Valley, New York, pages 14 and 161.

Clive Hicks for 'Cornucopia' enlarged from: 'A border of Green Men from a devotional work on the ways to Heaven and to Hell. Augsburg 1518', published in *The Green Man* by William Anderson and Clive Hicks, HarperCollins, London, Sydney, Auckland, Johannesburg, 1990.

New Knowledge Books, Horsham, Sussex, pages 94, 95 and 185.

The Philosophical Research Society, Inc., page 101.

Verlag am Goetheanum, Dornach, Switzerland, page 161.

Floris Books, Edinburgh, pages 167 and 171, and colour plate 11.

Mark Curtis, for his picture of a DNA helix on the right side of colour plate number 7. A similar picture of his was commissioned for the Millennium postage stamp in 2000.

Joy Hancox for the Globe (1599)—schematic design, colour plate number 19. Author of *The Byrom Collection*, Jonathan Cape 1992.

All the other illustrations are from the author's private collection.

Index

Page references in **bold** refer to illustrations